UTSA DT LIBRARY RENEWALS 458-2440
DATE DUE

GAYLORD

PRINTED IN U.S.A.

GLOBALIZATION AND REGULATORY CHARACTER

Advances in Criminology
Series Editor: David Nelken

Titles in the Series

Globalization and Regulatory Character

Regulatory Reform after the Kader Toy Factory Fire

FIONA HAINES
Department of Criminology
University of Melbourne, Australia

ASHGATE

Published by
Ashgate Publishing Limited
Gower House
Croft Road
Aldershot
Hampshire GU11 3HR
England

Ashgate Publishing Company
Suite 420
101 Cherry Street
Burlington, VT 05401-4405
USA

Ashgate website: http://www.ashgate.com

British Library Cataloguing in Publication Data
Haines, Fiona
  Globalization and regulatory character : regulatory reform
  after the Kader Toy Factory fire. - (Advances in
  criminology)
  1.Kader Industrial Toy Company - Fire 2.Factory laws and
  legislation - Thailand 3.Industrial safety - Law and
  legislation - Thailand 4.Globalization - Social aspects -
  Thailand
  I.Title
  344.5'930465

Library of Congress Control Number: 2005929612

ISBN-10: 0 7546 2563 X

Printed and bound in Great Britain by MPG Books Ltd, Bodmin, Cornwall

Contents

Lists of Figures and Table

FIGURES

TABLE

Author's Preface

The key research for this book is 'How has globalization affected safety standards in the rapidly industrializing context of Southeast Asia?' Researching this question brings together crucial debates on globalization and regulation. In particular, the book challenges regulatory scholarship to take account of the complexities of globalization and regulation in newly emerging industrial states. By necessity, it engages with competing debates on globalization and their often contradictory predictions about the future of safety standards in countries such as Thailand. While the impact of globalization would seem an obvious concern for scholars of regulation, most research and writing to date has focussed on advanced industrial and post-industrial states. Within the burgeoning regulatory literature solutions are prescribed and argued to be appropriate for raising standards. However, a significant number of countries exhorted to use the methods developed are *industrializing* rather than *industrialized*, and face their own quite different and unique economic, political and historical challenges. Few scholars have tried to explore the applicability of prescriptions widely accepted in the industrialized context to Southeast Asian countries. It is this gap that this research on the regulatory aftermath of the Kader Toy Factory fire in Thailand addresses. Reforms introduced after the Kader fire attest to the importance of context (or regulatory character) in any research and theory which assesses 'progress' in a country in terms of the international spread of laws and regulations. Pronouncements about *how* to regulate in the face of rapid economic, political and cultural change must be grounded in *where* the regulation is taking place – and *by what process* reform is achieved.

Acknowledgements

This book and the research that underpins it underscores both the privilege and the challenge of academic research. For me, the question about how we play our part in protecting and enriching the lives of all on this small planet found expression through understanding the Kader fire and its aftermath. This book is the culmination of that journey. I certainly did not travel alone, either physically or intellectually, and I owe a debt of gratitude to many.

This was the proverbial research on a shoestring. I am indebted to the University of Melbourne in providing some 'seed money' for that elusive major grant that would solve all my budget woes. It was not forthcoming and so I leant on friends, colleagues and acquaintances to a far greater degree than is decent. First and foremost amongst these was my research assistant and friend Cate Lewis, who gave enormously to the project with her time, intellect, understanding and emotional support. Not satisfied with her friendship alone, I also drew on the resources of her husband, David Lewis, whose knowledge and contacts in Thailand were invaluable. My sincerest thanks are owed to them both. I am also indebted to Peter and Sandy Renew for their kind hospitality and to all at the Christoffel-Blindenmission in Bangkok.

This research would not have been possible without the generous time of those who explained what had happened since the fire and provided me with the information and insight that forms the basis of this research. Many of these people have found their way directly into the book. In particular, I would like to thank Voravidh Charoenloet, Bundit Thanachaisethavut, Jaded Chouwilai, Dr Chaiyuth Chavalitnitikul, Phil Robertson, Waradom Sucharitakul, Tom Kanathat Chantrsiri, Somyot Pruksakasemsuk and Apo Leong for their participation in this research. Grateful thanks must go also to Roong Poomipug, not only for her skills of language and cultural interpretation, but also her considerable insight into the challenges faced by Thai workers.

Many contributed to the intellectual development of work outside of the field. In particular, I would like to thank David Nelken, whose enthusiasm for the book and critical comments were both most welcome. Also, to those at the Southeast Asia Research Centre at the City University of Hong Kong, in particular Kevin Hewison and Stephen Frost, many thanks. Kevin's comments on earlier drafts of the manuscript were much appreciated, as were those of Kit Carson. Asking extremely busy colleagues to read a whole manuscript places considerable extra pressure on them, and yet their comments have made real improvements to the work; I offer my thanks to them both. I would also like to thank Richard Mitchell, Sean Cooney and members of the Centre for Employment and Labour Relations Law at the University of Melbourne for their support whilst writing up this research, and members of the Asian Law Centre at the University of Melbourne for their helpful feedback. Any remaining errors, of course, remain my own.

There are also formal acknowledgements that need to be made. I am grateful for the permission of both Christopher Hood and Oxford University Press for allowing the reproduction of Table 1.1 (p. 9), 'Four styles of public management organization: Cultural theory applied', from Christopher Hood's (1998) work *The Art of the State: Culture, Rhetoric and Public Management,* Clarendon Press, Oxford. I am also most grateful to Sage for permission to draw on my work published in *Social and Legal Studies* in 2003 as 'Regulatory Reform in Light of Regulatory Character: Assessing Industrial Safety Change in the Aftermath of the Kader Toy Factory Fire in Bangkok, Thailand' (Vol. 12, No. 4, pp. 461–87). My thanks too, to both Cate Lewis and the Sydney Institute of Criminology for permission to draw on 'Kader, compensation and justice: the need for a comprehensive analysis' in Sharon Pickering and Caroline Lambert (eds) (2004), *Global Issues, Women and Justice,* Sydney Institute of Criminology Series No 19, Institute of Criminology, pp. 230–58, in the introductory chapter of this book.

I have been most fortunate with assistance in the publication of this book. This assistance was made possible through a publication grant from the University of Melbourne. This allowed me to obtain the valuable editorial services of Kerry Biram (kerry.biram@bigpond.com). To both parties my grateful thanks.

It is often said that academic research relies on the support of families. This research and this book are no exception. The love, support and forbearance of Bruce, Chris and Tim are all anyone could wish for. International research holds particular challenges for those at home, and I am very grateful for their emails, thoughts, hugs, banter and everything else that they did whilst I worked on this book.

This book is dedicated to the families of those affected by the Kader Fire.

List of Abbreviations

ADB – Asian Development Bank

ADPC – Asian Disaster Preparedness Centre

AFL-CIO – American Federation of Labor – Congress of Industrial Organizations. Peak US Union body

AMRC – Asia Monitor Resource Centre. International NGO based in Hong Kong

APPELL – Awareness and Preparedness for Emergency at the Local Level

BMA – Bangkok Municipal Authority

BOI – Bureau of Investment (in Thailand)

BVQI – Bureau Veritas Quality International. Accreditation and auditing company with specialization in safety

CCHSW – Campaigning Committee for the Health and Safety of Workers

CP – Charoen Pokphand Group. Thai-based conglomerate

CSKW – Campaign for the Support of Kader Workers

DIW – Department of Industrial Works (Thailand)

DNV – Det Norske Veritas. Accreditation and auditing company with specialization in safety

DOI – Department of Industry (Thailand)

EGAT – Electricity Generating Authority of Thailand

FES – Freidrich Ebert Stiftung. Peak German union body

GTZ – Gesellschaft für Technische Zusammenarbeit (Society for Technical Co-operation)

ILO – International Labour Organisation

IMF – International Monetary Fund

INGO – international non-governmental organization

ISO – International Organization for Standardization

ISO 9000 series (includes ISO 9001 and 9002) – Family of International Organization for Standardization standards for quality of products and services. Includes model for quality assurance in design, development, production, installation and servicing, also the model for quality assurance in production, installation and servicing.

ISO 14000 series – Family of International Organization for Standardization standards related to quality management for the environment

MASCI – Management System Certification Institute (Thailand)

MLSW – Ministry of Labour and Social Welfare (Thailand)

MNC – multi-national corporation

MOI – Ministry of Industry (Thailand)

NFPA – National Fire Prevention Association. US-based NGO that develops standards related to fire prevention

NGO – non-governmental organization

NICE – National Institute for the Improvement of Working Conditions and Environment (Thailand)

NSC – National Safety Council (Thailand)

OECD – Organisation for Economic Co-operation and Development

OHS – occupational health and safety

PFT – Peasants' Federation of Thailand

SA 8000 – Social Accountability standard aimed to support fair working conditions. Standard of SAI

SAI – Social Accountability International. NGO aimed to support fair labour standards

SME – small and medium-sized enterprises

TIS 18001 – Thai Safety Management Standard

TISI – Thai Industrial Standards Institute

WIND – Work Improvement in Neighbourhood Development. ILO programme aimed to increase safety in agriculture

WISE – Work Improvement for Small Enterprises. ILO programme to increase safety in small and medium-sized enterprises

WTO – World Trade Organization

Series Preface

Fiona Haines is a leading writer on the subject of business crime and the regulation of safety. Having made important contributions to these topics here she turns her attention to a more difficult task. How far is the literature of white-collar crime and regulation applicable also to the understanding and resolution of such problems in the setting of rapidly developing countries like Thailand? Are the de-contextualized 'best practices' this literature recommends equally applicable – or feasible – in these situations? Is globalization the problem or the solution? In a globalizing world, problems of environment, health and safety and the human costs of economic development can no longer be circumscribed by place. The recent terrible tragedies caused by the Tsunami in Southeast Asia, in which many Western tourists also lost their lives, show, if such further proof were needed, the implications of this increasing interdependence. It is likely that with appropriate preventive measures and a different type of economic infrastructure thousands of lives could have been saved. But technical know-how alone is not enough; insight into the social realities that make change possible is also essential.

This book provides us with this sort of understanding, which is made to emerge from the story of a massive fire in the multinational Kader toy factory in Thailand. We are given an original and detailed examination of what the author calls 'Thai regulatory character' as it influences the efforts at reform that follow the fire. We see how culture is shaped by – and itself shapes – the larger Thai context as well as its effects on Thailand's role in the world economy. This book shows the considerable effort that must be made in order to understand the relevance to regulatory processes and outcomes of social, economic, political and cultural differences. The author is careful at all points to steer a course between assuming similarities and exaggerating differences. Some parts of the account may seem familiar to those who know about the early stages of factory or environmental regulation in the industrialized West: the role of scandals, the passing of legislation without much in the way of enforcement, inter-organizational conflicts and special interests, the connection between regulation and state building, even tripartism – the negotiated relationship between government, business and unions. Other parts of the account will be strange, unexpected and even counter-intuitive: the place of the military, the importance of patriarchal norms, both for good and ill, the special role of women, the contrast between ideologically-motivated bureaucrats and others, the significance of self-reliance in Thai culture.

But this book's arguments and ambitions go well beyond providing a satisfactory description of scandal and reform in a foreign culture (which would be an achievement in its own right). It develops a key concept – that of 'regulatory character' – which transcends the present study and promises to be relevant to the increasing number of comparative socio-legal studies and research on legal transfers which come up against the vexing question of deciding what importance to be given to 'culture' as an explanation. For Haines (drawing on the work of Christopher Hood and Mary Douglas), regulatory character is framed by an understanding of the form authority takes within a particular place, the interaction between norms and laws set against an understanding of the rationale underpinning the relationship between individual and institution, and the subjective and objective reality of a given regulatory context. The ideal-typical elements she identifies as central to Thai regulatory character (albeit in tension and subject to change) may in many respects be specific to that context or at least to Southeast Asia more generally. But the idea itself is not.

As with all successful comparative enquiries, greater understanding of how matters go together elsewhere also provides invaluable insight into what is taken for granted 'at home' (though it would be equally important to see how scholars based outside the G8 countries explained the local 'cultural' and other causes of the difficulties developed capitalist countries have in dealing with business crime). Fiona Haines' excellent study may come to be seen as a pioneer in qualitative research into the nexus between comparative regulation and comparative criminology. I hope that it will stimulate more scholars to face up to the challenge of thinking globally whilst acting locally.

David Nelken
Series Editor

Chapter 1

The Tragedy of Kader

At 8.00 a.m. on 10 May 1993,[1] over 3000 workers began their day's shift at the Kader Industrial (Thailand) Company's soft toy factory in an industrial zone in Nakhon Pathon province near Bangkok. Nearly 1500 workers took their places in Building Number 1, one of a factory complex of four buildings. The factory produced a range of toys: everything from 'stuffed toys to plastic Father Christmases,' under licence for a range of toy companies. These included world-famous brands such as Arco, Hasbro, Toys-R-Us, Fisher-Price and Tyco. Kader itself was no 'hole-in-the-wall' enterprise. The Bangkok factory was part of a joint venture between the Hong Kong-based, Chinese-owned Kader Company and the Thai-based CP (Charoen Pokphand) Group, largely controlled by the powerful Thai Chaeravanot family.[2] CP remains one of the largest Southeast Asian conglomerates.

Most of the workers who took up their positions at machines or on the factory floor that day were women and girls; some were underage, having borrowed ID cards to get a job at the factory. A number were from the remote and poverty-stricken north-eastern provinces. Traditionally, daughters in Thailand contribute to family income, so it is common for young women from rural families to migrate to areas of employment and repatriate money (Busakom, 1993; Ungpakorn, 1999). Many of the women at the factory were the main or essential wage earners for their

---

[1]   I am indebted to Cate Lewis for her assistance with the narrative of the Kader Fire. There are several sources for the description of the factory and the fire, including Voravidh Charoenloet, (April 1998) 'The situation of health and safety in Thailand', Dossier no. 5, Asia Monitor Resource Centre Toy Campaign; International Confederation of Free Trade Unions, (undated) *From the Ashes; A Toy Factory Fire in Thailand: An Expose of the Toy Industry*, Belgium: ICFTU; Casey Cavanagh Grant and Thomas J. Klem (1994) 'Toy Factory Fire in Thailand Kills 188 Workers', *National Fire Prevention Authority Journal*, January/February: 42–9. Peter Symonds (1997) *Industrial Inferno: The Story of the Thai Toy Factory Fire*, Bankstown Australia: Labour Press Books; T. Chua and W. Wei Ling (1993) 'Help! Is there a way out?', *Asian Labour Update*, 12:1–8; Asia Monitor Resource Center (1997) Report on Regional Meeting 'Remembering Kader: Promoting Occupational Health and Safety, Workers Rights and the Rights of Industrial Accident Victims in Asia', Bangkok, May 10–13 1997; Asia Monitor Resource Center (1998) 'Toy Campaign: The People United will never be Defeated', April, Dossier No. 5 Compiled by the Hong Kong Toy Coalition and the Asia Monitor Resource Center.

[2]   CP's relationship to Kader is not direct nor entirely clear. There were a number of intermediary companies between the interests of the Chaeravanot family and the Kader factory; see Symonds, 1997, pp. 46–7.

extended family, either as single parents or with dependent or poorly-paid husbands or relatives. There were also a number of school and university students, working to earn extra money for their education costs.

Women such as the Kader workers seek employment in factories because it offers real advantages. Factory work can result in a progressive development of women's lives from their traditional situation, with greater personal freedoms (Foo and Lim, 1989). Many choose factory work because they wish to save and to contribute to family income, thus increasing their personal economic independence (Porpora, Lim and Prommas cited in Ungpakorn, 1999). Factories offer the companionship of fellow workers and an environment that appears safer than the dangerous and more physically demanding alternatives of construction, scrap metal collection, domestic work or street vending. Further, factory work is better paid than these alternatives with the possibility, in some factories at least, of increases in payment as skills and output improve (Symonds, 1997; Ungpakorn, 1999).

Nonetheless, conditions at Kader were still harsh. Only a minority of workers enjoyed full-time employee status under Thai legislation, entitling them to receive the minimum wage. The rest were contract labour, with many earning less than the minimum wage. This was not uncommon in Thailand, with official government figures showing that, in 1989, 47 per cent of employers did not pay the minimum wage (Symonds, 1997). Compulsory overtime until midnight and even up to 5.00 a.m. was common when orders had to be filled. Supervisors could set quotas for the day, with pay docked if workers could not meet the quotas. Conditions inside the factory were basic; for example, on the fourth floor there were only eight toilets for the 800 workers, and requests to leave due to sickness were often met with shouting and harassment, while lint, fabric, dust and animal hair filled the air in the production room. Critically, flammable materials were ubiquitous.

Soon after 4.00 p.m. workers heard cries of 'Fire! Fire!' Supervisors ordered that work continue, insisting that it was a false alarm. When workers finally began running towards the exits, they found the doors blocked by raw materials and other people trying to get out. By then, the lights had gone out and all was 'commotion and confusion'. As they crowded the stairs to the single exit and clambered over the bodies of those piled up behind the exit door, the building collapsed. Desperate workers trapped in the upper levels began leaping from the third and fourth floor windows onto the cement below. 'I didn't know what to do,' a survivor said. 'Finally I had no other choice but to join others and jump out of the window. I saw many of my friends lying dead on the ground beside me. I injured my legs but I came out alive.'[3] Another described the horror of the situation: 'In desperation ... I went back and forth looking down below. The smoke was so thick and I picked the best place to jump in a pile of boxes. My sister jumped too. She died.'[4]

---

[3] Tumthong Padthirum, quoted in International Confederation of Free Trade Unions (Undated), *From the Ashes; A Toy Factory Fire in Thailand: An Expose of the Toy Industry*, p. 10.

[4] Laman Taptim, quoted in International Confederation of Free Trade Unions (Undated) *From the Ashes; A Toy Factory Fire in Thailand: An Expose of the Toy Industry*, p. 8.

Officially, 174 women and 14 men died that day and 469 were injured. Many of the survivors owed their lives to the fact that the bodies of co-workers broke their fall. However, casualties were possibly much higher. It took rescue workers 20 days to clear debris and pull out human remains and bodies. For a chaotic two weeks after the fire, relatives faced the task of identifying decomposing bodies, many burnt beyond recognition. Kader refused to release a list of workers, so many relatives, particularly those from the provinces, did not know if their loved ones were at the factory or not.

Kader was the worst industrial fire globally of the twentieth century. A government inquiry found that the extent of the tragedy was exacerbated by many factors, all utterly preventable.[5] Building 1 collapsed within 20 minutes of the fire starting, giving little chance to escape. The steel framework of the building was not fireproofed, so that in the extreme heat generated by the fire the steel melted, causing the collapse. Highly flammable raw materials stored to ceiling level gave off poisonous fumes that compounded the hazard of the fire. Fire protection was rudimentary, with limited fire protection equipment and fire fighting water distributors available on each floor. There were no sprinkler systems and the fire alarms in Building Number 1 did not work. The building lacked separate fire exits, so many workers were trapped, while stairwells and freight elevators acted as channels for heat, smoke and fumes. Further, the lack of fire drills or training in fire fighting led to panic. Local firefighters had to get water from a nearby ditch because there was no water inside the factory. The horrific nature of the fire resulted from multiple elements, which, when combined, escalated the severity of the fire and compounded the suffering of all those involved.

In June 1993, I heard a first-hand account of the fire from one of the survivors, who was travelling with a group of activists in order to garner support for a campaign against Kader, a campaign aimed at ensuring the company paid adequate compensation to victims and their families. Hers was a harrowing experience. At 15 years of age, she had left work on a road construction crew to work at the Kader Toy Factory as she felt that such work would be safer than working on the roads out in the heat of the day. She had only been working at the factory a short while when the fire occurred. Her life was one of those saved by the bodies of co-workers, which broke her fall when she jumped from a fourth-storey window to escape the fire. At the end of her short talk, a discussion arose as to how to help. A boycott seemed obvious, yet the target was unclear, since nowhere on the product

---

[5]   Illustrated by the fact that there had been three fires at the factory prior to the tragic event, yet nothing had changed to prevent future fires or to stop the spread of fires beyond their ignition point. To claim ignorance about how this tragedy could have been prevented was not possible, since it was not an event without precedent. Accounts of the Kader fire comment on its eerie similarity to the Triangle Shirtwaist Factory fire in New York nearly a century earlier (Symonds, 1997; Grant *et al.*, 1994, pp. 45–7). The Triangle fire had generated considerable knowledge about fire prevention, knowledge that could and should have been in place at Kader. In a fire prevention sense, there was nothing new about Kader. Each element that acted as a catalyst to the spread of the Kader fire (lack of fire exits, poor housekeeping and lack of adequate fire fighting equipment) was well understood.

was there any indication that the toy, a Bart Simpson doll, was made by the Kader factory. Many manufacturers were involved in the production of the same line of toy, so separating out Kader from the rest was impossible. It seemed that the complexities of global production had made bringing those responsible to account even more difficult. Certainly, the consensus of the audience was that the evils of globalization lay at the heart of the problem, a problem that meant that conditions like those at Kader were on the rise.

Yet, in the aftermath of Kader there was reform. The awful reality of the fire led to a public outcry in Thailand demanding something be done. This, combined with a long intense international activist campaign, resulted in the Kader workers being paid the highest compensation in Thai history. The payment was made not from the rudimentary government scheme but directly from the company itself (Voravidh,[6] 1998; Lae and Voravidh, 2000).

Regulatory change was also forthcoming. In the compensation area, worker access to the state compensation fund was broadened to include all businesses that employed 10 workers or more. New building standards were drawn up and fire prevention standards were being updated and translated by the bureaucracy from the US model developed by the National Fire Prevention Authority (NFPA). In the state-based OHS regulatory regime, an annual Safety Day was introduced along with health and safety committees and prohibition notices. Further, changes occurred beyond traditional OHS regulatory mechanisms, with the development of an OHS management standard (TIS 18001), a market-based approach to raising safety standards. However, not all demands for reform were successful. Despite protest and initial co-operation from government, the momentum towards enactment of a dedicated health and safety act faltered and ultimately lapsed.

How can the pessimism of protest around the evils of globalization make sense in light of the changes that did occur in the aftermath of the Kader fire? Are the reforms alluded to above (and expanded on in Chapter 4) simply a charade, a house of cards ready to fall at the first demands by companies that they will move offshore if safety improvements go too far and eat into profit? Or should they be read optimistically as real signs of improvement, an indication that rapid industrialization fuelled by the global market will be accompanied by better conditions? This book demonstrates that both views are seriously limited, although both would find ample evidence to suit their own point of view. The mistake often made by the globalization literature is that global economic pressure has an unmediated impact on local context – either for good or ill. This research shows the importance of understanding how laws and regulations are understood in their local context. In short, the reforms following Kader, whilst recognizable to regulatory policy makers in the West, must be understood in terms of the place in which they occur. The relationship between law and practice, between law and social norms, is central to understanding the potential of the reforms, following Kader, to improve safety.

---

[6]   The academic convention is that Thai authors are denoted by their first names. This convention is followed here.

The first challenge to be met in order to understand the impact of globalization on regulatory reform is to comprehend local 'regulatory character', the relationships between individuals, social norms and laws. Regulatory character allows an assessment of whether laws and regulations are a tool to raise standards, an irrelevancy in everyday work life or perhaps a threat to jobs and good relationships with those in authority. Regulatory character is the lens through which the significance or lack of significance of reform can be understood.

This book brings together debates on globalization with those of regulation through a serious assessment of how the reforms following Kader came about, what motivated government to act, and then how the new laws were used, abused and ignored. It is motivated by a desire to make regulatory scholarship more reflective of the impact of our ideas. These questions are not just academic. Through forums such as the Organisation for Economic Co-operation and Development (OECD), the World Trade Organization (WTO) and the International Monetary Fund (IMF), the ideas of regulatory scholars, amongst others, are being debated and – in some cases – mandated through structural reforms which accompany financial assistance. Regulatory scholarship is then part of globalization in a very real sense, and as such deserves some scrutiny in the context of that debate. Regulatory scholars are increasingly asked to provide control solutions that can ameliorate the harms associated with the market, whilst maintaining the benefits (Haines, 1997; IMF, 1999; Haines, 2000; OECD, 2002; Sutton and Haines, 2003). It is critical, then, that regulatory scholars take better account of how disparate places understand, read and use laws – including those seen as 'best practice' by our global institutions. Indeed, recent world events make it more likely that the regulatory prescriptions of the West will be transplanted to very different contexts. Understanding regulatory character provides a way of assessing the impact of global policy-making on local contexts.

A second task is to make sense of the globalization debate in terms of its implications for regulation and regulatory reform. Research on this book began in the early 1990s when debates on the subject of globalization were at their height. The academic literature burgeoned simultaneiously, with the aim of defining the phenomenon and assessing its significance. For some, including those who attended the meeting with Kader victims in Trades Hall, Melbourne in 1993, globalization was the source of deep and widening divisions within the global community. That small group was certainly not alone. A significant literature sees globalization as responsible for continued and worsening divisions between the 'haves' and 'have nots' in the global community. Yet this evaluation competes with other powerful accounts of the significance and impact of global change. Certainly, much economic reform is predicated on globalization resulting in significant benefits for all. Others argue that the significance of globalization is overstated, that such changes are 'nothing new', rather are simply a continuation of economic and political inequality that make up the 'north–south' divide. Yet other voices suggest that the complex of social forces that constitute globalization provide new opportunities for change and progress.

Chapter 2 analyses how Kader is to be understood in light of the 'globalization debate' and concludes that whilst useful insights can be gained, there are limits on the degree to which debates on globalization can provide a useful account of either the nature of industrial disasters or their ability to generate reforms that improve safety. Globalization debates most often reside at a macro level of analysis with implications drawn from the global to the specific, and from the specific to the global, in ways that ignore or downplay the significance of local factors to change. In C.W. Mills' terms, globalization is often debated at a macro-level analytical frame that has lacked a useful micro level complement. Certain global pressures, though, are important. Clearly, the demand for market-based reforms, and with them the rise of competitive individualism as a normative good, is a significant influence on local reform. Important, too, is the growth of rule making and standards development at the international level, a phenomenon Giddens (1990) labels 'global rationalism'. Finally, the choices that individual states make in terms of their acceding to or rejecting global economic and political pressures to 'open the borders' to international trade – the so-called 'sovereignty response', as Mittleman (1994) describes it – is important to understand.

Yet the quality and significance of this 'sovereignty response' in the regulatory context is underdeveloped. What does sovereignty mean when it comes to regulatory reform? Further, is there an identifiable group of regulatory prescriptions that can be equated with progress? As a regulatory scholar, my first thought was to combine globalization with the insights provided by regulatory theory, a theory more used to dealing with micro-level dynamics. Disasters often play an important role in spurring regulatory reform, with both the content of reform and the reform process being important sites for analysis. What constitutes positive reform is critical to understand, however, since regulation itself can be counterproductive. Regulatory scholarship has grown as an endeavour to provide fresh ideas on how to reduce market failure whilst retaining the dynamism necessary for economic development. Such expertise appears at first glance to be a useful source for evaluating the worth of regulatory reforms after disaster events, and a suitable complement to broader macro levels of analysis. The second part of Chapter 2 reviews the potential of ideas such as responsive regulation, tripartism or meta-regulation to provide the relevant 'micro-level' analytical tools with which to review and understand the significance of the changes following the Kader fire. However, whilst regulatory theory has widened the debate on useful regulatory strategies to a considerable degree, its largely normative focus is problematic. Indeed, in positioning itself ultimately as a largely technocratic endeavour, normative prescriptions on 'positive' reform may unwittingly obfuscate the centrality of political will and economic demands as fundamental elements in determining what reform will occur. Studies specific to the reform process itself highlight the importance of economic and political context, in both the shape reform takes and the likely success of reform measures. This context becomes even more important when rules are appropriated from one particular setting to another. Without understanding the relationship between social norms and laws, the writing on regulation is seriously limited. Simply highlighting desirable reforms, as regulatory scholarship has tended to do, glosses over the specific ways in which context moulds regulation and compliance. Comparative work demands that reforms be understood as those appropriate to context, not as some contextual 'best practice' benchmark.

Chapter 3 expands on the potential for the concept of 'regulatory character' to provide a sufficient grounding in economic, political and cultural context to understand the nature and effectiveness of regulatory change following the Kader fire. As sketched out above, regulatory character is the summation of three relationships critical to how regulations interact within its economic, political and cultural context. These relationships are: (1) between individuals and social norms, (2) between norms and laws, and (3) between individuals and laws. They shape how regulations are viewed and how they are used. Regulatory character highlights the importance of the authority that flows from normative values and the complex relationship between those norms and written laws. How individuals negotiate their place, whether they draw on normative resources at work or legal processes illustrates how regulatory reform will, or will not, lead to significant improvement in safety at work.

Regulatory character is both a theoretical and empirical construct. Theoretically, it draws from Mary Douglas' cultural theory as adapted by Christopher Hood (1998). Cultural theory provides a useful starting point as it specifically addresses the importance, or lack of importance, of laws through the concept of the 'grid' dimension of a society. Differences between contexts in terms of emphasis on the group as a whole or the individual is explored through the 'group' dimension. Taken together, the combination between these two dimensions, 'grid' and 'group', provides insights with regards to a society's emphasis on hierarchy and authority, individual rights and responsibilities or egalitarian group-centred norms. These norms are not just central to small group settings; Hood (1998) has demonstrated the value of this analysis to the regulatory context and the way control bureaucracies both interpret failure and prescribe reform. Nonetheless, there are problems with cultural theory, particularly in its reification of culture and its under-emphasis on economic and political constraints. Chapter 3 shows how these problems can be overcome by consideration of *relationships* within a given context. Drawing on Weberian insights, Douglas and Hood's grid dimension becomes a mechanism to explore the interaction between norms and laws in a given setting, whilst the group dimension is used to explore the relationship between individuals and social norms. These relationships are necessarily influenced by economic constraints and political considerations. Regulatory culture is transformed into regulatory character by including an understanding of how attitudes and beliefs (central elements in culture) are moulded and shaped by the economic dependencies and the political environment. Regulatory character extends Selznick's (1992) notion of organizational character as it relates to the regulatory environment. Just as his concept of organizational character takes account of economic and political factors, regulatory character understands that the form regulations take and the nature of their implementation depend upon cultural assumptions of right action and moral worth within an environment, which are in turn shaped by economic dependencies and the political pressures.

A study of regulatory reform, then, must understand the regulatory character of a particular place. In the case of Kader, to understand Thai regulatory character requires an understanding of the Thai economic, political and cultural context in order to flesh out the relationships between individuals, norms and laws within an industrial safety context. This is no easy task, since there are, as in any environment, competing norms and competing views. However, it is possible to ascertain 'ideal-typical' forms of character that exert influence on reform. Academic literature on Thailand suggests that the dominant or 'traditional' ideal-typical form of Thai regulatory character is essentially patriarchal with a corresponding emphasis on the self-reliance of individuals. In Hood's terms this is hierarchist. How these hierarchical norms interact with law (i.e. the grid relationship) is complex, with laws both aimed to consolidate control, but also to act in a formalistic manner to convince outsiders of Thai capability. This literature also suggests that regulatory character should be understood as dualistic. Elements of Thai regulatory character, such as patriarchalism, can be interpreted both as expressing certain moral values and as a means for strategic advancement. In Weber's terms patriarchalism can be understood either as value rational (as a moral order) or strategically rational (as a means to exert control). Critically, the expectations for men and women differ, as their experiences of the moral and strategic order differ. Further, the Thai history of protest demonstrates that this traditional form of Thai regulatory character has been and continues to be under considerable challenge from those with alternative visions of a 'good' society, particularly from those with more egalitarian values. The result is that Thai regulatory character is in a state of flux, nonetheless it is a state in which traditional forms of that character exert significant influence.

Part of the reason for this state of flux is that regulatory character is interdependent with the global context. Pressures from the international market and from global rule-making bodies are felt by regulatory character, but are also interpreted by that character. Economic globalization, with its emphasis on competitive individualism, interacts with the self-reliance within Thai regulatory character. The characteristic qualities of self-reliance, including a need to focus on immediate survival, appears perfectly suited to an economic form that increases the uncertainty associated with employment, such as short-term contracts and casualization of the workforce. Equally as important to regulation, however, is the interaction between global rationalism, the plethora of rules and standards that accompany global trade, and the formalism inherent within Thai regulatory character. Chapter 3 ends by setting the framework for understanding the response to Kader, first in terms of Thai regulatory character and then in terms of the impact of globalization on Thai regulatory character.

This analysis of Thai regulatory character drawn from the academic literature is then tested and brought to life through the interview material on the response to Kader. Chapter 5 explores the relationship between patriarchal norms and self-reliant individuals shaped by what reforms were considered 'appropriate for Thailand'. Importantly, patriarchal norms could further reform, particularly when the 'moral goodness' of those in positions of authority was emphasized. The obligation of paying compensation and the development of a bureaucratic and economic service ethic amongst some public servants were important to some reform initiatives. However, the emphasis on status within a patriarchal world-view could also be problematic, particularly when the need to retain control (and thus status) was given priority in key decisions. Radical reform aiming to streamline safety regulation and increase its efficiency was stymied because of departmental demands to retain control of budgets and service areas. Further, tripartism (the negotiated relationship between government, business and unions) under patriarchal norms could be framed to retain the status quo and keep critics out, rather than act as a conduit for collaborative input.

The ability of those in authority to retain control, however, could be understood without its counterpart, namely the corresponding emphasis on the self-reliance of ordinary people. To be self-reliant was to build relationships with powerful others who can protect you in times of need. There are expectations within this relationship of reciprocity (see Woodiwiss, 1998): allegiance to a person in authority will be met with benevolence. This in part explains why worker demands for compensation from the company to Kader victims were given some public support. The patriarchal relationship, though, has a more problematic relationship to common Western prescriptions for good safety standards, such as the setting up of formal safety committees and an emphasis on prevention and safety awareness with OHS regimes. These practices are more allied to individualistic or egalitarian forms of regulatory character. Safety awareness requires an individual apprehension of, and behavioural response to, risk as a discrete concern. In contrast, self-reliance had as a primary concern the maintenance of key relationships. Acknowledgement by workers of safety hazards could threaten patriarchal relationships, and so a robust health and safety emphasis in the workplace was much more difficult under traditional Thai regulatory character.

Chapter 6 reviews the challenges to traditional Thai regulatory character through an analysis of activist demands for reform. Activist demands, particularly those aimed at a radical reform of OHS regulation, brought into sharp relief the problems inherent in the relationship between patriarchal norms and the law. Kader support groups, activists and others were well aware of the need for reform that could extend beyond the law, ultimately to 'character reform'. The long history of protest within Thailand had brought together a diverse range of people who demanded greater egalitarianism, where the voices of workers, particularly those with illness and injury, could be heard. There were many challenges. The patriarchal value placed on status for its own sake, the heavy-handed nature of control through tripartite committees and bureaucratic hierarchies, and the fragmented nature of safety regulation were a constant drag on substantive change. Whilst reform undoubtedly did occur, there was a consensus that little had changed. Chapter 6 shows how 'nothing has changed' can be understood as the persistence of traditional Thai regulatory character in the face of sustained protest and some regulatory reform.

The challenges to Thai regulatory character were not only local in origin. Chapter 7 explores the impact that globalization had on both Thai regulatory character and safety reform following Kader. It demonstrates how globalization, with the emphasis on individuals and markets, intersected with self-reliance within

Thai regulatory character. Reform consistent with both globalization and self-reliance emphasized using market mechanisms to raise standards. Market mechanisms comprising self-regulatory schemes, often developed by non-governmental organizations (NGOs) outside of Thailand, aimed to use consumer pressure in Northern markets to raise corporate standards. Ironically, the role for government in these schemes was secondary, merely to promote various accreditation schemes as the way of the future as a regulatory form compatible with opening up a particular industry to international market forces.

The impact of globalization on Thai regulatory character, however, could not be restricted to analysis of the way international trade valorized initiatives aimed at increasing self-reliance. The chapter also explores the additional emphasis on global rationalism, the development and transplantation of rules to guide how trade was to be conducted. Global rationalism emphasized the importance of rules over relationships, with relationships within the capitalist market viewed as potentially or actually corrupt. Global rationalism and the development of an international awareness of 'the rule of law' worked at many levels. Multinationals, particularly those well known to Western consumers, were well aware of their responsibility to abide by the law. These multinationals were seen by some to take their responsibilities, under Thai law at least, seriously. At another level, global institutions such as the International Labour Organisation (ILO) would try to stay ahead of market-based regulatory change and seek to influence its direction by developing rules for others to draw on.

Regulatory character was intrinsic to the way these international initiatives became part of the Thai system. Thus, whilst international initiatives might wish to promote individualism, traditional forms of Thai regulatory character dictated otherwise. Chapter 8 demonstrates how 'sovereignty' was re-established through the contours of regulatory character. Standards brought in were regularly picked up from a variety of overseas destinations and translated into the Thai regulatory system. This could, on the one hand, result in literal translations that looked good, but had no engagement with local context and, on the other, standards where elements were reordered so patriarchal control retained. Activists working on the global level that challenged Thai regulatory character are also considered here. Local activist groups would work together with international counterparts and scour the globe for regulatory examples more in keeping with their philosophy of active engagement. Recent protests by activists also had seen institutions like the World Bank attempt to draw in groups to assist them in shaping the future. This led to some tension. For some activists these institutions constituted 'the enemy', so any form of engagement was to be eschewed. Others were more open, yet still these overtures of some institutions were viewed with suspicion since the reason for an institution's request for engagement was not always clear and could lead to more demands being made on scarce NGO resources.

The intention of the book, though, is not to argue either that change will not happen, or that the reforms following Kader are unique, or that the research is somehow only pertinent to reading the Thai context. Change will take place, and it will be influenced both by the egalitarian demands of local activists *and* the individualistic orientation of the 'free market' championed by international institutions. The insistence that safety standards must follow industrialization if safety is to improve is clearly a legitimate, but also a highly complex, demand. Regulatory reform is not unique to context, but neither can regulation be abstracted to a set of 'best practice' forms that will simply need reiterating in each national context. Along with innovation, there must be a corresponding emphasis on empathetic readings of place in regulatory scholarship. Regulatory character provides one way to guide comparative studies of regulatory policy and practice. The particular form regulatory character takes shapes how reform occurs and how the resulting laws, regulations and techniques are used. An emphasis on regulatory character also brings to the fore the importance of reform as a process, one underpinned by normative assumptions of 'good' and 'bad' change. The imposition of preformed techniques could perhaps be viewed as a new form of colonialism: regulatory colonialism. In some cases this may actually be effective, but in other cases it will lead to superficial change, making little impact on the everyday realities of workers or the potential for future disaster. Scholars wishing to promote innovation and development in the form of regulatory reform must take account of context in a real and ongoing way. The tragedy of events such as Kader demands that this analysis be done and that it be fed back into proposals and theories to guide the future.

Chapter 2

Industrial Disasters, Regulatory Change and Globalization

The study of industrial disasters and the regulatory reform they generate brings together two separate academic debates: those of globalization and of regulation. Industrial disasters are a link between reflections on the new global order and its potential for future wellbeing, and pragmatic debates about how to reduce the risks of industrial processes. In the globalization literature, industrial disasters are often seen as evidence that the new globalized order brings with it an unpalatable and unacceptable dark side. For the radical literature, catastrophes such as Kader are argued to create untold suffering whilst the benefits of a 'trickle down' of wealth remain a sham for the bulk of the world's poor. Such a reading is contested, though, within the globalization literature. The literature is divided between those who view disasters such as Kader as being likely to increase, those who argue that change will bring improvements, first in living standards, then in industrial safety, and finally those who view globalization as a complex process with contradictory outcomes. This latter – and growing – group sees the response by various nation states to global economic and political pressures – the so-called 'sovereignty response' (Mittleman, 1994) – as critical. Each view of globalization brings with it ideas of what should occur to reduce the likelihood of a repeat of the Kader fire.

This diversity of analysis about what globalization is and what policies are required to reduce the risk of future disasters poses a challenge for regulatory scholars to identify 'what works'. Here regulatory scholars develop, test and disseminate models of regulation that succeed on the local level and can be 'globalized'. In doing so, they themselves become part of globalization, in this case the globalization of methods of 'good regulation' that can pare the risks from the benefits of globalization such that the rewards proliferate and the risks are controlled. Assessing the aftermath of Kader, in terms of what techniques were picked up and used, could then provide a useful method of identifying the impact of globalization on industrial safety. The generalized debates around globalization could be fused with the 'benchmarking' findings of regulatory theory to assess which of the predictions of the globalization theorists are right. Yet, as promising as such an approach may seem, there are limitations in combining a globalization literature that is often highly politicized, with the normative and apparently apolitical stance of much regulatory theorizing.

Industrial Disasters and Globalization

For many, Kader is symptomatic of the evils of globalization. It is a classic example of how the exploited suffer, whilst the global elite not only escape sanction, but also continue to reap substantial rewards from an economic system rigged in their favour (Mander and Goldsmith, 1996; Greider, 1997). For such commentators, global capitalism lies at the heart of the new world order where footloose capital can roam the globe in search of the easiest gains at the lowest cost. Low-cost products and services for the global rich are paid for in full by the global poor. The current economic system, premised on the benefits of free trade, systematically benefits the global elite. This process, supported by the policies and practices of institutions dedicated to upholding free trade, abet capital in the process of exploitation. Institutions such as the International Monetary Fund (IMF), World Trade Organization (WTO) and World Bank are instrumental in maintaining economic globalization and thus remain responsible, in large part, for the resulting devastation in its current form (Mander and Goldsmith, 1996).

For others, economic globalization is not merely an expansion of national or international forms of capitalism. It has fundamentally restructured the form of capital relations (Harvey, 1989) with inequality once defined according to the 'north–south' divide now reconstructed into 'core' and 'periphery', in line with international markets. The economically powerful cut across national borders. Kader's relationship with the major toy companies illustrates the form of the globalized core of economic power. Workers form part of the periphery, which is both dependent on, but exploited by, the core. Marginalized workers, too, know no national boundaries, with the marginalized as likely to live in the ghettos of New York as the shanty communities of Klong Toey in Bangkok. The irony for these commentators is that the proponents of the new economic system argued that 'trickle down effects' would raise the living standards of the poorest nations, but instead it has reconfigured winners and losers in a manner that deepens rather than softens inequality (Harvey, 1989; Mitter, 1994; Martin and Schuman, 1996; Bauman, 1998; Bello, Cunningham and Poh, 1998). 'Core–periphery' inequality is every bit as pernicious as the 'north–south' inequality that preceded it. This reconfiguration, though, has an added edge in that systems of power and resources ordered around core and periphery challenge the legitimacy and relevance of the nation-state (Waters, 1995; Strange, 1996). Market disciplines cut through national borders as multinationals, not nation states, wield greater and greater power. Global institutions are seen to hasten this process; a cardinal example was the IMF structural adjustment packages of the 1990s, replete with measures that freeze social security measures and force contracting out and privatization on unwilling and progressively weaker governments (Martin and Schuman, 1996; Bello *et al.*, 1998). Such austerity measures place constraints on the Third World that mirror the constraints of the colonial era. The emphasis by the IMF and World Bank on measures such as 'good governance' hides a reality of control and intrusiveness that leave the weak with fewer and fewer resources with which to survive (Anghie, 2000).

This powerful critique of current global policies and practices paints a dark picture of not only the present, but also the future. Here, globalization is a phenomenon, the direction of which is determined primarily by its economic core, and the result of which is manifest in its economic effects. It is a simple but powerful message that fuels protest and animates debate. The dual emphasis on the primacy of economics and the global shape of the effect of economic policy and practice forms one trajectory, within what Held, McGrew, Goldblatt and Perraton (1999) describe as the 'hyperglobalist thesis'. The emphasis of this view of globalization is on the fundamental reorientation of the social order away from states to individuals and markets. For those who might be termed 'pessimistic hyperglobalists' (discussed above), this transformation foreshadows a bleak future.

Others, who also may be characterized as 'hyperglobalist', share a belief in the economic core of globalization. Yet, for commentators such as Kenichi Ohmae (1995) and Milton and Rose Freidman (1996) the future is far from bleak. Indeed, a powerful consensus has argued that the transformations taking place as a result of economic change will produce optimal outcomes for all. (For a useful analysis see Dunkley, 1997.) This optimism has infused policies within the World Bank and International Monetary Fund, whose prescriptions rest on the fundamental good, as they see it, of economic globalization and, in particular, neoclassical economic views of free trade (Gill and Law, 1988; Dunkley, 1997; Anghie, 2000; Hewison, 2002a). Such 'optimistic hyperglobalists' share a similar understanding of the economic processes of globalization, but their vision of the future stands in stark contrast. Globalization based on free trade and the integration of nation states under an economic global order has the potential to reap substantial reward for all. For optimistic hyperglobalists, the wealth and dynamism created by globalization will, over time, create a trickle-down effect of wealth and economic development from the core to the periphery. All nations are capable of developing their own unique competitive advantage and thus increase their access to world markets. Unlike the pessimists, there need not be winners and losers (although there may be temporarily); rather the size of the 'pie' itself can be enlarged.

Much of the early debate about globalization revolved around this hyperglobalist view (Higgott, 1999), and certainly many of the protests over globalization are engendered by the fear of losing control to a faceless globalized elite. One might be tempted to say that optimistic hyperglobalizers meet within the luxurious hotels of Seattle, Geneva and Barcelona, whilst pessimistic hyperglobalizers protest at the door. Yet, as Held *et al.* (1999) outline, this hyperglobalist reading is far from hegemonic, even if it is perhaps the most popularized and publicly debated version. Both the economic core of the process and its impact in terms of fundamentally reshaping human societies worldwide has been challenged. For those Held *et al.* (1999) term 'sceptical', the economic core of globalization is retained, but its novelty dropped. Globalization is a myth; current trends reveal a continuation of history rather than a radical break from it (Hirst and Thompson, 1996). Old inequalities remain. Sceptics draw on an historical analysis that emphasizes the longstanding nature of internationalization (as distinct from globalization), measured in terms of centuries not decades. Further, according to their analysis, current forms of internationalization are neither the most extensive, nor the most intense and the state remains central (Hirst and Thompson, 1996; Weiss, 1998). A critical unit of analysis remains the nation-state. Economic interests are dominated by some states (Western, primarily the US) and it is the states of the global south that continue to suffer.

The primarily economic focus of analysis links both hyperglobalist and sceptic. At odds between the two is the centrality of the state, and with it the view of a process that is primarily international, a process between states (the sceptic view) with one that is transnational (the hyperglobalist view). Not all, however, are comfortable with a debate on globalization that revolves around a primarily economic core. The third group within the globalization debate, those Held *et al.* (1999) label 'Transformalists', point to a complex, contradictory process comprised of not only economic changes and related political activities, but also communicative and social elements (Giddens, 1990; Castells, 1996; Sassen, 1998). These combined forces of modernity are primarily driving change that reaches through the geographical and political boundary of the state. For the transformalists, the development of national policy and action must take account of global dynamics and global policies (for example, those of the WTO and IMF) to a far greater extent than was previously the case. Further globalization is a contested process, not simply determined by global capitalist processes, and is one where NGOs influence outcomes alongside more traditional international players (Castells, 1997). The nation state remains central to understanding the current world order in the transformalist view, but can no longer be thought of as a unitary geographical and political entity. It is rather a unit of sovereignty that marshals its political, economic and social resources to position itself on the global stage. This positioning is necessarily relative, since globalization means that the state cannot view itself as independent from the world. A state may align itself in a position arguably best able to gain benefit from the new order (such as accepting the policy prescriptions of global institutions) or actively reject the overtures of the global hegemony as tainted or evil (Mittleman, 1994).

This study of the aftermath of Kader provides a unique opportunity to explore whether and how the economic and political realities that are wrought by globalization influence safety standards in a rapidly industrializing context. From this literature base, the central question to ask is whether there is evidence that globalization can be blamed, or credited, with the change in the safety of working conditions in a rapidly industrializing environment. By ascertaining the content and the reasons behind reform, research into the aftermath of Kader can explore the economic and social processes of globalization, the nature of sovereignty, and how the interaction between the two affected the reform process.

The disaster is thus a heuristic device able to explore the validity of the various analyses of globalization in a particular context. Certainly, from the contrasting debates on globalization described above, divergent expectations concerning its potential impact on safety standards can be suggested. For pessimistic hyperglobalists, globalization provides exactly the economic and political conditions whereby improvement in the wake of the Kader fire is unlikely. The strength of capital over labour, the weakening of unions, the diminishing power of the nation state and the need for the withered state to prostrate itself to the need for capital do not augur well for improvement in safe working conditions. Rather, such analysts would anticipate that political attention would be drawn to the needs of capital over labour.

It is important, though, in a study of regulation not to confine research questions to expectations, but also to understand what would be seen as an optimal outcome. For pessimistic hyperglobalists a good outcome would be one in which individual capitalists were made accountable for their crimes. Secondly, tight controls would be placed on working conditions so that the safety of workers could be assured, with strong union involvement to make companies accountable to workers. Finally, for some, the best outcome would involve a diminution of the free trade agenda, to be replaced by one that placed human, not economic, values at the centrepiece of global relations (Bello *et al.*, 1998). Various social clauses inserted into the rules of international trade would be a welcome first step.

For optimistic hyperglobalists, the desires of their pessimistic counterparts are their worst-case scenario. Optimistic hyperglobalists have always had a strong ambivalence towards regulation. From a strict neoclassical economic standpoint, one that underpins the philosophy of free trade, regulation, and particularly social regulation should be viewed warily. Regulation always has the possibility of 'regulatory capture' (Kolko, 1963, 1965; Stigler, 1975). Regulatory capture is one form of 'rent-seeking behaviour' that clouds the ostensibly social goals of regulation. Powerful corporate actors influence government to design a regulatory framework that suits their own agenda to keep out competitors. For Stigler (1975), rules that appear concerned with protecting the consumer, the environment, or the safety of workers are really a disguise for market control, since their primary purpose is to form barriers to market. (See also the discussion in Trebilock and Howse, 1999, pp. 500–22). The same argument is made against powerful states that push for social clauses to be inserted into the rules of trade. Here again the powerful are bending the rules of the market to protect their own self-interest. In both the national and international arena, regulation advantages the powerful to the detriment of the powerless (see Baumol and Blinder, 1988, pp. 380–406; International Monetary Fund, 2002; Trebilock and Howse, 1999, pp. 441–63; Block, Roberts, Ozeki and Roomkin, 2001). Access to the market must be protected against special pleading and regulation assessed by its impact on competition. From such a viewpoint, disasters are risky in that they threaten to divert enthusiasm from economic reforms that, in the long term, will create the greatest good for the greatest number. Any regulatory change may place long-term benefits in jeopardy. The best-case scenario for optimistic hyperglobalists, then, is where the disaster does not detract attention from the benefits of free trade. Economic values are those that allow human values to flourish. As development proceeds, safety will improve, but through the working of the market and economic growth, not through regulatory intervention.

In many senses the expectations from the 'sceptical' view of globalization would mirror the pessimistic globalists, namely that the capital of the powerful would prevail. The key difference would be in the international as opposed to the global nature of the reasons why capital would be expected to prevail. Western economic interests (as opposed to those of the 'core') would be well represented in any reform. Success would be achieved by holding states of the global north accountable for the abusive business practices of their companies, particularly where those practices affected the global south.

Research expectations from the transformalist thesis are clearly more complex. The modernization thesis at the heart of this view would suggest several interrelated hypotheses. Certainly, the expectation might arise that the response to Kader would be informed by a global resource base. Regulatory reform could draw from global expertise as an example of what Giddens (1990) has termed 'global rationalism': the increasing global quality of rule-making systems (see also Haines, 2000). Secondly, global systems, including but not restricted to markets, would penetrate national boundaries to which the state would respond to re-establish its sovereignty. This re-establishment of sovereignty would take one of two forms: either alignment with global forces (including, for example, the adoption of key regulatory standards and codes) so as to benefit from them, or a rejection of them so as to reassert sovereignty and legitimacy. The response would encompass not only politicians and bureaucrats but also an increasing array of non-governmental actors seeking to institutionalize their values. Finally, the range of positive outcomes would be quite diverse since the literature is broad. To an extent, positive outcomes might well be described as some sort of 'third way' of a new means of bridging the disparate needs of a country to both attract capital and treat workers well. The substance of this, though, may well vary from place to place.

Juxtaposing the aftermath of Kader with current debates on globalization in order to explore the diverse expectations outlined above promises a rich study. Kader, acting as an instrumental case study (Stake, 1998) could link together the broader dynamics within globalization with the grounded realities of the aftermath of the disaster. However, there is a critical weakness in combining macro-sociological debates on the nature of globalization with micro-processes of safety reform following disaster. In particular, such a study could well fall foul of a confusion of levels (Mills, 1963) where macroscopic level dynamics are assumed to have a direct, unmediated impact on day-to-day decision making. What may appear to result from global transformations may instead result from more mundane considerations. In short, too much might be asked from research and consequently little of value gained.

Industrial Disasters and Regulatory Reform

To overcome this problem of a 'confusion of levels', an analytical framework is needed, separate from that of globalization, more attuned to dealing with the grounded realities of disasters and their regulatory aftermath. Disasters have long been associated with close-grained analyses of what went wrong, and how to prevent future occurrence (Reason, 1997). As Weber ([1948] 1991, p. 220) commented, the reality of human tragedy makes a mockery of rules, and at their base regulations are rules (Teubner, 1998a). Post-disaster enquiries are most often concerned with immediate causes of a disaster, and with preventative (that is, regulatory) solutions (Paterson, 2000). In contrast to the macroscopic debates analysing the connection between globalization and disasters, the literature on how to frame regulations to reduce the number and impact of disasters tends to be microscopic – a concern with immediate weaknesses and errors. Reduction of identifiable risks is seen as paramount, whilst general debates about the impact of broader socio-economic factors fades in importance (see, for example, Reason, 1997, pp 15-18).

Yet clearly, post-disaster reform takes place within a charged political environment. In the aftermath of disasters a 'regulatory crisis' can be precipitated (Hancher and Moran, 1998). Human and other resources are brought to bear on a particular problem to ensure this 'does not happen again' and a regulatory solution ensues. Sociologists of disasters have noted that in the case of disasters (including industrial ones) public reaction tends to be 'prosocial', in contrast to the devastation caused by riot and civil unrest, adding to the possibility of positive reform (Quarantelli, 1993).

The paradigmatic case is perhaps the Triangle Shirtwaist factory fire in New York in 1911. Before Kader this had the dubious honour of being the largest factory fire in recorded industrial history. It was also one that changed the regulatory landscape in the US. Despite, or perhaps because of, their awfulness, disasters can spur progress. In the case of the Triangle fire, the public moral outrage spurred government reform in the form of regulatory change (McCluskey, 1998). Many governmental initiatives in the US concerned with fire prevention and health and safety can be traced to this one event. Further, non-government technical organizations, such as the National Fire Prevention Association (NFPA), grew out of the event, providing much-needed technical expertise to prevent future industrial fires.

However, a progressive response to industrial disasters is not inevitable. Economic and political realities can block regulatory change, change that would lessen the risk of future disasters (Curran, 1993). In order for change to occur, disasters need to be seen as a social problem by those in a position to change the regulatory framework. Whilst sociologists of disasters have long argued that disasters are rooted in the social structure (Quarantelli, 1995), there must be 'openness' within that structure to change how hazards are viewed and risks reduced. Part of this may well involve political protest as the Triangle case itself demonstrated (Symonds, 1997; McCluskey, 1998).

It is also not safe to assume, then, that reform following disasters will be effective. Indeed, as we have seen above, a neoclassical economic perspective can see regulation itself, not the market, as the danger (Stigler, 1975). For such commentators, it is the experience of market failure – disasters included – that will spur greater awareness of risk so that employers, workers and consumers will mould their choices so as to reduce the risk of recurrence. Market failure has an important educational role (Haines and Sutton, 2003).

In the case of disasters such as Kader, this perspective is hard to justify. For many, this view is not only naïve, but immoral, as it ignores the suffering of the weakest members of society, those with little choice but to work in substandard conditions. Surely, disasters such as Kader are a graphic example of why market failure should be seen as a reason to regulate? Further, the devastation at Kader was easily avoided; the reason loss of life was so great was because simple strategies, such as clutter-free fire exits, did not exist. Even if over-regulation and market distortion are possible, there must be a way to ensure that basic safety standards exist.

It is in this gap between the political desire to gain the benefit of the dynamic competitive market and the appeasement of the public demand for safety and certainty, that the appetite for regulation and regulatory reform has grown (Haines and Sutton, 2003). Regulatory scholarship has developed in concert to provide relevant expertise on the most efficient and effective form that regulation and regulatory enforcement should take. The challenge for regulatory scholarship is well defined: design a regulatory framework that can obviate the need for market failure, whilst retaining the dynamism of the market. In the pursuit of their goal, regulatory theorists have ventured beyond traditional 'command and control' punitive regulatory forms deemed necessary by pessimistic hyperglobalists as an indication of progress (Ayres and Braithwaite, 1992; Grabosky, 1994a, 1994b; Gunningham and Grabosky, 1998). Such a view, they argue, is both too narrow (i.e., it does not take account of the creative use of the market to regulate in the majority of cases) and does not account for the overall development of societies as they reap the benefits of economic reform and free trade.

Regulatory theorists argue that regulatory techniques, if designed correctly, can be the vehicle by which the public good and private interest can be combined (Burk, 1988). The market can and does regulate, and can be encouraged to do so by third parties seeking to influence social outcomes of business behaviour. In the hands of skilled policy makers, the deficiencies of the market can be deftly healed through a plethora of regulatory techniques from meta-risk management (the regulation of self-regulation by companies) to pyramidal enforcement strategies based on trust and assurance (see, for example, Ayres and Braithwaite, 1992; Gunningham and Grabosky, 1998; Baldwin and Cave, 1999). In short, the market can regulate well. Its inherent creativity and dynamism can often reduce risk in a manner that is unimaginable to the regulatory authority, and hence beyond prescriptive purview (Grabosky, 1994a, 1994b). Other private actors as well as third parties, including consumers, insurers and banks, can stimulate the creativity of companies towards overall risk reduction and regulatory improvement.

The view of globalization within this analysis is primarily optimistic. Globalization is transformative. The interconnectedness of various societies means that the dispersal of 'best practice' is more easily assured, prompted by the demands of various non-governmental organizations (NGOs) (Braithwaite and Drahos, 2000). As noted above, there is, largely, congruence between the aims of regulatory scholars and proponents of market reform. Indeed, some of the most creative work in the area has come from scholarship aimed at devising regulatory measures that ensure a competitive market (for example, the work of John Braithwaite; see for example Ayres and Braithwaite, 1992, pp. 15–16). This pragmatic approach of some of the regulatory literature has seen the ideas of regulatory scholars considered as ideally suited to the new globalized environment. The dynamics of the market can regulate in a similar manner to that within a state. As trade becomes global in its orientation, so too can regulation.

Not surprisingly, work in this area has emphasized the possibilities of self-regulation with consumer oversight, and in particular the value of codes of conduct. Examples here include the work of Fung, O'Rourke and Sabel (2001) on Realizing Labour Standards, Gunningham and Grabosky (1998) on Responsible Care, and Meidinger (2002) on Forest Stewardship. Analyses of labour standards focus on differing forms of codes of corporate conduct, essentially forms of self-regulation, where consumers, unions, NGOs or auditing firms take on the oversight role previously afforded by the state (see Diller, 1999). Such regulatory techniques emphasize the importance of understanding market relationships in order to extend control. Under the concept of 'chains of responsibility', the regulators demand that the major partner in any industry has responsibility for the safety and wellbeing of others in the contracting chain (Haines, 1997; Haines and Sutton, 2003). State oversight and monitoring of each company is reduced by transferring responsibility to the dominant market player. In conceptualizing good regulatory techniques in this way, regulatory theory resonates with hyperglobalist views of the transformation of markets in a move away from state control towards markets that are constructed around core and peripheral elements. Good regulation is that which can encourage the core to take care of the periphery.

This resonance of regulatory theory with hyperglobalism can mean that solutions are stripped of political content since the concern is on finding solutions, of rising above politics. This emphasis of regulatory theory on efficient and effective techniques tends to gloss over the very real influence politics has on regulatory reform (Hancher and Moran, 1998; Reichman, 1998; Haines, 1999), what techniques are acceded to and the reasons that lie behind adoption or lack of adoption. Regulatory theory's foray into the global arena provides a useful example of how proposed techniques, rather than being neutral, have the potential to bolster the prevailing political order or conceptions of the public good. Corporate codes of conduct and consumer oversight of market behaviour have been cited by regulatory theorists as holding considerable promise for the improvement of corporate behaviour globally (Grabosky, 1994a, 1994b; Braithwaite and Drahos, 2000; Fung, O'Rourke and Sabel, 2001). For Fung, O'Rourke and Sabel (2001), such codes are seen as the first step in a 'ratcheting up' process at work within labour standards regulation. To a greater or lesser extent these codes see the state as relatively powerless, with little influence either to promote safety standards, or to stymie them. However, the potential for codes to be effective when independent from a strong state regime is yet to be proven. Research in Australia suggests that voluntary codes work best as an adjunct to, but not a replacement of, traditional forms of government regulation (Gunningham and Johnstone, 1999). Yet, they are being promoted as a useful technique in the industrializing world as a method of improving behaviour in the absence of a strong state-based regime. There is little evidence to date of the effectiveness of this strategy; self-regulation enforced by non-state actors has yet to prove its credentials. Indeed, many reports suggest considerable problems with compliance with codes of conduct by multi-national corporations (MNCs) (Diller, 1999; Murray 2001a).

Further, these calls for a greater role of MNCs in their own regulation through application of various codes of conduct, together with a variety of 'overseers', have tended to see the international sphere as 'empty' of regulatory influence (Murray, 2001b). As Murray points out, the regulation of working standards was amongst the first to have had a presence in the international arena, most prominently through the vehicle of the International Labour Organisation (ILO). There is a tendency in those advocating novel regulatory forms (such as company codes or mechanisms for 'ratcheting up' regulatory standards) to downplay or even ignore the work of the ILO (but see Braithwaite and Drahos, 2000). In doing so there is the possibility of letting go previous hard-won gains. Whilst there are clear problems with the ILO, not the least of which is bureaucratic inertia and lack of accountability by those nations ratifying various conventions (Cooney, 2000), there are clear lines of representation and a rich history from which to learn. Central to the ILO paradigm, however, is the necessity for the nation state to be at the centre of any regulatory framework.

Because of this paucity of political analysis there is then a mixed potential for regulatory theory to provide insightful analysis of the reasons behind and effectiveness of regulatory reform following the Kader fire. Certainly, there would be a demand on behalf of these theorists for any analysis to go beyond an analysis of command and control regulatory forms. Also, such analysis would expect accelerated learning and uptake of solutions from other parts of the globe to be evident in the aftermath of disasters in rapidly industrializing contexts. However, such theorizing is largely silent on why certain regulatory forms might be taken up, and what might be effective in a given economic and political context.

Studies of regulatory reform, in contrast, tend to emphasize the political nature of regulation in general and reform in particular (Curran, 1993; Haines, 1997; Reichman, 1998; Paterson, 2000). This political quality of reform is particularly prevalent in the context of disaster. There are two aspects to the importance of political concerns: namely the role politics play in engendering momentum for reform, and secondly, the political elements that lead to adoption of one set of reforms as opposed to another. Dan Curran's (1993) work, for example, emphasizes the importance of the former in understanding reform. His work argues that both an economic and a political logic direct reform progress. Reform requires both a scarcity of labour supply coupled with industry dependence on a given source of skilled labour, and secondly a strong union committed to safety reform.

More recent work, however, complicates drawing unequivocal conclusions as to what constitutes effective reform. Despite the apparent solid foundation for reform generated by the intense scrutiny after disaster, reform that does occur may not equal progress. Paterson (2000), in his analysis of the impact of successive disasters on regulation of the offshore industry in the North Sea, illustrates how political demand for reforms following one disaster can overcompensate for problems uncovered in post-disaster inquiries. Inquiries following subsequent catastrophic events implicate this overcompensation as critical to failure. Typical to this overcompensation is the pendulum that swings between detailed prescriptive rules and general rules. Part of the reason for the failure of reforms may lie in incompatible views of what constitutes necessary change. Reforms can reflect the competing interests of law, politics and economic actors as they struggle to exert regulatory authority (Reichman, 1998; Haines and Sutton, 2003). Further, there may be miscommunication between different systems (i.e., legal, political and economic) as to the purpose of new regulations. Each system then re-scripts the regulation to suit their underlying world-view (Teubner, 1998a; Paterson, 2000). Regulatory techniques brought to life after industrial disasters are not exclusively tools for the reduction of risk and harm as conceived of by pragmatic approaches to regulatory scholarship. Rather, the evidence from reform studies suggests that they are political or bureaucratic manoeuvres aimed to entrench particular worldviews.

Reform and the Specific Contribution of Place

Whilst these studies of regulatory reform cited above point to the centrality of politics to reform, appreciation of the unique contribution of place to regulation and its reform still tends to be in its infancy. International comparative studies, for example, often compare one regulatory form with another to identify successful forms of regulatory regime (see, for example, Gunningham, 1991; Gunningham and Grabosky, 1998), which once identified can be promoted internationally. Where context is included, it tends to be in the form of generic variables, such as the mix of small or large companies, or the form competition takes within a market (Gunningham, 1991). Differences in regulatory styles between the US and Japan are a good example here, with the negotiated consensus model of Japan contrasted with the legalistic orientation of the US (Aoki and Cioffi, 1999; Kagan, 2000; Kitamura, 2000). Here, a primary concern for many scholars is to ascertain the most successful form of regulation and hence encourage its general application.

Within studies of regulatory reform a related process takes place. Here, rather than identify 'good examples', the aim is to develop meta-theories – overarching paradigms that also can be used to evaluate outcomes, irrespective of context. Curran's (1993) work, for example, points to a structuralist Marxist paradigm, whilst Paterson and Tuebner's work directs attention towards systems theory and its explanatory power as a catalyst for juridification.

There remains the possibility, however, that context is critical to understanding both how reform occurs, and how effective is its outcome. Certainly, the importance of an intrinsic appreciation of a given setting is supported by an alternative stream of writing (e.g. Bierne, 1983). The work of Nelken (1994) has extended this need to take account of place to the area of regulation. Nelken (1994) argues that culture plays a critical role in evaluating the worth of regulatory techniques aimed at controlling corporate conduct. He contrasts the prescriptive punitive regime of Italy in the case of corporate harms with the compliant, self-regulatory orientation of the UK. In contrast to other commentators, Nelken asserts that the value in such analyses is not so much to enable an evaluation of 'good' and 'bad' regulatory practice, but rather to develop an appreciation of how regulatory frameworks intersect with particular economic, political and cultural contexts. Caution thus needs to be exhibited in evaluative assessments of the 'worth' of the two regimes. In this case, 'best practice' is better thought of as 'appropriate' practice. It is possible to argue, for example, that the punitive regime in Italy is better suited to combat financial misdealing, and the persuasive regime more suited to the UK. Different national settings produce differing regulatory regimes because of their different legal and cultural framework, and any evaluation of these regimes must appreciate how these regimes work within the local context, either to promote compliance or, in some cases, to provide the means for continuing non-compliance (Nelken, 1994, pp. 229–39).

This caution would be supported by those who see real problems in so-called 'legal transplants' – the taking of a form of law from one context and enacting it within another (Kahn-Freund, 1974; Teubner, 1998b; Cooney, Lindsey, Mitchell and Zhu, 2002). Bold assertions by analysts of the need for regulatory reform to follow 'best practice' are, in a different setting, viewed by them as yet another experiment in 'legal transplantation'. Given historical precedent, such transplants stand a good chance of being ineffective. For commentators such as Kahn-Freund (1974), success or rejection of a legal transplant rests on the similarity between the political systems of the donor and the recipient. Greater similarities between the two political systems are more likely to result in a successful transplant.

For many Asian nations, the phenomenon of, and problems with, legal transplantation are familiar, since much law in the East Asian region is based on the law of the colonizers. The gaps that arise between the letter of the law imposed by the colonizers and the local everyday practice are diverse (Harding, 2001). Change can and does occur, but the nature of that change and its relationship to improvement intended by law reformers is less clear. Both normative orientation and legal structures need to be brought to centre stage. Tanase's (2001) analysis of Japan is instructive here. He argues that the modern framing of the Japanese law and the legal rights enshrined within it sit somewhat uneasily with the traditional sense of morality of Japanese citizens (but see also Nottage, 2001). Importantly, Tanase is not arguing that nothing has changed, but that it is much more gradual, generational and dependent on pre-existing norms and values than reformers often suggest.

Clearly, the role and interests of the state in law reform must also be recognized. Law reform, for example, may result from 'palace wars' – the need to gain or entrench political power (Dezalay and Garth, 2001) – as much as from any intention to improve a given situation or modernize. Thus, the aim of any reform may be as much a political aim rather than an instrumental one, and the impact on everyday behaviour limited. Cooney *et al.* (2002) argue that differing conceptions of the role of the state and the purpose of law within the region further complicate the success of any transplants. In particular, the same authors point to law in Asia as being seen as an instrument of the state, not a means to protect the individual from state abuse. They emphasize the different methods by which this is achieved. In particular, they point to repressive laws where the will of those in power is imposed forcefully on the individual, versus legal frameworks that exert power through invoking corporatist forms of control. Business and nominated labour groups are brought under the aegis of the state in the development of laws and policies 'in the national interest'. Creation and reformation of law is premised on the need for regime stability. The repression of independent unions is an oft-cited example where a particular government will invoke the need to maintain 'political stability'. The problems associated with regulatory reform within a Western industrialized context are thus compounded within a non-Western industrializing context. Cooney and Mitchell (2002), extrapolating from Teubner (1998b), argue that legal reform in these cases should be viewed more in the vein of 'legal irritant'. In their analysis, the system communication failures familiar within a Western context are exacerbated within an Asian setting. An investigation of the content of law reform following disaster needs to be associated with an assessment of the nature of the 'gap' between the law and actual government and business practice. Such a gap may well take on a radically different contour than that experienced within a Western industrialized context. As Cooney and Mitchell (2002, p. 267) state, 'The impact of regulatory interventions in the field of labour law [within Asia] is likely to be considerably less predictable than in Western countries (and of course they are already unpredictable there).' In short, they argue, the burgeoning literature on regulation must become more sensitive to context if useful conclusions are to be drawn about the relevance of its insights to a non-Western setting.

Conclusion

The enormous size of the task of adequately accounting for reform following the Kader fire should now be clear. There are critical elements that must be taken account of, from literature on both globalization and regulation and its reform. Globalization brings with it several analytical challenges: assessing the impact of economic reform aimed at creating a global market based on 'free trade', as well as the degree to which international regulatory regimes (or 'global rationalism' to use Giddens' (1990) phrase) shape regulatory reform. More recently, this literature highlights the importance of sovereignty, specifically how concerns about national sovereignty influence national responses to global overtures and strictures. Yet, to avoid Mill's (1993) 'confusion of levels' literature, this chapter has argued that debates emanating from the globalization literature need complementary approaches more attuned to local context. Such approaches can be used both to assess changes that do occur in the wake of disaster as well as to help identify local factors that influence the reform process. Pragmatic regulatory scholarship provides a way forward in evaluating change, with a loud call that any assessment must go beyond 'command and control' regulatory forms to take account of the way the market can itself be made to regulate to produce safe outcomes.

A focus on normative solutions provides little, however, with which to understand the dynamic of change. Here, regulation and regulatory reform needs to be appreciated as an interaction between law, regulation and context, not simply a process of scientific identification of useful techniques and their implementation of a given legal framework. Literature that does address change specifically points to the centrality of 'regulatory crises' (Hancher and Moran, 1998, p. 160), crises that are quintessentially political in nature. Political and ideological pressures are not only involved with engendering reform, but also shaping the 'appropriate' response. Further, techniques and regulatory methods may be suited to a particular cultural context and not readily transferable. Certainly, the pitfalls of simply mapping regulatory change and from that assuming some sort of behaviour change are well illustrated by the rich history of socio-legal studies tracing the problems of 'legal transplantation'.

Chapter 3

Regulatory Character

The challenge for this study is to conceptualize the regulatory context in a meaningful way, one that can answer Nelken's challenge of recognizing the uniqueness of context and its specific interaction with regulatory frameworks. Certainly, the importance of this is highlighted in a study of Kader, since the context of Bangkok – Thailand – is not one heavily drawn upon by regulatory theorists. In evaluating the worth of regulatory reform in Thailand, the challenge for this chapter is twofold. Firstly, to develop a means by which regulatory theory itself can be sensitized to context, and secondly, to apply this method to understanding the uniqueness of the Thai environment so that this can be taken into account when understanding the response to Kader. Finally, however, the means to characterize regulatory context must not come at the expense of sensitivity to global change and its impact. This chapter argues that using 'regulatory character' as a conceptual framework to understand the impact of context on reform provides a way forward.

Regulatory Context and Culture

Making regulatory theory responsive to local context might usefully begin with a cultural analysis, where culture is understood as a conceptual framework of ideas, beliefs and values that interpret both the significance of events and how they are properly responded to (Geertz and Geertz, 1975). A cultural approach brings to the fore the way significance is attached to particular events, as well as what reform might be seen as legitimate, and what might be seen imposed and foreign. Cultural analyses are not new to regulation (see Haines, 1997), with Hood's (1998) work, *The Art of the State*, arguably the most comprehensive attempt to deal with the influence of culture on regulatory context and as such a useful starting point. *The Art of the State* draws on Mary Douglas' cultural theory adapted to suit the public management environment. The book argues that administrative contexts, similar to groups or communities, can be categorized according to the dimensions of 'grid' and 'group'. The grid dimension captures the extent to which public management is conducted according to well-understood general rules. The group dimension refers to the extent to which public management involves coherent collectivities institutionally differentiated from other spheres of society (Hood, 1998, p. 9). Administrative contexts thus can be assigned to one of four types: hierarchist, fatalist, egalitarian or individualist (see Table 3.1 below). Hierarchist administrative styles are high on both grid and group dimensions, having a socially cohesive, rule-bound approach to organization. Fatalists are low on co-operation yet retain a rule-bound approach, thus are low on the group dimension but high on the grid dimension. Egalitarians invest in participation and thus are high on the group dimension; their adherence to a rule-bound approach, though, is low and so are considered low on the grid dimension. Finally, individualists are low on both group and grid dimensions, with an atomized approach to organization and outcomes not determined by rules, but by negotiation and bargaining.

Table 3.1   **Hood's (1998) four styles of public management organization: cultural theory applied**

Grid	Group	
	Low	High
High	*The Fatalist Way* Low-co-operation, rule-bound approaches to organization. *Example*: Atomized societies sunk in rigid routines (Banfield, 1958).	*The Hierarchist Way* Socially cohesive, rule-bound approaches to organization. *Example*: Stereotype military structures (Dixon, 1976).
Low	*The Individualist Way* Atomized approaches to organization stressing negotiation and bargaining. *Example*: Chicago-school doctrines of 'government by the market' (Self, 1993) and their antecedents.	*The Egalitarian Way* High-participation structures in which every decision is 'up for grabs'. *Example*: 'Dark green' doctrines of alternatives to conventional bureaucracy (Goodin, 1992).

Source: Table 1.1 (p. 9) from *The Art of the State: Culture, Rhetoric and Public Management* by Christopher Hood (1998). Free permission from Oxford University Press (www.oup.com).

Throughout his analysis, Hood (1998) adapts cultural theory in ways central to the regulatory context. He demonstrates, for example, the way in which the four approaches differ in their interpretation of public management disasters, both in terms of assessing causes and prescribing solutions. In the face of disaster, hierarchists point to lack of planning and procedure, whilst fatalists emphasize the fickle finger of fate, individualists emphasize the lack of incentive structures, and egalitarians the way the power structure worked to hide latent problems (Hood 1998, p. 26). Each approach also has favoured responses, from tightening procedures and processes (hierarchist), the ad hoc responses of the fatalist, the public accountability mechanisms of the individualist, and finally policies to increase participation and encouragement of whistleblowers (egalitarian). Those familiar with industrial disaster scholarship will find much that resonates with that literature. Equally as important, though, in Hood's analysis of how each type has inherent weaknesses, are some that can engender future public management crises (Hood, 1998, p. 28). The analysis questions the linear 'progressiveness' inherent within much regulatory literature, instead pointing to the way approaches are (re)discovered anew.

Hood's (1998) work can also be extended to explore regulatory change within a given cultural framework. Regulatory change following disasters would be expected to follow a given cultural understanding of the safety problems that led to the disaster. So, a hierarchist culture might be expected to develop greater specificity in regulatory requirements; a fatalist response would see tokenistic change; an individualist culture would emphasize the need for punitive enforcement mechanisms aimed at promoting individual responsibility, and an egalitarian response would argue for greater tripartite access.

As appealing as the notion of culture is to regulatory scholarship, there is a strong antipathy by scholars, particularly in the field of Asian studies, against the use of a cultural analysis (see for example Keesing, 1991; Hewison, 2001; Lindsey and Dick, 2001), with the blunt warning of Roger Keesing (1991, p. 50) that 'Cultural explanations too often are non-explanations or seductive disguises.' For this reason, their concerns must be looked at in some detail to ascertain whether Hood's (1998) analysis remains useful for an analysis of Kader, or whether some modification is required. Further, for our purposes, the introduction of cultural theory analysis must not disregard the complexity and dynamism necessary for an interactional understanding of regulatory change and regulatory effectiveness. That is, it must be able to help explain not only stability, but change. Further, it must explain the 'law–practice' gap – that is the relationship between formal law and actual behaviour – and not assume that law arises in evolutionary fashion from underlying norms.

There are several elements to the critique of scholars of Asian law against a cultural approach. A first concern is the way a cultural analysis is used as a short cut to explaining different outcomes. Lindsey (2002, p. 1), for example, argues that for too many commentators culture has become 'a grab bag of everything the foreign law reformers do not know or are unable to find out about the target jurisdiction' (Lindsey, 2002, p. 1). It is a convenient tool for 'orientalizing' behaviour in lieu of developing a sustained analysis. Rational strategic reasons for behaviour are ignored, and in its place the 'black box' of culture is imposed. In this way, culture becomes an explanation for irrationality. This provokes an equally unhelpful response by elites within some Asian nations of the superiority of so-called 'Asian values' that results in a form of reverse cultural imperialism used as a political weapon to deflect criticism both of occidental and internal kinds (Lindsey, 2002). Overall, these debates tend to reify culture as unitary and consensual, where in fact there may be a considerable diversity of values and positions within societies concerning core values and beliefs. Culture is also seen as static, separated, closed and self-referential that denies the reality of cultural change, plain to most serious analyses (Keesing, 1991; Lindsey, 2001). Finally, a cultural analysis can simply gloss over economic realities. A focus on culture can merely become a focus on superstructural elements of society, ignoring the more important economic and class drivers of change (Hewison, 1989; 2001; Hutchison and Brown, 2001; Williams, 2002). This final critique can be extended to criticisms that see in a cultural analysis a justification for ignoring the real catalysts of local change, those that reside in the economic and political realities of a particular place or system (Keesing, 1991; Wallerstein, 1995, pp. 162–75).

The dangers, then, revolve around two axes. Firstly, cultural analyses tend to both unify and essentialize notions of culture, which then allows the writer to orientalize behaviour as foreign and irrational. Secondly, cultural analyses tend to ignore or downplay the importance of economic and related political drivers of change.

Both these criticisms of cultural analyses also resonate with regulatory scholarship. The first concern of essentialism and consensus would be shared by many writers within the regulation field who point to the conflict in values within the regulatory sphere (Teubner, 1998a; Paterson, 2000; Haines and Gurney, 2003). Downplaying the importance of economic and related political drivers of change would similarly resonate with many writers (Pearce and Tombs, 1990; Curran, 1993; Hopkins, 1995; Haines, 1997). However, ignoring cultural influences also has problems, since it may lead to analyses that ignore the importance of subjective meaning and interpretive norms that influence what authorities and individuals consider should be done to ameliorate harm. How individuals and groups make sense of the world has a material effect on the shape, meaning and effectiveness of systems of authority and law (Poggi, 1990; Selznick, 1992; Cotterrell, 1998, 2001; Sewell, 2002). Maps of cultural meaning significantly influence the importance and value placed on events, and understanding cultural norms allows insight into 'how things are done around here' (Haines, 1997). In light of this, the alternative hypothesis that culture is merely epiphenomenal, a direct product of contemporary economic and political circumstance alone, seems equally problematic.

Dealing with Criticisms of a Cultural Analysis 1: Unity and Essentialism

Nonetheless, the criticisms must be addressed. Perhaps the easiest aspect to dispense with is the problem of 'orientalizing' behaviour. Clearly, attempting any sort of cultural analysis, especially of countries other than one's own, is hazardous. However, the strength of Hood's (1998) approach and of cultural theory in general is that it does not see culture as 'out there', but intrinsically bound up with how all societies make meaning of their environment. Indeed, both Christopher Hood and Mary Douglas see cultural ordering as a feature of all societies, not peculiar to 'other places'. Christopher Hood's (1998) book specifically is concerned with the use of cultural analysis to reform within Western developed contexts. Mary Douglas herself has written extensively on the importance of cultural understanding of risk to the practice of regulation in the West (Douglas, 1992), not only the relevance of cultural analyses to explain behaviour in 'other peoples'. Culture and the norms guiding culture affect us all.

A related concern, that cultural analyses divide the world into 'rational' and 'irrational' (read 'cultural') responses can also be addressed within a cultural theory framework. The ubiquitous influence of cultural values on regulatory frameworks brings the 'irrationality' of all systems of regulation to centre stage when viewed from a competing paradigm. Where, to be rational, means to behave according to carefully thought through means (e.g., punish/persuade) to some mutually agreed upon goal (to be safe), much regulatory behaviour in the industrialized West might well be viewed as irrational (Beck, 1995). Hood (1998) illustrates well in his book that the perceived need to regulate and the method by which it is institutionalized has more to do with political perceptions of danger than with an accurate or objective calibration of risk. This does not make such regulation irrational.

Cultural theory goes further than this, however, and argues that it is important – and not simply reductionism or poor scholarship – to view culture as creating dichotomies of 'order' and 'disorder'. Mary Douglas (1966) argues that a central element of culture is the way a given society understands order and place, belonging and not belonging. Cultural norms 'resolve' both complexity and dissonance by assigning roles, positions and 'proper' places. Dissonance may still exist, but a cultural frame allows for members of a society to continue to function despite the inevitability of events that challenge the norms of cultural order. Importantly, however, cultural theory does not assign intrinsic value to one set of cultural values over another but allows for an insight into the complexity of possible 'rational' responses to events, namely through the four 'master categories' of order/disorder (hierarchism, fatalism, individualism and egalitarianism). Each of these master categories can be broken down or 'stretched' further into subcategories (using the same dimensions of group and grid), should the need arise (Hood, 1998, p. 20).

Cultural theory, then, can address Asian legal scholars' concerns around the use of the concept of culture as a tool to 'orientalize' behaviour. Nonetheless, problems of essentialism remain. These problems are threefold. Firstly, the ability of a cultural theory approach to cope with both complexity and dynamism, as well as stability, within a regulatory context still is not clear; secondly, there needs to be an appreciation of the complexity of what constitutes rationality (and thus the potential incommensurability of cultural theoretical forms) that underlies the insights of systems theory; and thirdly, the need to incorporate the insights of socio-legal studies and their appreciation of the 'law–practice gap'. Each of these will be taken in turn, before turning to the final challenge of accounting for the importance of economic factors in determining regulatory forms.

The first problem, of accounting for complexity, is dealt with to an extent within cultural theory. However, the way in which complexity is accommodated tends to undermine the capacity of the theory to explain dynamism and change. In terms of complexity, Hood refers to the 'stretchability' of cultural theory; namely the way it can be subdivided further and further, using the same dimensions of grid and group, until a suitable level of analysis is reached (Hood, 1998, p. 20). In terms of dynamism, the analysis is less specific save for observations that public management gurus tend to underestimate the problems in 'new' styles as well as an observation that that the longer a particular master trope has held sway, the more vehement the eventual move in an opposite direction (pp. 189–92). However, it may well be that the real problem is dealing with complexity and dynamism as separate issues, rather than a single concern. This is because the categorical analysis that lies at the heart of a cultural theory approach depends upon further sub-categorical analyses in order to 'fix' the right level of specificity and accuracy that quickly can descend into a focus on the minute detail. In this process, dynamism is sacrificed.

This problem is overcome if cultural theory is seen as an ideal-typical (rather than categorical) form of analysis. Ideal types differ from categories in two important ways. Firstly, an ideal type is the description of an idealized form, one never found in its full splendour, but one with sufficient gravity that it can encapsulate the dynamic within a given setting (Weber, [1948] 1991, pp. 323–4). That is, an ideal type gives a sense of the vector (i.e. movement in a given direction) or gravitational pull within a given social setting, but will not explain all its various complex elements at any one point in time. An ideal type then is suited to explaining both dynamism and change. Complexity can be accommodated, however Weber went to considerable lengths in his comparative studies to explore the ways in which within a given setting data diverged from an ideal type (Weber, [1947] 1964, pp. 109–12, and see, for example, Weber, [1922] 1993, pp. 28–31). Nonetheless, the description of specific examples did not come at the expense of exploring the underlying gravitational pull of a dominant ideal type within a given setting. Further, complexity could arise from the way in which competing ideal types were found in a particular context. This often led to tension, and with tension the potential for fluidity and change.

Secondly, a Weberian understanding of rationality can also help explain the tension within a given regulatory setting and the interaction between individual and institutionalized explanations and expectations. Cultural theory, as outlined by Hood (1998), does not explore in any particular depth the way rationality can take different forms (not just adhere to different values or result in different approaches). Critical to regulation is the tension between three forms: means/end rationality or instrumental rationality, value or substantive rationality, and formal or legal rationality. The rationale underlying each is different, and with it, the justification for behaviour. Means/ends or instrumental rationality is legitimated by the end to be achieved; value or substantive rationality by invoking the need to adhere to the specific value itself; and formal or legal rationality by recourse to the law, that is, it is right if it is sanctioned by law. Each of these is 'rational' and behaviour can be predicted once the rationale is understood. However, there is considerable antipathy between each form, whilst at the same time some (such as formal rationality) lend themselves more easily to an institutionalized framework. For this reason, substantive rationality, over time, becomes institutionalized through rule-setting processes (or 'rationalization') that transform substantive justification into a formal rationality with its dependence on rules (Weber, [1948] 1993, p. 220; Giddens, 1995, pp. 40–50; Haines, 1999). This rationalization process, however, sees the purpose or value 'leeched out' and lost in an obsession with rules. Over time, the antipathy of substantive rationality towards formal approaches, seen as devoid of values or 'spirit', sets the scene for a charismatic break towards a more substantive appreciation of the central values of that society or community (Haines and Sutton, 2000).

What this suggests for Hood's (1998) work is that each cultural type holds within it a tension between the values of the particular ideal type and their institutionalization in a set of rules. The dynamism within regulation may be as much aimed at recapturing a particular value, rather than at changing values; the latter in Weber's view is a far more difficult proposition (Weber [1948] 1991, pp. 152–3). Protest may be as much aimed at 'recapturing' some notion of a past moral order, one that has been sullied by strategic political manoeuvrings, as it is at changing that order. Dynamism and change, then, may arise both from a change in values or the tension between values, as well as from the problems inherent within the institutionalization of a set of values within a legal framework and a demand to recapture the values of yore.

An excellent example of the value of this more comprehensive view of rationality which assists in the understanding of regulation and reform is Wendy Espeland's (1998) work *The Struggle for Water*. At the heart of this book is an exploration of the impact of a conflict of rationalities on policymaking. The book explored bureaucratic and political decision making with regard to increasing the access to water in the arid environment of Arizona. The preferred option to increase the water supply was to build a large dam, the Orme, at the confluence of two major rivers. Yet this would have meant flooding the traditional land of the Yavapai Native American people. Of interest here is how the conflict was resolved between the Yavapai, who protested against the dam, and 'old guard' civil engineers within the Bureau of Reclamation with a longstanding experience of dam building and who saw dam building as an honourable and desirable process. Despite a 'rational' analysis producing a solution that enabled both adequate water and saving the native land, neither Yavapai nor the 'old guard' engineers were happy. The new policy resulted through the efforts of a 'new guard' of environmental engineers within the Bureau of Reclamation, whose modus operandi was to perform instrumentally rational calculations that offset the environmental cost of the Orme Dam against the economic benefit. These calculations showed that a number of smaller, less-intrusive dams delivered the same water outcome and so were substituted for Orme, and appeared to be a classic 'win/win' outcome. On means/ends criteria, both Yavapai and the 'old guard' should have been happy: the Yavapai had saved their land, and the engineers had a cost-effective solution that delivered equal water outcomes. Yet neither party was content. The disappointment of the Yavapai appears most difficult to understand from an instrumental view of rationality, since they were victorious in their protest against the dam. From a value rational position, however, the source of their angst is clear. Their victory was premised upon a cost/benefit analysis, where the state placed a price on their attachment to their land (for them something of ultimate value), a calculation they found abhorrent. Land was not commensurable. The engineers' disappointment might have been instrumentally rational, except that the alternative plan provided identical, if not better, water supply outcomes. Again, their position can only be understood by way of their values, in this case the pioneering values associated with water reclamation. Espeland's study is a priceless example of the need for an understanding of not just objective outcomes, but an empathetic analysis that takes account of subjective meaning.

What is argued here, in light of the discussion above, is for an extension of Hood's (1998) work where an analysis of a given regulatory context, or 'regulatory character', would explore the ideal-typical cultural form or forms present. A key aspect of this exploration would be identification of the form(s) of rationality that infuse each ideal type, which can provide a way of understanding the regulatory dynamic in a given locale as well as the tensions between different ideal types present.

The dynamism of regulatory context might be enhanced further by use of the dimensions of group and grid as a means to explore, within a particular context, the interaction between social norms and formal laws (the interaction within the grid dimension) and the interaction between individuals and social norms as well as between individuals and formal laws (the interaction within the group dimension). Regulatory character is thus a series of interactions essential to understanding the generation of regulations and the nature of regulatory compliance. This is schematically outlined in Figure 3.1 (below)

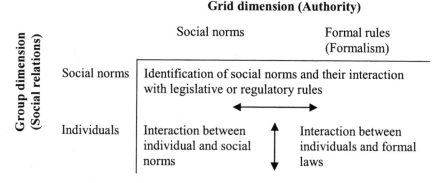

Figure 3.1   Dimensions of regulatory character

The use of the 'group' and 'grid' elements to explore dynamism and interaction – not simply as a means to categorize and differentiate one sub-group from another – makes sense from a Weberian perspective. The 'group' dimension of cultural theory as shown in Figure 3.1 captures an understanding that rationality encompasses two different levels of analysis, namely at the subjective or individual level, as well as at an institutionalized or objective level. Weber himself emphasized the importance of both a subjective (individual) and objective (institutionalized) rationality (Levine, 1985, pp. 152–62; Giddens, 1995, pp. 40–50) as separate, but interrelated levels. Weber's methodology emphasized the need for both a subjective as well as an objective understanding within a given context

(Weber, [1947] 1964, pp. 88–112). For regulatory character, this opens the analysis to the potential of exploring the interaction between the subjective rationality of the individual and the institutionalized rationality of organizations, both public and private. Rather than categorize a particular regulatory environment as 'high' or 'low' on the group dimension, the purpose of an ideal-typical analysis would be to understand both subjective (individual) and objective (institutional) dimensions of social or regulatory order, that is the interaction between individuals and social norms.

The 'law–practice gap' is central to the 'grid' dimension since it points to the tension and interrelationship between rules, norms and authority. However, as with the group element above, this axis also is not used in a categorical or sub-categorical manner (i.e. to denote a context as 'high' or 'low' in its use of norms and laws), but rather it is used to explore the means by which authority is legitimized, institutionalized and expressed. The purpose is to explore the *interrelationships* between individuals, norms and laws. There are two facets of this. The first is the way norms are related to formal rules. The second relationship is between individuals and formal rules, that is, how individuals use or do not use formal rules to achieve their goals. Clearly, this is central to the regulatory arena. Longstanding debates about 'deterrence' versus 'compliance' models (Reiss, 1984) or 'punish' and 'persuade' (Braithwaite, 1985) hold within them assumptions about the degree to which the written law stands as the primary source of authority – and should be used as a first resort – or whether the norms of reciprocation guide compliance behaviour. This points to different ways of exerting authority as understood by Weber in his analysis (Weber, [1947] 1964, pp. 328–63; Weber, 1971). A particular regulatory character may emphasize norms, with laws relegated to a secondary role (as in Weber's understanding of traditional authority), or regulatory character may emphasize rules or laws, where the written law designates what is permissible and has independent authority over individuals in positions of power. An emphasis on the former sees legitimation through recall of norms, the latter legitimation through invoking the law. In each case, however, there is both an interaction as well as a tension between norms and laws. Exploring regulatory character in this way provides a means to understand the nature of authority and the relationship between norms and the authority of law.

Finally, this sensitivity of regulatory character to rationality also brings with it possible insights into the regulatory reform or law-making process. This process, which Weber labelled rationalization, is essential to regulatory reform. Competing ideas of what reform 'should' occur (based on egalitarian, hierarchist, individualist or fatalist norms) must be translated into a regulatory framework. An understanding of the three relationships that form regulatory character, between individuals and social norms, social norms and formal rules and individuals and formal rules together with their rationality (in the Weberian sense) can assist in understanding how regulatory reform unfolds.

Dealing with Criticisms of a Cultural Analysis 2: Regulatory Character and Economic Context

Whilst Figure 3.1 provides a useful heuristic device with which to explore regulatory context, the analysis above still has not dealt with the major outstanding concern of critics of a cultural approach, namely the way cultural analyses tend to ignore or downplay economic and related political drivers of change. Even with the changes to cultural theory to suit a regulatory context outlined above, undertaking an analysis predicated on culture alone would simply reverse the bias of economic and political approaches. Where one argues that economics and politics explains all, the other responds that culture can do the same.

A possible resolution to this, without dispensing with culture altogether, is to combine an analysis of culture with an economic and political analysis in a 'characteristic', as opposed to cultural, analysis. The understanding of character is an extrapolation of Selznick's (1992) use of the term in understanding organizational behaviour. In his words, character as it relates to an organization is:

> ... a broader idea than culture. Culture is the symbolic expression of shared perception, valuation and belief ... The character of an organization includes its culture, but something more as well. A pattern of dependency – for example on a particular labour force, a market, or particular suppliers – may have little to do with symbolism or belief. The character of a company or trade union owes much to the structure of the industry, the skills of employees or members, the alliances that can be fashioned, and many other practical limits and opportunities. Attitudes and beliefs only account for a part of an organization's distinctive character. (Selznick, 1992, p. 321)

A characteristic analysis understands strategic, pragmatic responses to a given set of circumstances. Cultural norms themselves can be used as strategic resources. More critically, economic and political realities that constitute 'a pattern of dependency' are not ignored. But, it also does not preclude the possibility that economic and political strategies are in turn informed by cultural perceptions and values.

What I am suggesting is that a similar form of analysis that Selznick (1992) uses to understand organizational character can be applied to regulatory character. The limitations of culture are overcome by a focus on regulatory character, since within a characteristic analysis culture exists in relation to economic and political realities. Regulatory character particularly as it relates to industrial regulation, like Selznick's (1992) organizational character, is shaped by its dependencies on particular labour forces or markets. The nature of this dependency may differ, depending on the extent to which a particular market allows for the rules of competition to include regulatory considerations. As was outlined in *Corporate Regulation: Beyond Punish or Persuade* (Haines, 1997), critical differences in regulatory outcomes may relate not only to culture, but to the room a particular company has within a market both to comply with regulations and to remain profitable. In that earlier analysis, I explored how this explained the difference between small 'low status' companies reliant on contracts with other companies for their survival, and large 'high status' organizations with the capacity to dictate market rules (Haines, 1997, pp. 131–59). A characteristic analysis would then focus on economic and political demands facing a particular regulatory context alongside a cultural milieu that moulds understanding of the possible and the desirable.

With the introduction of economic and political dependencies, the relationship of culture to economic and political history needs some clarification. I would argue that regulatory character could be viewed as a distillation of economic, political and cultural history. Each place thus develops a particular regulatory 'character' that draws on one or more of the ideal types (hierarchist, fatalist and so on) identified by Hood and Douglas that mould the interaction between individuals, social norms and formal laws. Regulatory character provides the resources for both understanding and acting within a given set of circumstances and critically establishes the means to exert power and influence. A characteristic analysis does not alter economic realities that may be faced, such as the need to retain investment or win a contract (Selznick, 1992), but it may shape how these demands are responded to, including provision of characteristic resources to exert power through exploiting economic and political circumstances, should the opportunity arise. In this way, the essentialism within a cultural analysis is overcome by a focus on regulatory character, as in a characteristic analysis norms are seen to exist in relation to economic and political realities, as both an historical product, but also an independent influence on the present.

The introduction of a characteristic analysis, over and above a cultural analysis, has one final advantage. A characteristic analysis introduces 'openness' to regulatory culture, which can incorporate economic and political dependencies arising from the international as well as the local sphere. In doing so, it provides a means to understand how the 'macro' environment ('globalization') intersects with and is incorporated into the local environment. Regulatory character is a particularly appropriate means to explore globalization and its effects, particularly globalization associated with external catalysts for local change.

Exploring Thai Regulatory Character

How, then, might regulatory character be used to explore the regulatory aftermath of Kader? The first step is to use the theoretical parameters of regulatory character as outlined in Figure 3.1 and ground them in the Thai context, to move from a theoretical concept to an empirical reality. To do this is to answer the following questions: What is the interaction between social norms and legislative or regulatory rules in the Thai context? How do individuals relate to and interact with social norms? And finally, how do individuals use and respond to legislative and regulatory responsibilities? To answer these questions requires some familiarity with Thai economic, political and cultural context as presented in relevant literature. This forms the first part of the discussion of this section. It is not my purpose, however, to give either a definitive account of Thai cultural norms, or a comprehensive account of Thai economic and political history; there are clearly others more qualified to do this (see, for example, Wyatt, 1984; Hewison, 1989; Suehiro, 1989; Pasuk and Baker, 1995, 1998, 2000). Rather, my aim is to highlight those features that give an insight into the nature of authority and the form of social ordering that appear most critical to understanding Thai regulatory character. In particular, the analysis should help uncover possible ideal-typical influences within the Thai regulatory sphere that help understand the response to Kader.

The second task is to sketch Thai regulatory character from the features identified in Figure 3.1 and the elements of the Thai context discussed below. Thirdly, the way in which globalization might interact with Thai regulatory character is explored. In particular, the discussion maps out which elements of Thai regulatory character are valorized by the dynamics of globalization, how Thailand might be expected to reassert sovereignty, and the potential implications this has for regulatory reform and effectiveness. The section concludes with the major research questions arising from Thai regulatory character and its relationship to globalization.

Cultural Norms

The exploration of culture as a facet of regulatory character aims to explore the 'map of meaning' within which regulatory reform and compliance takes place. It is not an exploration of legal culture *per se*, but social norms that might influence the reform process and the effectiveness of new regulations or laws in the safety sphere. Secondly, the presentation is clearly aimed at uncovering what 'order' and 'disorder' might mean within a Thai context, since it is an understanding of this that Douglas (1966) has argued to be central to a cultural analysis. Conceptions of risk and danger are, as Douglas (1992) reminds us, intimately concerned with cultural norms of order, both within Western and non-Western contexts. Because risk and danger are so closely involved in debates of regulation and regulatory reform, an attempt at understanding rationality and social norms within a particular place is critical to understanding regulatory character.

The description below relies heavily on one author, Niels Mulder (2000). The reason for this is that Mulder's analysis tries to capture the cognitive ordering process within Thai society and so can give some insight into a subjective (individual level) analysis. Other accounts (e.g., Unger, 1988) tend to remain external and descriptive, consequently are less useful for the purposes of understanding regulatory character. Mulder (2000) explores the duality of 'inside' or 'outside' within Thai culture that relate to different spheres of action, with the 'inside' relating to the sphere of moral goodness (*khuna*), and the 'outside' to power (*decha*). It is not possible, however, to conceptualize the political and bureaucratic (and by extension the regulatory) context as purely in the realm of power, since whilst these spheres loosely relate to 'family' and 'other', there is considerable interpenetration between the two. Rather, Mulder (2000) argues these spheres relate more to social distance. Close relationships are within the sphere of moral goodness, and distant relationships relate to *decha*. *Khuna* is characterized by *bakhun* or moral goodness, gratitude and obligation. Such expectations can be found in the public sphere, where there is an interpenetration of the two sorts of social relations. *Decha* at the extreme is characterized by chaos and immorality. At the level of interpenetration, the emphasis is on the 'good leader': those in authority who should be dependable and reliable, exemplified in Thai society by the King, but also present in the 1997 Constitution that emphasizes the importance of good leadership alongside democratic accountability (Laird, 2000, pp. 163–208; Connors, 2002; McCargo, 2002a, pp. 9–12; McCargo 2002b, p. 255–6). Under interpenetration, there is also an expectation of reciprocation (Mulder, 2000, pp. 34–5). The pursuit of power, however, remains both desirable and dangerous. To pursue power in the public sphere is to make oneself vulnerable and to need protection, a function fulfilled either from religious symbols or patrons. In Thai society, order and hierarchy are seen as important elements as a defence against chaos; hierarchical relations thus protect individuals against danger, capriciousness and revenge. The duality of normative expectations of social relationships points to different ways the authority and influence can be exerted: the first (under conditions of interpenetration) acts within an understanding of moral imperative (*bakhun*); the second (*khuna*) as a more clearly goal-directed, strategic endeavour.

The work of Yoshifumi Tamada (1991) on power complements that of Mulder. Tamada contrasts the nature of formal power, *amnat,* with that of *itthiphon,* informal power or influence. There are two important elements of Tamada's work. First, that *itthiphon* works through reciprocity. Individuals without formal political power are nonetheless able to exert considerable influence because they are able to make themselves indispensable to those in official bureaucratic or political positions. Those with official power reciprocate by taking account of those with *itthiphon* when they discharge their official duties. Secondly, his work shows that the rule of law may not be as strong as the legislature suggests (Tamada, 1991, p. 14), because of the way *itthiphon* works to mould how legal mandates are responded to. In Tamada's work, *itthiphon* relates in large part to the use of money and donations by business to both politicians and bureaucrats, and clearly links in with work on corruption (see also Pasuk and Sungsidh, 1994; McCargo, 2002a, 2002b). However, rather than simply label *itthiphon* as networks of corrupt practices, it is important to understand that it also points to the nature of obligation and reciprocity within Thai society.

A critical element for our analysis, however, is to understand the place of the individual and their relationship to this authority structure with its hierarchical norms. Whilst Thailand has been characterized as individualistic and loosely structured by some (Unger, 1998), Mulder disagrees. Individuals need to be understood in light of the broader society. Rather than individualistic, he argues that individuals are self-reliant,[7] a skill critical to enable each person to understand their position in the broader society and act accordingly. The individual uses their skills, namely recognition of the status of others and using status symbols and

---

[7] It must be emphasized here that 'self-reliance' needs to be seen in terms of the individual skills inherent in maintaining social networks and social harmony, not in the sense of being able to survive independently from sources of social support or networks as is understood within some usage of the term. This latter definition is unhelpful in understanding what is meant here by 'self-reliance' in the Thai context.

systems of patronage, in order to maintain or enhance their position (see also Laird, 2000, pp. 245–9). Patronage can be found through those with official power, *amnat*, but also through business people with *itthiphon*, or influence (Tamada, 1991). Everyday interaction depends on a mutual recognition of position, accompanied by appropriate presentation of the self, which allows for smooth relationships (Mulder, 2000, pp. 43–9).

A smooth or pleasant relationship, though, does not then necessarily indicate commitment of one person to another or a commitment to a given institution. Neither does a smooth relationship necessarily mean agreement. Moral obligation does arise, with respect to particular 'inside' individuals, but is not uniformly present. The public sphere that comprises regulation and its enforcement is complex. Mulder (2000, p. 36) argues that Thais allow everyday experiences including contradictory, opposed or complementary elements to remain unresolved, particularly in the power-related *khuna* or 'outside sphere'. Order is re-established in understanding the dichotomous nature of reality. Further, those who challenge these hierarchical norms in essence put themselves at risk; they lack the protection that hierarchy affords and are both admired and feared.

A cultural analysis, though, cannot be complete without recognition of a gender dimension to conceptions of 'order' and 'place'. There are clear gender implications of this dichotomous dimension to culture. Mulder (2000, p. 72) argues that *khuna* relates in particular to the role of mother, whilst *decha* is seen as masculine – the world of risk, politics and prestige. In terms of expectations, Mulder argues, women will be practical and reliable. He writes:

> Where many men often appear to be wishy-washy, spoiled, cocky and carried away by the greatness of their scheme, the women are generally hard working, responsible and conscientious. They can, and do, take a lot. In spite of this, they normally maintain their good humour, and their grace, contributing to the mystique of Thailand as the Land of Smiles. Let nobody be mistaken, though. In the male dominated world of Thailand, a smile may mean anything, from defence to submission, from politeness to subservience, and behind smiling female grace and elegance, one often finds powerful, go getting women. Nevertheless, even given all that the Thais appreciate grace and elegance; things should be beautiful to be in order, yet this order also requires hard work and dependability. Which is why it is women who are at the heart of Thai life. (Mulder, 2000, p. 73).

This reliability of women can be seen from their historical role as the stable point in the life of the family. Whilst men may have spent some time as monks in the local monastery, or spent long periods of time away from their children working in other regions, women have assumed the greatest responsibility for the raising of children and providing both financial and social stability (Pasuk and Baker 1998, pp. 150–152; Doneys, 2002). However, the position of women in Thai society is complex, with land inheritance, for example, historically matrilineal (Timm, 1992). Yet, the position of women has been restricted within the political sphere, despite a traditional role in breadwinning and agriculture (Doneys, 2002). The large number of young women, daughters leaving their villages to find work in the factories of Bangkok, then, should not be seen as unique, but as a continuation of their role.

Nonetheless, the political influence of women historically has not been great, and remains restricted despite the 1997 Constitution emphasizing equality (Doneys, 2002).

Regulatory character, then, must be sensitive to gender. The way regulatory character shapes the understanding of disaster and the responses to it may act in different, unequal or paradoxical ways when viewed from the vantage point of the men and women involved. Certainly, in the case of Kader, most of those involved were young women: mothers, students and wives. A concern for the research then, is the way 'self-reliance' may hold different implications for women, when compared with men.

This presentation suggests certain cultural elements that may be important in understanding regulatory character. Firstly, recognition of a separation between moral suasion and strategic power, where relationships are guided either by moral obligation or, in the case of *decha*, used for strategic advancement in status, may be expected. This suggests that regulatory character is dualistic, with both *khuna* or *decha* dimensions. These can be usefully understood as emphasizing different forms of rationality, where *khuna* relates to a value-based or substantive rationality, whilst *decha* encapsulates an instrumental, or more accurately strategic form of rationality. Secondly, the discussion above points to the protective quality of hierarchy and the emphasis on smooth interaction. Regulatory character appears from this analysis as clearly within a 'hierarchist' frame of reference in Hood's (1998) analysis. However, this ideal type may well be based on hierarchist norms of interaction that rely heavily on individual self-reliance and knowledge of such norms. The relationship between norms and laws may well not be simple. Finally, Mulder's analysis alerts us to the reality that the experiences of men and women are likely to be very different.

A characteristic analysis, though, would emphasize that it is not helpful to see these cultural elements *ex nihilo*, but rather as intimately entwined with political and economic facets of character. Whilst Mulder's (2000) analysis of culture sketches a preliminary understanding of the subjective components of regulatory character, political elements, in particular, are important to grasp as they may give a clearer indication of the objective or institutionalized dynamic of regulatory character.

Political Context

Five elements of Thai political history stand out as important in their potential to influence regulatory character. The first of these is the historical legacy left by the monarchy, particularly with respect to the reform of the state administrative and legal structure as a defence against the threat of colonization in the early twentieth century. The second element is the role of the military in the replacement of the absolute monarch in 1932, the successive periods of military rule and military influence in government. The third element is the competing role of the civil elite in shaping Thai politics over the same period of 1932 to the present. The fourth element is labour history, including the role of protest in the political reform process. Finally, the nature of contemporary Thai politics needs to be understood, with its emphasis on individual personalities and a presence of multiple competing political parties.

Monarchy, the response to the threat of colonization and its legacy. Thailand is unique amongst its neighbours in that it was never a colony of the West. This provides a sense of independence and 'Thai-ness' that is an important feature of contemporary Thai politics. Equally as important, however, is the manner in which colonization was averted. Siam[8] was clearly under threat from both French and British interests in the early twentieth century, with some Thai regions appropriated by both the British and the French, specifically in the regions of contemporary Myanmar and Cambodia. That colonization did not go further is largely due to the accommodation of colonial interests (Hooker, 1988) and the bureaucratic and political reforms of the monarch, King Chulalongkorn. Reform was undertaken both as a response to the threat of colonization and to the opportunities provided by the weakening power of provincial rulers in the region. The reforms established royal sovereignty across the region at the expense of local rulers (Pasuk and Baker 1995, pp. 228–43, but see Riggs, 1961). Local rulers were brought under control, although administrative reforms gave regional bureaucratic administrators considerable local authority, accompanied by the prestige such positions afforded. The practice of 'self-remuneration' from local populations in addition to receiving royal salaries increased their desirability.

The centrepiece of recognition by foreign colonial powers, however, was not so much in the changes to actual administration and power relations. The justification for colonization was removed by the Siamese monarchy in the development of a bureaucratic administrative system, a legal and constitutional system modelled along European lines (Riggs, 1961). Through this mechanism, Siam was recognizable as a legitimate sovereign nation. This meant that foreign powers were unable to colonize Siam under the pretence of establishing the rule of law since the Siamese state was pre-emptively constructed along the same (constitutional) principles as the European powers (Hooker, 1988, p. 549). Andrew Harding (2001, p. 22) has described this as a process of 'inoculation' against colonialism. 'Foreign' laws have found their way into Thailand, but the relationship between law and practice is complex (Harding, 2001). An example here is Riggs' (1961, p. 100) argument that the elements of constitutional change aimed at legitimating authority in Thailand remained formalistic, that is, they satisfied external (i.e., Western) scrutiny in terms of what constitutes legitimate authority or legitimate rule, but did not relate to how authority was actually justified or exerted from within. This does not mean change did not take place, rather that legal change did not have an easy relationship to underlying social change. Taken as a whole, the formal structure of power, including legislation and administrative structure, did not bear simple relation to the way power was actually wielded, or political will made manifest.

General scholarship in the area of legal transplants contains vibrant debates about the legacy of transplanted law (whether the transplant was initiated by invaders, or imported as in the case of Thailand) (see Nelken, 2001, for an analysis

---

[8]   Siam was the official name of the country before 1939 (Wyatt, 1984, p. 252).

of these debates). Contributors to this debate demonstrate that the effect of these transplantations, how they influence the relationship between law, power and behaviour, needs to be appreciated at two separate levels: both how individuals assert their legal rights, and how those in positions of power use the law (Garth and Dezalay, 2001; Jettinghoff, 2001; Nottage, 2001). In the Thai context, Engel's (1978) study *Code and Custom in a Thai Provincial Court* provides an in-depth account of how disputes were most often resolved through drawing on the services of local leaders through some sort of mediation. The formal courts and legal system, when they were used, were used so as to augment their position in extra-legal negotiations. Further, courts were most likely to be drawn on by those who did not have access to local leaders who could resolve the issue. The court and formal legal system was then used as additional leverage to resolve the dispute.

The institutionalization of political power through the legal system is similarly complex. Throughout recent history, the political debate and struggle to establish popular and political legitimacy, which could be enshrined in constitutional form, has proved challenging. Thailand has had repeated constitutional change, with 16 different constitutions since the end of the absolute monarchy (McCargo, 2002a). Mulder (2000) argues that the level of constitutional upheaval has not led to significant change in the way authority and power is wielded in Thailand '... sixteen constitutions and sixty years of discussion have not much changed the exercise of power and have contributed little to the realization of effective popular control ...' (Mulder, 2000, pp. 41–2). For others, this is a clear oversimplification; political change has occurred (Laird, 2000; Connors, 2002; McCargo, 2002a), yet the reality of constitutional change points to the complex relationship between authority in Thailand and the constitutional formal legal system. The emphasis within the current constitution itself, for example, is on government by 'good people', independent from the legal framework continuing the traditional emphasis on the nature of the person above the expectations of the role (Hewison, 2002b). Constitutional change itself has been argued to contribute to the difficulty of constitutional mandates themselves engendering significant change with McCargo (1998, cited in McCargo 2002a, p. 3) arguing that constitutionalism is 'a political "disease" that paralyses and distorts Thai public life' as public individuals compete to make their mark on history through membership of successive constitutional committees.

Thai political history suggests, then, that the relationship between norms and laws within Thai regulatory character is complex. Authority may well flow from hierarchist norms, but formal laws may bear only an indirect relationship to how power is wielded, and the ability of ordinary people to access the law may be somewhat circumscribed. Further, extra-legal means of resolving disputes, through negotiation via people in positions of authority, may be preferred. Nonetheless, laws may play an important role in placating an audience (as was the case with colonial threats), by their very presence.

The role of the military. The second political element of importance relates again to authority and its legitimate use, this time with respect to the military. The military has a long history of political influence within Thailand. In the period following the transition from absolute to constitutional monarchy, it was the military, under Phibun, that finally gained control of the political sphere (Pasuk and Baker, 1995, pp. 266–75). Their justification was their stability as an institutional force in Thailand and from this, their ability to work for the long-term interest of country. Military leaders, in particular Phibun, saw the military project of rightful authority and the national project of Thai independence and success as closely aligned. Military leaders had a critical role in shaping the economy, both in terms of the degree to which Thailand was involved in import substitution or the degree to which it was open to foreign trade (Hewison, 1989; Pasuk and Baker, 1995, pp. 323–66). This included a close relationship to the private sector, including a direct involvement through ownership of state-run enterprises (Suehiro, 1989). During the first half of the twentieth century there was considerable hostility by the military to the Chinese private sector, which was seen as a threat (Suehiro, 1989, pp. 108–109) however, this declined as the Chinese became integrated into the Sino-Thai elite (Suehiro, 1989, pp. 122–30). Since the 1980s and the opening of Thailand to free trade, the military has continued its historic influence within the private sector, albeit somewhat reduced, through the practice of high-ranking military figures taking positions on the boards of major businesses (Pasuk and Baker, 1995, pp. 277–81, 331–2; Chai-Anan, 1997).

The role of the military as 'rightful leaders' has had a mixed history with respect to relations with the monarchy. The rise of General Phibun during the 1930s saw the monarch, Prajadhipok, move overseas and then abdicate in 1935[9] (Pasuk and Baker, 1995, p. 281). In ideological terms, the military saw themselves as replacing the monarchy. Nonetheless, after a period of some negotiation with key royalist elites, the (then) ruling absentee monarch, King Bhumibol, returned to Thailand from Switzerland in December 1951 (Pasuk and Baker, 1995, p. 281–5; Kobrua, 2002). The ideology of 'Nation, Religion, King' as the defining element of Thai identity reappeared for the first time since 1932, an ideology that was enhanced considerably during the rule of General Sarit, with the combination of military and monarchy seen as the way to provide the stability and core values that Thailand needed.

The nationalist project pursued by the military has often involved suppression of key groups, in particular organized labour, and in earlier periods the Chinese (Pasuk and Baker, 1995, pp. 174–207; Brown, 1997; Pasuk and Baker, 1998, pp. 136–44; Brown, 2001). The resumption of military dictatorship after a period of democratic rule was often justified in part as a curb on communism, corruption and self-interest (Pasuk and Sungsidh, 1994, p. 51).[10] Once in place, the policies pursued included the repeal of labour rights, such as freedom of association, on the justification of communist infiltration or 'Thai for the Thais' (Pasuk and Baker, 1995, p. 197). This rationale is better understood when it is realized that Chinese workers in the 1920s were amongst the first to organize and flex industrial muscle

---

[9]	The government immediately chose a successor, Prince Ananda Mahidol, who was at school in Switzerland. For the next 15 years there was no resident reigning monarch.

[10]	Pasuk and Sungsidh (1994) argue, however, that corruption was actually greater during periods of military rule.

in the pursuit of better conditions. Military rule and the suppression of labour rights also received support from the US during the period of the Cold War, Thailand being seen as a friendly country in a vulnerable region. The power of the military has subsided somewhat since the end of the Cold War, and particularly since the failed military coup in 1992 and the development of a new constitution. However, their influence remains, albeit it more indirect ways. In keeping with other areas of Thai society there is fluidity and change; the ex-military can become civil politicians and powerful business people. The military as an institution has strong corporate interests, from which it receives revenue (Chai-Anan, 1997).

Bureaucratic elite. Even during its heyday, military hegemony was never absolute. The bourgeois revolution (Ungpakorn, 1999) that led to the end of the absolute monarchy resulted as much from dissident bureaucrats as it did from the military. Their major complaint, highlighted by worsening economic conditions, was the staffing of the bureaucracy according to the rules of patronage and privilege, rather than skills and effectiveness of administrative tasks. Patronage and privilege were defining features of the bureaucracy under the absolute monarchy. In contrast, reform-minded bureaucrats, educated in Paris in the 1920s, envisioned for Thailand a future that was broadly speaking both idealist and socialist. The result of the revolution was, though, a compromise where socialist policies were largely absent and the status structure of the bureaucracy largely retained (Pasuk and Baker, 1995, p. 252). The contemporary bureaucracy contains within it two distinct elements: the historic status-oriented structure, as well as elements of the modernist ideal of efficient policy implementation.

Labour history. Labour history and the politics of protest in Thailand comprise the fourth strand of political context. The history of protest spans both the industrial action of Chinese labour, and the protests that led to the overturning of military dictatorships in 1973 and 1992. Industrial action by Chinese immigrant labour was prominent from the 1920s to the 1940s (Hewison and Brown, 1994; Pasuk and Baker, 1995, pp. 173–207; Brown, 1997). During this time the Chinese had considerable political leverage stemming from their control of key positions in the city (such as the ports) and the general scarce supply of skilled labour (Pasuk and Baker, 1995, pp. 175–7). Industrial action from that time has been characterized by violence and tactics by business to undermine organized labour, and by government – both military and civil – to co-opt the labour movement.

There are several distinct strands of Thai labour and labour organization. These strands are divided according to the type of industry and the relationship between the labour organization and government (Pasuk and Baker, 1995, p. 190). First there is the state enterprise sector. Historically, labour organization in this sector has been the strongest, in line with their considerable industrial power. Over time, this group has gained pay and conditions considerably above other sectors of the economy. Their achievement has been gained to the detriment of some private sector workers. This is due in part to the joint agreements between union leaders in this sector and military governments, who then enjoyed the benefits of patronage by the military elite (Pasuk and Baker, 1995, p. 189). The second group are those who work for what Pasuk and Baker (1995, p. 190) term the 'more sophisticated' large businesses. Enterprise unionism and paternalistic management practices in these (particularly Japanese) companies have brought with them above-average pay and conditions. For the third group, the majority of private sector workers, conditions are bleaker. Companies exploit workers in the sure knowledge of a plentiful supply of labour. Hours of work are long and pay is well below the minimum wage, implemented through exploiting loopholes in the law, such as employing workers on temporary contracts and paying piece rates through subcontracting out work (Hewison and Brown, 1994; Pasuk and Baker, 1998, pp. 136–44). Attempts by workers to organize have been met by sacking the responsible employees or, worse, imprisoning them as 'communists' (Pasuk and Baker, 1995, p. 191). Finally, there is the informal sector, where opportunities for organization revolve around non-government organizations as opposed to unions (Naruemon, 2002).

Protest against military regimes is an important feature of Thai activist politics. This activism penetrated deeply into Thai society, beyond organized labour. In 1973, student protest was central to ending the 15 years of military rule begun by General Sarit. At that time, disaffection had been growing, particularly in rural areas. This disaffection was given a voice through the increasingly articulate and vocal student movement, centred on Thammasat University. Growing activism led to a major demonstration that ended on 14 October 1973, in which 100 students lost their lives. This tragedy led to the resignation of the military government (Pasuk and Baker, 1997, p. 302) and was considered by many Thais to be a watershed, marking the beginning of a period of extended student political activism. Thai history was re-read in light of Marxist insight, and the communist party of Thailand joined forces with the urban student movement and the organized peasant movement, the Peasants' Federation of Thailand (PFT). The protest was defined by its rejection of military rule, a rule seen to take from the population more than it gave. The alternative of a liberal vision of the rule of law, however, was not strong; more often the vision was a socialist one, or a return to traditional rural values (Pasuk and Baker, 1995, pp. 300–14). These competing visions gave rise to considerable political conflict during this period (Hewison, 1996; 2002b).

The repression in 1976 that followed this liberalization involved the destabilization of the PFT through the assassination of 18 leaders and a campaign to divide the left by the use of the epithet of 'communist' (Pasuk and Baker, 1995, pp. 307–8). Nationalism was reasserted again under the banner of 'Nation, Religion, King', during which time the role of the King was expanded and oriented towards rural development. The protest of 1992 followed a much shorter period of military rule, from a 1991 coup, justified by the military leaders on the grounds of anti-corruption. It was an unstable affair, with Thailand vulnerable to the poor image that a coup sent to overseas investors and trade partners (Pasuk and Baker, 1995, pp. 355–61; Hewison, 1996). Cold War support for the military was waning. The protest that led to the downfall of the military was characterized by the middle class and NGOs, dubbed by the press as *mob mu' thu'* (mobile phone mob). From

17 to 20 May 1992, the army moved in to disperse the demonstration. Official figures state the number who died to be 50, but many suspect the figure to be more than 100 (Pasuk and Baker, 1995, p. 360).

Partly because of this history, Thailand contains a vibrant but diverse sector of non-governmental organizations (NGOs), however, not all NGOs, including unions, are working to change the status quo (Ungpakorn, 1999). NGOs can be aligned with particular political agendas, but companies also set up NGOs to assist outworkers. NGOs do not have a single political position; indeed they may differ markedly in their emphasis of the importance of traditional values, or of education, or in their demand for political change and the need for the rule of law (Hewison, 2002b). The union movement has changed also. The powerful state enterprise unions have been weakened by privatization and, although some companies still retain a paternalistic style towards employees and encourage enterprise unionism, the majority continue to undermine any attempt to organize workers.

Contemporary Thai politics. Contemporary Thai politics, the fifth and final element, is dynamic. In contrast to party political contests in the West, historically it has largely been driven by battles between individuals, not between parties. It is not unusual for key political figures to change party allegiance, or to split away from a party and develop a new political party. Individuals, their charisma and connections are as important, if not more important, than party platforms (McCargo, 1997; Surin and McCargo, 1997). The mobility of individual politicians is assisted by the existence of multiple parties encapsulating similar views, in particular three parties of the right championing royalist, conservative views. In addition, 'transfer fees' often have been paid to electable individuals to encourage their defection; this is a problem for parties of every political hue (McCargo, 1997). There are parties that began as a champion for political reform, most notably Palang Dharma, but since the mid 1990s have become professionalized. Palang Dharma began as a radical[11] Buddhist-based party under the charismatic leadership of Chamlong, a Santi Asoke Buddhist monk, but by the mid 1990s was headed by Thaksin Shinawatra, a telecommunications tycoon and technocrat (McCargo, 1997). Thaksin Shinawatra then formed his own party, *Thai Rak Thai*, in 1998, which rapidly gained ground, bolstered by mass defections from opposition parties; Thaksin was elected Prime Minister in February 2001 and re-elected for an unprecedented second term in February 2005. The emphasis on individuals as opposed to parties means that an individual's network of support can be critical to their political success. This network covers a range of relationships, from those that are based on reciprocity and mutual interest between the politician and their patrons, to those where the politician is a mere 'decoration' for the patron (Tamada, 1991, pp. 12–13). The connection between individual politicians and *jao pho* (loosely, 'godfather') has been the focus of comment and study (Pasuk and Sungsidh, 1994; McCargo, 2002a). Such connections are often important for bankrolling political campaigns, particularly in crucial rural areas. Corruption is

---

[11] 'Radical' here refers to its opposition to mainstream Buddhism, rather than a political orientation.

often publicly debated, indeed one notable Prime Minister, Banharn Silpa-archa, was known as the 'walking ATM' as a result of his method of achieving and retaining power (Pasuk and Baker, 1995, p. 345; Pasuk and Baker, 1997). As much as this is an indication of corruption, it is also illustrative of the freedom of the press and openness of debate in Thailand, despite some curbing during military regimes (Thitinan, 1997). Notwithstanding the problems associated with the individual-centred Thai political sphere, the relational dynamic of Thai politics also underlies successful public interest projects such as environmental protection, where the support of individual high-ranking officials can ensure project success, independent from the legal basis for activism (Prudhisan and Maneerat, 1997).

Politics and Thai regulatory character. How might this diverse political history shape Thai regulatory character? There are several potential elements that extend the preliminary sketch outlined from the cultural analysis. Certainly, the hierarchist nature of regulatory character would be confirmed; however, which group of individuals or what institution is at the apex of this hierarchy is less certain. Perhaps, from the view of the military elite their ideal might be for the values of 'Nation, Religion, King' to infuse an institutionalized 'moral' social order. The success of this, however, is certainly open to challenge and the existence of multiple hierarchies may be more accurate than envisioning Thai regulatory character as unitary in the sense of a single hierarchy or normative order. Further, political history highlights the importance of networks and relationships to establish control. One example here is the relationships between the military and the monarchy, or between key unions and the military. Another is the link between the *jao pho* and politicians. Certain families dominate certain locations, and their dominance results in part from tactics such as vote buying (Surin and McCargo, 1997; McCargo, 2002a, 2002b). Known as 'godfather politicians' these powerful individuals and families are intensely disliked by the middle class in Bangkok. Electoral abuse, including vote buying, occupies much of the time of the Thai Electoral Commission (McCargo, 2002a). The emphasis on control, in the Asian studies literature (Cooney *et al.*, 2002) referred to in Chapter 2, within a Thai sphere is likely to take corporatist forms; that is, the emphasis is on the maintenance of relations between key groups in order to marginalize 'outsiders'. However, these relationships may not simply be institutional, but may well relate to key individuals or factions within institutions, since contemporary Thai politics illustrates the importance of the individual, over and above the institution. This extends beyond the visible democratic political arena to the importance of relationships outside of that arena, including relationships with the *jao pho* (Pasuk and Sungsidh, 1994; Surin and McCargo, 1997; McCargo, 2002a).

Understanding Thai political history also allows insight into the complexity of the relationships between norms and laws. There are two elements to this. The first is the dynamism of legal change, illustrated by the multiple changes in the Constitution. This suggests a desire to enshrine authority in constitutional law. The fact of so many changes, however, suggests that this is a difficult achievement, and that norms and relationships might often be more authoritative that the formal law. The function of the law, however, has an important second dimension: as a demonstration of legitimacy. The form the law takes may have more to do with the audience (whether local or international) than with its effective implementation.

The final element of importance is the impact of protest, both against the military and for industrial rights. The strands of protest are many, with some elements of protest and radical thought aimed at the development of the rule of law, and others aimed at reinstating traditional rural values or replacing traditional authority structure with socialism. Actual institutional change often has not lived up to the expectations of sizeable minorities of the population, one example here being the lack of institutionalization of socialist values in the replacement of the absolute monarchy. Further, the monarchy has often played a pivotal role in 'nudging' political reform in a direction that retains 'traditional' Thai character (Hewison, 1997). Nonetheless, Thailand has an open and vibrant level of political debate, albeit often tied to individual personalities.

Economic Context

The final concern is to understand the Thai economic context, and with this the relationship between economic and political power. Historically, the Thai economy has been characterized as a tripod structure, with state, domestic and foreign capital intersecting around a royal or military core (Suehiro, 1989, pp. 273–86). In this structure, economic and political powers were closely allied. The control of economic power by the political elite could be both indirect, by alliances and legislative control of national and international capital, or by direct ownership of the means of production. Even after the decline of the Sakdina,[12] the monarchy owned substantial economic resources, and stimulated nascent domestic capital development through the Privy Purse Bureau (Suehiro, 1989, pp. 90–3). Expansion of the state into the economy occurred after the fall of the absolute monarchy in 1932. Phibun, as Prime Minister, set a pattern for close connection between political position and control of economic resources under his programme of 'Thai Economy for Thai people.' The result of this was the concentration of wealth and power in both the bureaucracy and the military, as Suehiro (1989, p. 130) states: '… whatever the original intent, "Thai people" later did not come to indicate either the common people or Thai farmers, rather it came to mean the government officials or a specified political group.' This expansion of the state-owned sector increased the influence of both state and military official in business affairs, a situation that persisted throughout the twentieth century (see also Hewison, 1989, pp. 206–14). It is important to note, too, that Thailand (Siam) has a long history as a trading nation. Before colonial expansion, forest goods (namely timber and related forest produce) formed the basis of export, with weapons and luxuries the major imports (Pasuk and Baker, 1995, pp. 91–2). Siam's forestry trade was restricted however, due to the colonization of neighbouring regions and the colonial practice of trading only with other colonies and the mother country. In response, Siam developed rice as a major commodity, for both internal

---

[12] Loosely understood as the feudal system, nonetheless one where control of people was more important than ownership of land (Suehiro, 1989, p. 278).

consumption and trade. The monarchy was aware that the surrounding colonies did not have the agricultural base to grow sufficient rice, and so Thailand expanded in this commodity, becoming a central part of the 'rice bowl' of Asia (Pasuk and Baker, 1995, pp. 97–101; Pasuk and Baker, 1998, pp. 12–13).

This expansion of the rice trade drew Thai labour to the rural areas, with the consequence of a shortage of labour in the city. The monarchy responded by encouraging Chinese immigrants to work in urban areas. During the 1920s, Chinese labour migrated to Thailand, mainly settling in the urban areas to fill the labour shortage in the cities. Pasuk and Baker (1998) refer to these early Chinese migrants as 'pillow and mat' capitalists in recognition of the paucity of capital with which they arrived and their ability to generate a dynamic business environment.[13] Chinese business interests soon became a dominant force in the city. First involved in small business and petty trading, many went on to form large Thai firms, including the ubiquitous Thai conglomerate CP, with family members controlling CP subsequently diversifying into a range of different businesses; with some members having a financial interest in the Kader factory. Over time, ethnic Chinese were further integrated into the Thai elite through strategic business and family alliances. So, whilst the inter-war years were characterized by small business 'shophouse capitalism', the post-war years saw the development of larger business comprising both Chinese and Thai interests.

The post-war years saw the development of the banking and finance sectors, with agreements with both the US and Japan assisting this development (Hewison, 1989, pp. 104–8). In the 1970s there was a steep rise in investment, mainly from Japan (Suehiro, 1989, pp. 211–17), with Japanese investment in Thailand taking advantage of the weakness of the baht as compared to the yen, as well as allowing manufacturers to curb escalating costs of production at home (Pasuk and Baker, 1998, pp. 33–8). This saw a shift from low- to medium-technology enterprises as well an increase, over time, of joint ventures between Japanese and Sino-Thai interests. The progressive overshadowing of technological production by multinational corporations saw a shift to the development of Thai heavy industry, as well as an expansion of investment in real estate and the financial sector. The structure of firms also changed, with a shift towards greater investment in subcontracting, particularly in the manufacturing sector (Pasuk and Baker, 1998, pp. 136–40).

In common with the experience in other countries, industrial development since World War II has been accompanied by a gradual shift of people from the country to the city. In Thailand, this movement to Bangkok, in particular, resulted from three interrelated factors: the influx of Japanese and other investment into urban-based industry, rising population levels, and poor prices for agricultural produce (Pasuk and Baker, 1995, pp. 198–9). Critically this shift involved increasing

---

[13]   It is important to recognize, though, that the Chinese were an influential force in the Thai economy from before this time. In the nineteenth century the Chinese had considerable influence through their tax, farming and trade interests. They often consolidated their interest through marriage alliances with the Thai royalty and the Thai elite (Suehiro, 1989, pp. 71–90).

numbers of women and girls moving to the city. In contrast to other countries, however, many workers returned to the countryside. There developed a regular migration of workers moving from country to city and then back again. Many made the trip more than once. Gradually, however, more people stayed, so that – in 1990 – slum dwellings in the greater Bangkok area housed over 1.2 million people (Pasuk and Baker, 1998, pp. 133–4). In more recent years the response to this overcrowding of Bangkok, coupled with the push for efficiency by the MNCs, has led to greater and greater levels of contracting out being undertaken in rural areas.

The Asian financial collapse assisted this restructuring of companies to a 'core and periphery' structure (Harvey, 1989) that atomized production between locations and companies. Multiple subcontracting chains are evident in many production processes within Thailand (Pasuk and Baker, 1995, pp. 199–204). Outworking is now common in many industries and is found alongside many in-house manufacturing plants. In addition, temporary employment is common, with continuous hiring on a probational contract an oft-used ploy (Pasuk and Baker, 1995, p. 201; Brown, Bundit and Hewison, 2002) with, as Kader showed, only those considered permanent employees being entitled to the minimum wage. Reviewing the Thai research, Brown *et al.* (2002) suggest that only 40% of registered factories comply with minimum wage standards, with workers within the rest, including the large informal sector, receiving less than the minimum wage. Subcontracted work is often paid by a piece-rate system. At the other end of the spectrum there is considerable wealth in the country (Pasuk and Baker, 1998), with the dominant Sino-Thai elite also having considerable economic interests outside of Thailand. Major Thai companies, such as CP, have factories and operations throughout Asia (Pasuk and Baker, 1995, pp. 164–6).

Constructing a succinct conceputalization of the Thai economy, even from the brief outline above, is not easy. What is clear, however, is that diversity rather than unity characterizes economic activity. The three 'legs' of the economy – the state, local capital and international capital – are each an important part of the picture. The link between economic and political power is evident through the historical role of the monarchy, the links between the Thai elite and the Chinese, and the enduring involvement of the state including the military in the economy. Further, it is important to understand that trade is institutionalized in Thailand; it is not of recent origin. Neither is trade restricted to relations with MNCs from the West; Asian, including Thai, conglomerates are also clearly part of the equation. Small and medium-sized enterprises are also well represented (Brown *et al.*, 2002), whilst self-employment and work in the informal sector continues to be a reality for many Thai people. However, the size of the business does not necessarily predict the nature of the employment relationship, since temporary and peripheral forms of employment remain common even in large, well-established businesses. There are many business relationships linking the various strands of Thai industry together, although some forms of work, such as street vending, lie outside of this. The countryside remains attractive to many, although it can no longer sustain the economic needs of the population. This pull of both rural and urban regions results in considerable internal migration in the search of work, both from rural regions to the city, and sometimes the reverse.

What are the implications of this brief description of the dimensions of Thai regulatory character? The importance of key individuals, or patrons, in positions of authority is evident, as is the relationship between economic and political power. This was given an added dimension with the influx of Chinese migrants, wooed to the country for their business skills and self-reliance. Business networks and social relationships, particularly between Chinese and Thai, but also between Japanese and Thai, are evident in economic history. What is striking in terms of economic policy is, until fairly recently, the directed nature of trade. Industry policy was concerned with the developing specific industries: small business, technology, heavy industry and so on. Economic history would alert regulatory character to the history of the close interrelationship between economic and political power.

Other elements also flesh out aspects of self-reliance. Self-reliance is characteristic of 'shophouse capitalism' – small businesses that exploit local business opportunities – as well as the presence of the informal economy. Self-reliance, though, needs to be understood as the ability to find patronage as much as, if not more than, self-sufficiency. Nonetheless, an important dimension to this is the rapid expansion of MNCs of both Western and Asian origin that thrive on multiple chains of contracting and subcontracting relationships. The tentative connection between self-reliance and 'core and periphery' industrial structure is mediated by patronage. Contracting out and self-employment may well reinforce the elements of self-reliance and patronage pre-existing within the Thai industrial milieu.

Thai Regulatory Character

How might the elements of Thai cultural, political and economic context discussed above frame Thai regulatory character? In particular, how might the generic tensions within regulatory character work in a Thai context? As outlined above, regulatory character requires understanding of three relationships: that between social norms, in particular norms of authority, and formal laws; the relationship between individuals and social norms, and the relationship between individuals and formal laws (see Figure 3.1). The first question element to be determined is the normative underpinning of authority. Certainly, from the discussion above, ideal-typical forms of regulatory character would appear to be hierarchist (see Figure 3.2 below). Throughout Thai history, both the monarchy and the military have justified their authority within a patriarchalist frame, which encompasses both the institutionalized social order as well as the normative form of authority. The second issue then, is to determine how patriarchalism relates to the formal legal structure. From the description of Thai politics above, it appears there is a complex relationship between the norms of patriarchalism and the authority of law. A framework of legislation, regulations and ministerial directives under a constitution indicates some authority vested in rules, albeit one that is vulnerable to considerable change. An individual's recourse to the law may also depend upon extra legal avenues for redress. Resolution of disputes may well take place between parties independently from the law in the first instance. The implementation of laws also may be difficult, because of the independent influence of both the bureaucracy and the influence or *itthiphon* exerted by business. Further, legal change might reflect the need to placate an audience, rather than to effect behavioural change. The term 'formalism' might be used to capture the uneasiness of the relationship between laws and norms.

Grid dimension

		Social norms	Formal laws (Formalism)
Group dimension	Social norms	Authority primarily exerted by individuals in positions of power (hierarchist/patriarchalist) who use laws to indicate legitimacy (a formalist use of law) or to exert control	
	Individuals	Individuals expected to be self-reliant and use networks of patronage	Individuals mainly ignore law, preferring to use social or reciprocal norms to express opinion or to exert influence

Figure 3.2   Generic dimensions of Thai regulatory character

At the individual level, there is a need to understand the nature of Thai self-reliance. Self-reliance relates to that element that incorporates a sense of order that is premised on the individual using their own resources to build networks that enable them to make their way in life. This draws on Mulder's (2000) analysis and incorporates studies that argue for a need to understand the individualism characteristic of Thailand. However, self-reliance is, for the reasons outlined above, a more insightful encapsulation of this element than individualism. Where regulatory character is animated by an emphasis on self-reliance, the principal concern for any individual is to gain patronage, with the result that webs of patronage order society. Patrons resolve personal and social problems. The patronage system, not the legal system, orders society and is the principal means to resolve problems. A weakness, though, of Figure 3.2 as a solid starting point to explore regulatory character and its impact in the wake of the Kader fire, is that it fails to draw on either Mulder's (2000) insights, or use an understanding of rationality to provide a more comprehensive account of the regulatory dynamic. Figures 3.3 and 3.4 expand on Figure 3.2, to illustrate the competing ideal types of regulatory character; one infused by a substantive rationality (Figure 3.3), the other a strategic orientation (Figure 3.4). Figure 3.3 is labelled 'interpenetrative' regulatory character to capture Mulder's idea of the interpenetration of *bakhun* to the public sphere. The two depictions take account of the dualism described above, namely in terms of whether relationships are expressed through *khuna* (moral goodness) or *decha* (power). Regulatory character is thus not unitary. Nonetheless, as in Figure 3.2, Figures 3.3 and 3.4 illustrate what might be tentatively termed 'traditional' Thai regulatory character, one subject to the political challenge and protest evident in Thai political history described above. As ideal-typical, their function is to allow insight into the regulatory dynamic and sources of tension.

Patriarchalism

	Social norms	Formal law (Formalism)
Social norms	Ideology of Nation, Religion, King. Leader expected to exhibit benevolence and 'good leadership'. Emphasis on smooth relationships based on hierarchical norms.	Law is a mechanism of protection of the good of society, an expression of benevolence and paternalism.
Individuals	Use of skills of self-reliance to acknowledge and work within the hierarchy. Individuals find their own place within the hierarchy and seek patrons. Potential for overt conflict due to different beliefs, values and ideas and attitudes reduced since reciprocation expected to follow social norms.	Use of formal mechanisms of law eschewed under emphasis on relationships and obligations. Dissonance and contradiction between law and social norms accepted.

Figure 3.3   Regulatory character (interpenetrative dimension)

In both Figure 3.3 and Figure 3.4, regulatory character is driven by the relationship between patriarchalism and self-reliance; formal law and formal regulatory mechanisms are secondary. In Figure 3.3, the ideals of Thai patriarchalism are expressed through an emphasis on 'Thai-ness', religion (Buddhism) and reverence for the monarchy. Leadership involves both personal authority and obligation. Good government requires good people in positions of power. These elements are supported in law. For ordinary Thais, linking in to systems of patronage through the use of personal skills is important. This self-reliance, though, should not be seen as either individualism or synonymous with self-sufficiency; rather it is an expectation that individuals will understand and act within the norms of patriarchalism. An individual acting in an appropriate manner will be supported through the presence of hierarchy and norms of reciprocation. Formal law is merely an expression of good leadership and is a mechanism for the execution of authority. The individual, then, does not resort to legal rights, but rather works through networks and obligations. The dissonance that arises between law and norms may not necessarily be openly acknowledged or seen as problematic.

Under conditions of *decha* or strategy, the obligations of leadership are replaced by the fruits of status and the need to retain control (Figure 3.4). Whilst repression in the pursuit of control is present in Thai history, as evidenced by the oppressive response to protest in Thai history, corporatist forms of control through building relationships and excluding dissenters are more common (Pasuk and Baker, 1995). Those in positions of authority in business, government, military, and to a lesser extent unions, join to establish control. Self-reliance means getting ahead by working strategically within the status quo. Formal law and formal regulatory mechanisms assume greater importance as tools for strategy. Formal law is a tool for retaining control as well as, following Riggs (1961), a means of placating various audiences.

Patriarchalism

	Social norms	Formal law (Formalism)
Social norms	Domination of the population by those in authority through corporatism. Roles used to increase status and social position. Relationships with other members of the elite a means of excluding those who threaten status quo.	Law as a strategy for extending control. This works in one of two ways: either laws are drafted to entrench those in positions of authority, and/or are designed to deflect criticism (i.e. be formalistic), whilst ensuring they are unable to function in a way that challenges the status quo.
Individuals	Nepotism characterizes patronage, with individuals rewarded for their ability to extend control of those in authority. Individual strategy aimed at increasing social position central to action. Those not in networks of patronage, or who challenge them, repressed and exploited.	Knowledge of hierarchy and social norms central to strategy of improving position, with law another tool to be exploited. Violent private confrontation possible if position is threatened.

Figure 3.4   Regulatory character (strategic dimension)

In exploring the way traditional Thai regulatory character influences the response to Kader, there are three critical elements to be kept in mind. First, as was clear from the cultural analysis above, the impact of either dimension of Thai regulatory character on women as opposed to men may be radically different. In particular, the quality of women as self-reliant, as well as being the source of care and security, may place on them extra burdens in the wake of a disaster such as Kader. Further, changes made to the law to enshrine equal opportunities may act only to placate activist groups, particularly those outside of Thailand. Secondly, these traditional, ideal-typical forms must not be viewed in isolation from the history of protest emanating both from labour and the bureaucratic elite. The reality of almost constant constitutional change (reflecting change from military to civilian rule and the reverse), as well as reform and repeal of labour laws (Pasuk and Baker, 1995, Ch. 6), means that Thai regulatory character at any one time is likely to be fluid and have the capacity for surprise. Nonetheless, those reforms that resonate with the character in Figures 3.3 or 3.4 might be expected to have greater currency.

Finally, the impact of rapid economic change has the potential to have an independent influence on regulatory character. In particular, it may introduce elements of fatalism into that character, where the obligations of patronage are consigned to history. Nonetheless, economic change may also consolidate ideal-typical elements of Thai regulatory character. This final element is explored more fully in the interaction between globalization and regulatory character below.

Globalization and Regulatory Character

This study began with the task of assessing the impact of globalization on regulatory change following the Kader disaster. We are now in a position to return to the debates on globalization and suggest ways that globalization might intersect with Thai regulatory character. In Chapter 2, several elements of globalization that might be critical to the response to Kader were discussed, in particular the conceptualization by Held *et al.* (1999) of the debate being divided between hyperglobalists, sceptics and transformalists.

For hyperglobalists, economic factors drive globalization. Whilst hyperglobalists differ (between pessimists and optimists) on the moral value placed on economic change, both understand those changes as associated with the expansion and promotion of capitalist policies and practices associated with free trade. These policies and practices focus on the product or service for export or import and ensure identical products are given equal chance within the global market, irrespective of its origin. The aim is for the market to become global, in terms of access and participation by each player. Regulations, including safety regulations, threaten this process if they increase the cost of the product or provide a means by which a government of an importing country might discriminate about the worth of one product over another, such as placing some kind of trade sanctions on products.

The neo-classical economic philosophy that underpins the global policies of free trade is premised on individuals in the market pursuing their selfish desires in the pursuit of profit (Smith, [1776] 1970). This individualist philosophy of the primacy of the individual within the market might reasonably be expected to augment and interact with self-reliance within Thai regulatory character. Further, from the emphasis of neo-classical economic policies and practices on strategic individualism (Freidman and Freidman, 1996) one might reasonably expect that it is self-reliance under conditions of external power or strategic self-reliance (as in

Figure 3.4) that has most to gain. Even so, this interaction between global economic policies and self-reliance should not be viewed as simple or unproblematic, since self-reliance, as has been explored above, exists in relationship within the existing power relations of Thai regulatory character. Economic globalization will be unlikely simply to augment the individualism within self-reliance; rather it may cause a flow-on effect to patriarchalist practices, for example. Nonetheless, if hyperglobalists are right, the influence of the nation state over regulations is likely to be diminished, with an emphasis on regulations that do not 'interfere' with free trade.

The second element of importance in the discussion of globalization was the growth of global rationalism, or the rules accompanying free trade (Giddens, 1990). These rules clearly take many forms – the first of which are rules associated with free trade itself. In addition, however, there are the rules and regulations developed to minimize risk associated with industrial production, not only health and safety law, but workers' compensation, fire safety standards and building standards. These rules, too, form part of global rationalism. Here the intersection with regulatory character might well be expected to take place through formalism – at the adjacent corner to self-reliance (see Figures 3.3 and 3.4). Again, the relationship should not be seen as simple. First, some rules may well have a national source (such as the US); others may be sourced from international bodies such as the International Organization for Standardization (ISO) and International Labour Organisation (ILO) (see Braithwaite and Drahos, 2000). The influence of one nation over others in the area of regulatory reform may well lend weight to the arguments of the global sceptics, that powerful nation states hold greatest sway over 'global' developments.

The third element discussed in Chapter 2 was the element of sovereignty; the argument of Weiss (1988) that countries do not act as a blank page in the face of global forces, but seek to establish their identity in their response. This may take one of two forms: either moving to align with forces in the hope of economic and political gain, or active rejection as an assertion that global imperatives are 'tainted' (Mittleman, 1994). The discussion of regulatory character (above), however, suggests a third option in addition to these extremes. Sovereignty may well be re-established through the contours of regulatory character. In this way, global influence is mediated through regulatory character. Clearly, there may well be instances where this character is changed in the process, and others where the changes may be more apparent than real.

Finally, the challenges to traditional Thai regulatory character evident in labour history and the protests against military rule also have their counterpart in the global arena. The final point of intersection is between local and global activists and traditional Thai regulatory character. Again, this relationship is expected to be complex. A key aspect of the data analysis will be to understand how the aspirations of Thai activists are able to draw support from global NGOs in a manner that is mutually beneficial.

Conclusion

This chapter has established a solid means to move to an analysis of reform following the Kader fire. Regulatory character is clearly developed from Douglas' (1966) cultural theory and Hood's (1998) adaptation of this within a public administration context. Cultural theory's strength is the way it is able to illustrate how responses to industrial disasters such as Kader are moulded by dominant cultural views. Limitations to cultural theory are minimized by a shift to the concept of regulatory character, a concept drawing heavily on a Weberian analysis of rationality and authority. First, a categorical analysis is transformed into an ideal-typical approach allowing for both dynamism and complexity within a particular context. Secondly, the dimensions of 'group' and 'grid' are transformed from variables to categorize particular contexts into axes to explore relationships within regulatory character. The group dimension is able to explore the interaction between the subjective (individual) and objective (institutionalized) elements of regulatory context, both with the norms of authority and formal legal systems. The grid dimension explores the nature of authority and legitimation of behaviour within a regulatory context and in particular the interplay between norms and laws.

Finally, the limitations of a cultural analysis in its appreciation of economic and related political elements are minimized by shifting to a characteristic analysis, drawing on Selznick's (1992) concept of organizational character. The key here is that culture is not hermetically sealed, rather it is shaped and moulded by economic and political dependencies. Regulatory character, likewise, takes on an openness that enables it to explore economic political dependencies as well as providing the means to explore the interaction between the local context and global influence. This interaction with the global arena in the aftermath of Kader is explored in Chapters 7 and 8.

The second part of the chapter explored regulatory character in a Thai context. Traditional Thai regulatory character was seen as hierarchist. This was termed patriarchalist to emphasize its normative (as opposed to formal or legal) base within Thailand. Further, the character was, following Mulder (2000), also argued to be dualistic, with one element emphasizing a substantive rationality of values, the other an instrumental or strategic rationality. The exploration of Thai regulatory character provides a clear rationale with which to explore the data following Kader, in particular the tensions between the two dimensions of traditional regulatory character: the substantive and the strategic. This is particularly important when exploring the nexus between patriarchal authority and self-reliance and has implications in particular for women, as their experiences under Thai regulatory character are likely to differ significantly from those of men. The analysis of the response to Kader in light of the patriarchal self-reliance nexus forms the basis for Chapter 5.

Secondly, the analysis pointed to the complex relationship between norms and laws. Legal authority appeared to have less emphasis within Thai regulatory character. Nonetheless, it had an important function when norms were challenged. This was particularly evident under the threat of colonization, where laws were created to ward off a threat by creating a basis of legal recognition of one power by another. This takes on new importance when considering the history of protest and challenge, both historically within Thailand, and critically any protest emanating from Kader. The way in which legal reform is aimed primarily to placate protest, rather than to create change, will be the basis for Chapter 6.

Chapter 4

Ripples in a Pond:
The Response to Kader

The first task in the presentation of the data is to outline the major features of regulatory response to the Kader tragedy. From the data collected, it is simply not possible to trace the development of one regulatory arena as archetypical of general trends in regulatory reform. In an industrial disaster such as Kader, multiple regulatory regimes are involved. In particular, the disaster highlighted weaknesses in regulations pertaining to workers' compensation, occupational health and safety, building standards and fire protection. Each area met a different fate in the wake of the fire. Some, such as the need for adequate compensation, received a higher public profile in the aftermath, whilst others, such as building standards, tended to remain outside public consciousness in the push for change. For those regulatory arenas at the forefront of public consciousness, pressure from non-governmental organizations (NGOs) and unions were critical elements in regulatory reform.

Those that remained outside the public gaze, such as building standards and fire safety standards, tended to develop through international collaboration at the governmental and elite level. Thai building standards set to be passed by parliament drew on standards developed in such diverse countries as the UK, Canada, Australia, Germany, Japan, Hong Kong, Singapore and China. The link to Kader of these reforms was not direct although the link to other contemporary disasters, such as the Royal Plaza Hotel collapse and the Royal Jomtien Hotel fire, was clearer. These latter disasters arguably had a higher profile, both in terms of the business elite within Thailand, as well as in the international arena.

Further, reforms could also involve private as well as public actors. For example, in the fire safety area improvements were promoted by the nascent fire protection industry, in particular companies involved in the production or distribution of equipment such as fire prevention technology, alarms, sprinklers, fire panels and the like. This could give rise to some conflict and difficulties, as fire prevention was also championed by local NGOs, who saw some problems with the involvement of for-profit organizations where businesses had little or no money.

The major focus of this research was on compensation and health and safety regulation. It was these two areas that had the greatest public profile. Certainly, the size of the fire in the centre of the capital galvanized the human response to suffering. The ensuing demands for compensation tapped into the public psyche about the need for reparation and support for victims and their families. Directly after the fire, the level of public support for victims meant that politicians felt compelled to respond. The then Prime Minister, Chuan Leekpai, went to the scene and promised a full investigation into the incident. Arrests were made; however one of these, the arrest of Viroj Yusak, a worker accused of lighting the fire by throwing away a cigarette, appeared more a case of blaming the victim. Nonetheless, company directors Julin Unaphum and Pichai Laukesem were also arrested, but later released. Charges were laid against these directors as well as a number of others involved in building and managing the factory.

Compensation

Immediately after the fire, an effective lobby group was created to push for compensation. The group was named 'Campaign for the Support of Kader Workers' (CSKW) and drew support from NGOs, unions and academics. It is important to note however, that it was not the Kader union itself that was instrumental in reforms. The Kader union was small (about 300) and weak. It disbanded soon after the fire and the members were dispersed. The major concern of the CSKW initially was to get compensation. Kader had paid into a compensation fund which entitled victims and their families to between 20,000 and 40,000 baht (US $520–1,040). Nonetheless the amount of compensation was woefully inadequate.

A decision was made to lobby Kader directly for additional compensation. This was a highly co-ordinated and creative campaign that travelled worldwide in order to raise awareness about the plight of Kader workers and their families. The focal point of the campaign was demonstrations in Hong Kong in front of company offices. The demonstration was wide-ranging, involving information, street theatre and videos to gain support of the local population. It was this part of the campaign that Voravidh Charoenloet, an academic activist and member of the CSKW, felt was the most important element in gaining further compensation. Eventually, after direct negotiation between the committee and the company, the government entitlement of 20,000–30,000 baht was supplemented by 330,000 baht (US $8,600) from the company. Part of this involved ongoing educational support for victims' children until they reached university level.

For this campaign to be successful, local NGOs needed to combine with their international counterparts to target the responsible company directly, since it was the company that was ultimately the subject of the protest action, and who paid the majority of the compensation, not the government. This strategy of targeting companies directly has since been repeated for high-profile disasters subsequent to Kader and has continued to prove successful. However, it was clear that this process placed certain injured workers at an advantage, but left many behind – those victims of multiple individual low-profile events that failed to reach public attention. Adequate compensation became a case-by-case affair, with those workers successful not because of the level of injury, but because of the high-profile nature of the event that led to the injury. A problem of those left behind was exemplified in the research which identified the problems of achieving compensation for victims of industrial disease, an ongoing and difficult problem. These victims not only faced an uphill battle of getting their ailment seen as related to their job, they also failed to gain a high international public profile in terms of their plight. Activists were forced to work through the government compensation system and little money was forthcoming.

Nonetheless, reform to government compensation schemes was also the target of some campaigns. Limited reform was forthcoming, with a growth in the number of companies required to pay into the compensation fund. Previously, only those companies with 50 or more workers were required to contribute. This changed in the wake of Kader, to a situation where companies with 10 or more workers were required to pay into the fund. However, making these reforms effective in terms of providing adequate payment – or indeed paying any compensation at all – proved to be more difficult. Further, the amount to which workers were entitled remained low and was inadequate to meet everyday needs. Victims could also find that once the company had contributed to the fund, lobbying the company for additional payment was made more difficult since the fund provided a means for companies to abrogate any further responsibility towards victims. There was an assumption by some companies that if they had paid into a compensation fund, they considered themselves absolved of further responsibility, despite the fact that such compensation was inadequate (Voravidh and Lae, 2000).

As a consequence, the amount of money in the fund was large and growing, since whilst individual payments both to and from the fund were small, few claims against the fund were successful. The cumulative assets of the fund rose from 34,150 million baht in 1995 to 88,560 million in 1999 (Annual Report, 1999) There was considerable incentive for the bureaucracy to keep the size of the fund increasing, as 22 per cent of the interest from the fund could be used for OHS promotion by the ministry administering the fund. With a large and growing fund, there were problems with adequate oversight, leading to the possibility of inappropriate or corrupt use of public money. The regional representative of the American Federation of Labor – Congress of Industrial Organizations (AFL-CIO) illustrated this with an example of inappropriate use of the money:

I'll give you a classic case, this group FES[14] they think 'Oh, wow, let's give them [officials from the Ministry] a study tour of Germany, they will see the light [about OHS] you know. So they [FES] took them on two study tours over a period of, I think, three years … Nothing changed, nothing changed. So the group [from the Ministry] then said 'Well we want to go on another study tour' and the FES says 'Well in fact you've gone on two study tours, you've met everybody, and despite all that you haven't changed your attitude or ideas one iota. Why should we send you on another study tour?' And they said, 'Well no, we really want to learn more', and the FES says, 'Well I'm sorry we don't have any budget available.' They said, 'Well that's OK, we'll pay ourselves. We want you to set up the tour and we've got business-class tickets.' Now what they were doing was taking money out of the fund. You've got to understand, see, that getting the money in the Civil Service System is very difficult in Thailand – so these people are sitting on a golden egg.

---

[14]   Freidrich Ebert Stiftung, the peak union body in Germany, which plays a role in educating both unions and government on health and safety issues in Thailand.

From a bureaucratic perspective, there is the very real issue of needing and retaining a budget. All government departments guard their budgets jealously, and Thai departments are no exception. The Asian financial crisis created further problems for government funding. As the regional representative of the AFL-CIO continued:

> ... The relevant group [Social Security Office] in the Ministry of Labour still want control because what they do, they get operating expenses out of the fund – plus any interest that gets earned by the fund, which is now huge, just disappears into that group ...

Local activists, however, were concerned that the money should be used for appropriate purposes, namely the prevention of occupational injury and disease. Their solution was to demand the creation of an independent occupational health and safety institute that would have oversight of the compensation fund to ensure that any interest gained from the money would be used for its proper purpose. The need for this institute formed a centrepiece of the campaign and is described in more detail below.

Before turning our attention to health and safety changes, one further element of the compensation regime is important. This is the effectiveness of the compensation that is actually paid. Analysis of the interviews suggests that once Kader had paid the compensation, they were able to regain the moral high ground and state they had done all they could reasonably have been expected to do. However, there was evidence from a research report of one of the most active NGOs in the area, the Arom Pompangan Foundation, that much money had not been paid and of that which had, there was evidence of misuse (Napaporn, 1997). For example, in one case the government promised a university scholarship for a high school student working at Kader, in order to get money for university. She was still unable to work and had not received any money to assist her in her studies. Further, even where compensation was paid, the inherent gender inequalities in society could mean that the money ends up in the wrong hands, or being spent in ways that do not advantage the victims. Most of the victims of Kader were women, many with children. The compensation that was paid, was paid to the husband. The foundation received reports of husbands depositing their children with the children's maternal grandparent before marrying again and denying ongoing responsibility for their children.

The long-term impact of the fire for victims was well summarized by Dr Voravidh, an academic activist:

> It appears that once the compensation was paid, there was no follow up. The government was happy that the conflict was resolved, the owner of the factory felt its brand name had not been tarnished. But the workers and their families still have to live with the situation every day. (Voravidh and Lae, 2000, p. 10)

Occupational Health and Safety

After the immediate concern with compensation, the CSKW turned its attention to health and safety reform. To reflect this new role it changed its name to the Campaigning Committee for the Health and Safety of Workers (CCHSW). The disaster remained an important rallying point. It was seen by the campaign as an opportunity for occupational health and safety (OHS) reform and consciousness-raising. The key demand was to set up a national Occupational Health and Safety Institute, which could provide independent oversight of the compensation fund and work towards comprehensive health and safety reform. A second demand was for a National Safety Day to raise awareness about health and safety and the plight of victims as well as improvement in the training and effectiveness of safety officers. Whilst there had been legislation allowing for safety officers within companies, these people had been poorly trained, were only part-time, and lacked the support of management and so feared losing their jobs if they were too critical. Finally, the CCHSW pushed for the creation of safety committees in each workplace.

Initial progress on the reforms was positive. The demand for a National Safety Day was acceded to, ministerial directives written into the regulations requiring the creation of safety committees in the workplace were drawn up, as well as improved training for safety officers. In addition, all parties agreed that comprehensive legislative reform to change attitudes towards workplace safety was necessary. The government set up a joint working party on reforms drawing on the expertise of NGOs as well as bureaucrats with expertise in the area, and a draft bill agreed to by both the Ministry of Labour and the CCHSW was finally drafted in 1997.

The centrepiece of this bill was the independent OHS institute. It was set up, as the CCHSW demanded, along a 'five-partite' model involving the traditional three groups (employer, union and government) along with victim groups, local victim-centred NGOs and academics. Activists saw this novel five-partite structure as a way of maintaining the central focus of reform on the health and safety of workers, not partial reform that protected the status quo or maintained the political interests of traditional tripartite members. Critically, the bill also stated that this new institute would control the compensation fund.

At the last moment, though, the Ministry replaced the negotiated bill with one of their own, one that excluded the independence of the OHS institute, and retained the existing management structure of the compensation fund. The bill required minimal re-organization of government departments. This led to an overall stalling of the reform, with neither act of parliament resulting. Indeed, a decade after the fire there remained no central Occupational Health and Safety Act in Thailand and thus no overriding duty of care on the part of employers.[15] Further, key bureaucrats who were considered to be pushing too hard for health and safety reform were 'moved sideways'.

---

[15] The need for an Act had been referred to the National Occupational Safety and Health and Working Environment Committee. The exact form the legislation will take was still the subject of protest at the time this book went to press.

There were some reforms to existing health and safety legislation, then, in line with CCHSW demands. On the whole, though, these changes were piecemeal, and the status quo remained, where responsibility for health and safety remained divided between a number of government departments. The responsibility for OHS regulation and enforcement remained divided between two major ministries: the Ministry of Industry (MOI) and the Ministry of Labour and Social Welfare (MLSW). Within the MOI, the Department of Industrial Works (DIW) retained responsibility for factory safety, whilst within the MLSW, the Department of Labour Protection and Welfare and its sub-bureaucracy, the National Institute for Working Conditions and Environment (NICE), continued to share responsibility for occupational health and safety and the safety inspectorate. Comprehensive OHS reform required one or other department to cede some control, something they were unwilling to do.

However, to limit the assessment of health and safety reform following Kader as purely that involving minor legislative reform would be a mistake. Reforms had taken place beyond the 'command and control' focus of either the MLSW or the DIW. A key policy initiative of the Department of Industry (DOI) was the development of an occupational health and safety standard by the Thai Industrial Standards Institute (TISI), a sub-bureaucracy under the Department of Industry. The standard, based on a draft International Organization for Standardization (ISO) standard, set out the key criteria for a health and safety management system. The system was voluntary. Companies could be accredited to the TIS 18001 standard as a way of improving their health and safety programme and demonstrating their commitment to health and safety. At the time of the field research, the initiative was still in its early stages and relied on companies seeing the benefits of a good health and safety programme in terms of increased productivity and retention of trained staff.

This initiative of the Department of Industry is consistent with global trends that emphasize the value of self-regulation and accreditation. It is interesting to note that the policy explicitly sets out to capitalize on market mechanisms for its success. Under guidance from the IMF, seed funding has been made available for three years to allow the DOI to set up an independent auditing institute, MASCI,[16] to audit companies accredited under the TIS 18001 programme. It was envisaged that MASCI would eventually become self-funding through revenues from industry keen to take advantage of TISI accreditation. IMF intervention was aimed at ensuring a shift to the private sector of elements of health and safety accreditation seen to be amenable to private sector control. Auditing was seen as one such element.

TIS 18001 accreditation was seen as flexible, allowing health and safety to remain abreast of rapid changes of corporate form and investment location. In the case of Kader this was important. The Kader operations largely shifted from Bangkok to the regions and, rather than relying on factory labour, production largely moved to a home-work environment. The increases in standards of the

---

[16]   Management System Certification Institute (Thailand).

product and of the working conditions were both addressed by accreditation systems. Quality of the product could be assured through ISO 9001 accreditation, and it was hoped that TIS 18001 would eventually form the assurance for health and safety of the workforce. Nonetheless, both remained voluntary.

Prosecutions Postscript

For activists, TIS 18001 was not where their main concern lay. A voluntary programme, particularly one without strong worker input, was seen to have limited effect. Bringing about more tangible changes that were compulsory and enforceable was central to their campaign. So, too, was the concern to bring individual directors to account for their contribution to disasters and to make them more responsible. After the fire, there was a great deal of concern expressed by activist NGOs and union groups that Kader and individual directors should be held to account. There was anger at the arrest of Viroj Yusak and a widespread feeling that he was made a scapegoat for the problems at the factory. However, keeping track of the court cases that arose out of Kader did not feature prominently in activist work since court cases tended to be long and to fall well short of activists' expectations of justice. Indeed, at the time of fieldwork in 1999–2000 some believed that the cases had lapsed and charges dropped; this was not the case. Prosecutions were brought against fifteen individuals at Nakhom Pathom Provincial Court. Amongst these were those against Viroj Yusak the worker accused of lighting the fire by smoking a cigarette, two directors of Kader, a building engineer and a company shareholder as well as Kader Industrial (Thailand) itself as a juristic entity (Penchan, 2003).

Some cases, such as that against Viroj Yusak, were protracted. Reasons for this included the fact that hundreds of witnesses were called, many of whom had returned to their provinces and were difficult to find. In addition, over the 10 years of the case there were frequent changes of judges and prosecutors. At each change the new court actors needed time to familiarize themselves with the case, prolonging proceedings (Prapaiparn, 2000). The witnesses called included injured workers, many of whom testified that they saw Viroj smoking in a cloth storage room. Engineers and architects were also called up, some as expert witnesses; others had worked for Kader and stated that they had been required by the factory owner to change the building specifications, namely to downgrade the steel materials to non-fire-resistant ratings and to reduce the number of fire exits. It will be remembered that both these factors considerably exacerbated the loss of life due to the fire.

The case finally concluded in January 2003, almost 10 years after the fire. Viroj Yusak was sentenced to 10 years jail for lighting the fire. Charges against all individuals associated with Kader including the directors and the engineer were found not proven. The Kader company was fined 520,000 baht.[17] Activist groups

---

[17] Approximately US $13,500.

expressed their dismay at the outcome. It was reported that the prosecution would appeal the case (Penchan, 2003).

Conclusion

This brief summary has shown that reforms were forthcoming in the wake of Kader. In the terms of Hancher and Moran (1998), it appeared there was a regulatory crisis in the wake of the disaster that generated reform. Further, the data show that in the case of Kader a range of regulatory arenas were affected, not limited to the high-profile areas of compensation and occupational health and safety. Building standards and fire safety standards were also drawn into the crisis and were in the process of reform. Secondly, the reform process involved a range of actors: politicians, bureaucrats, private companies, activists and standard-setting NGOs, such as the National Fire Prevention Association (NFPA) and the International Organization for Standardization (ISO). The range of actors involved varied from one regulatory arena to another, as did the accessibility of each area in terms of public understanding and public profile.

The involvement of the private sector and the interaction between the private sector and government was also notable in the aftermath of Kader. Firstly, the compensation for Kader victims was paid directly by the company, not the government. It was the company that was the target of vigorous protest. Secondly, recent reforms, specifically TISI 18001, sought to capitalize on private sector involvement and the need to improve their health and safety practice. Both of these are beyond the 'command and control' conception of the proper focus of regulation.

There were also significant reforms to traditional government regulatory structures. The compensation scheme was strengthened and a number of new occupational health and safety initiatives introduced or reworked. In many respects the reforms were familiar to an international audience, as were the problems. Internationally, the need for separation between compensation regulators from occupational health and safety policy and research is argued to be critical by some (Hopkins, 1995), whilst others see value in a joint approach (Industry Commission, 1994). Further, regulatory arenas often overlap and are shared by a number of agencies. Dangerous goods (hazardous substances), building safety, and fire safety are all areas where regulatory responsibility is often split between regulators and bureaucracies. Characterizing the regime in Thailand in light of its regulatory structure as either 'good' or 'bad' brings with it problems in terms of identifying an adequate or objective benchmark against which to compare the Thai regime.

The outcome of the court case highlights both the differences and similarities between Thailand and industrialized nations in their approach to safety. Certainly, the jailing of the worker for 10 years appears unjust and incongruous with the 'progressive' image Thailand would like to convey. In terms of safety management it is a classic case of 'blaming the victim' (for a US history of this phenomenon sees Sellars, 1997). It is unlikely that such a prosecution would be considered within industrialized countries. Indeed it can be contrasted with the public outrage expressed against Esso Australia in the Longford Gas explosion in Victoria, Australia, when the company tried to pass the blame onto one of its workers. It was felt that this, in part, lay behind the size of the fine levied against the company, AU $2 million (Australian Broadcasting Commission, 2001). However, Kader (Industrial) did not escape sanction. Further, a finding of guilt against a company with prosecutions failing against powerful individuals is a pattern common in the West (Ayres and Braithwaite, 1992; Wells, 1995).

Critically, then, the reforms in the wake of Kader must be appreciated in light of Thai regulatory character. This chapter has provided several examples, including but not limited to the court outcomes, which indicate the need to evaluate reform in context not as an abstract or technical exercise but one intimately connected to the local environment. The challenge of providing an effective compensation scheme, the worth of the activist push for a five-partite OHS regulatory framework, and the significance of TIS 18001, all require a grounded approach to evaluating the reforms in the wake of Kader. The next two chapters take up this challenge.

Chapter 5

Regulatory Character and Response: Patriarchalism and Self-reliance

Regulatory character, if it is to be a useful concept, should provide a means for understanding the significance of change, or lack of change, within the Kader reforms. How should the failure of significant change in occupational health and safety law be viewed? Are the changes that were made, such as safety committees and a Safety Day, a substantial step in the right direction for example? What of the failure of the reform bill? Was this a major setback, or was it better seen as an ambit claim, one that settled to an appropriate set of reforms? These next two chapters are primarily concerned with understanding the reforms in their local context. Chapters 7 and 8 then go on to explore how the changes should be understood in light of the challenges of globalization, with a particular focus on how regulatory character anticipates and is influenced by global processes. It is here that the moves towards positioning Thailand as a location for ethical investment will be assessed. Each of Chapters 5 to 8 relies heavily on the narrative of informants to the research. It was felt that this was the best way to communicate the complexity of character. These narratives provide the flesh and mind around the skeletal discussion of reforms in Chapter 4 and the theoretical framework of regulatory character.

Chapter 3 outlined a framework for understanding Thai regulatory character in some detail. Regulatory character is framed by an understanding of the form authority takes within a particular place, the interaction between norms and laws set against an understanding of the rationale underpinning the relationship between individual and institution, and the subjective and objective reality of a given regulatory context (refer Figures 3.3 and 3.4). The chapter argued that traditional Thai regulatory character emphasized patriarchal authority structures, where norms of society emphasized hierarchical relationships with power flowing down from individuals in positions of authority. This authority drew strength from the self-reliance of Thais as flexible and adept at understanding their place. Patronage and personal relationships were critically important, as were an understanding of a person's status. Smooth relationships were assisted by individuals consciously positioning themselves within the hierarchical social order, and assisting others to do the same. The authority of law, or formalism, was vested in the author of the law, that is, those in positions of authority within the hierarchy. Law was a device for asserting authority, or in the case of foreign threat or protest as a means for asserting independence or placating threats, rather than necessarily aimed at changing behaviour.

However, this form of Thai regulatory character was not without challenge. The history of protest within Thailand, particularly against military leadership, as well as the development of a civil elite, had made inroads into institutional structures and the development of a rule of law. Nonetheless, this emphasis remained tenuous, since the activities of both protesters and the civil elite could be targeted as much at the re-imposition of the ideals of a traditional Thai society, as one which was based primarily on the rule of law (Hewison, 2001).

In addition, Thai regulatory character was argued to have two sides, labelled interpenetrative and strategic. Interpenetrative regulatory character was character expressed through ideals of 'Nation, Religion, King', of deference to hierarchy and the responsibilities of the elite. Conflict was held at bay by recognition of place and obligation. Under the interpenetrative dimension of regulatory character, law protects the social order (see Figure 3.3 above). Strategic regulatory character, in contrast, used systems of authority for the purposes of control and domination (see Figure 3.4 above). Primarily this took the form of corporatist control, although violent repression could occur against those deemed 'outsiders'. Self-reliance was expressed through nepotism of strategic relationships between 'insiders' and repression of others. Law was explicitly a means of extending control or as a means of asserting independence. Under this guise, the fact of the law's existence was important, that is, it contained the right things, but not that it was workable in practice. Finally, strategy characterized individual relationships, with the ultimate purpose being of enhancing one's position.

Chapter 3 concluded with the statement that the experience of regulatory character would be likely to differ quite considerably between men and women. Women's experiences emphasized their reliability and responsibility and their role in providing social cohesiveness. Within a hierarchical frame, women were both strong and subordinate, with laws to enshrine equality likely to miss the fundamental reality of women's lives.

This chapter will explore the degree to which understanding the patriarchal/self-reliance nexus within regulatory character can enliven an understanding of the reforms following Kader. The focus is then primarily on the 'group' dimension of regulatory character, that argued in Chapter 3 to be the dominant relationship in the Thai context. The analysis below begins with an exploration of patriarchalism, both that exhibiting an interpenetrative hue and that demonstrating the impact of a strategic face. The exploration of self-reliance follows a similar pattern and rounds out the 'group' interactions of Thai regulatory character. Clearly, this dimension is dualistic. Interpenetrative patriarchal forms emphasize values, whilst strategic patriarchalism shows the results of political manoeuvring and control strategies aimed to maintain the status quo. Interpenetrative self-reliance, in contrast, involved trust in authority, albeit one that required hard work. Strategic self-reliance on the other hand involved a much more active process of using institutions – government, private and NGO – for personal gain.

Patriarchalism

Patriarchalism and Interpenetration

Waradom's personal story is an accessible beginning point for understanding patriarchalism within Thai regulatory character. Waradom, a fire safety consultant, was a member of the elite, with a strong desire, following his experience of Kader, to develop a fire safety regime in Thailand. His was a story of privilege. At the centre of his understanding of the obligation his privilege brought with it, was the example set by the King Bhumibol of service to Thai people. As he stated, 'I admire my King very much. If you ask Thai people, we all love our King, because our King dedicates his life for our Thai people.' Waradom was certainly not alone in expressing this feeling, indeed the importance of the King as an example was commonly expressed. Yet as Waradom's story below illustrates, for him there was more than the usual reason for such feelings of obligation. He was both distantly related to the King and had benefited from education at the royal school. Waradom began by explaining his relationship to the Royal family:

> ... The first generation of my family is related to the queen of King Rama VI ... She didn't have kids. That's why we're just related ... But this helps me a lot in Thailand, because I have this last name – Kosotarakoum ... My father's father, my grandfather, is the brother of the Queen of Rama VI and also my grandmother on my father's side is the sister of the first Prime Minister of Thailand. So my father's side is quite strong.

This relationship provided opportunities for his family, in particular for his father, and also meant that he also could benefit from the family relationship to royalty in the form of an elite education:

> ... My father is a policeman, a general in police cadets, police force, police department, OK, and my mother is a housewife. We have two children in my family, myself and my sister ... When I studied in primary school I'm suddenly in the King's palace. It has about eight levels at that time ... I stayed very close to the King's house, King's palace. This school they started for the prince and princess to study, we have the same friends ... [we] all graduated from the school at that time. This school had eight levels, each level has only one class, and one class always forty students. So the eight levels had three hundred something students at that time ... very small. We have a lot of teachers and we talked about the people, the student and teacher ... one teacher covered maybe ten students, something like that. So we're proud to stay in this school.

He was not, however, entirely impressed by the activities of those from a privileged upbringing. He felt many had squandered their opportunities, an example he did not wish to follow. His sister had proved that more was possible:

> Right now my sister is a judge and myself, I'm going to accomplish my dreams ... I'd like to help people ... That's my dream. Since I was a child my mother always tell me, 'You should be somebody. You help people' ... the great generation cannot cover the second, the third and the fourth generation. We were treated so well. So most of my family, not myself and my sister but another one, just stay on the assets of the previous

generation. And I think this happen from all over the world when you were born in the well-to-do families. Wealthy people, they don't know what to do … when you are born in too rich a family, you just do nothing, except spend money.

Finding the means to serve took him first to engineering school and then on to the Army. A position in the Army provided the authority needed for change in the public good; as he stated below, in the Army, 'Nobody can touch you; you can do many things.' Waradom continued:

> … And after that I go to the engineering school … In Thailand also we have to take what we call entrance examination. It's also quite difficult to pass through the area that we want. OK. Finally I got to engineering school and I study electrical engineering for four years. After I graduated from engineering school, I go to Royal Thai Army, work as medical engineer, designing medical systems for Army buildings. It's requirement for all men in Thailand to get involved with the Army. But myself, because I study in engineering school in the university, I already passed these requirements. OK, so I don't have to go to the Royal Thai Army. But, in Thailand in the past, everyone who worked with the Army or for the people. In our country, it helps something. Nobody can touch you; you can do many things in our country.

However, by the time Waradom had joined up, the Army was no longer the dominant force for change it had once been. Waradom realised his dreams were not to be found in the Army: 'right now many things change,' he recounted. Further education seemed a better means of advancement. For reasons beyond his control, education outside Thailand, a normal course for Thais of his status, was not open to him and he settled for an MBA in Thailand. It was here at graduate school in Thailand that he became aware of the realities of study for the majority of Thais, those without his privileged background:

> So I work in our Army and together I study Master degree in Business Administration [in Thailand] … At that time, to study in the MBA school is quite difficult. It's about 6000 people in the examination, only 137 pass. So luckily I passed the examination. [I was] really happy at that time … So when I study with these people in the Masters degree, I realise they're all very good at studying, in working. So I found something from this people I could compare back to my high school … the palace children cannot do anything because of their parents. But these [MBA] people work very hard. They start from zero, even minus. They have to pay [for] their house, [their] course – even pay their parents! But myself, I pay nothing. I found that these people work very hard but don't have opportunities or chance to step higher. So I compared this to previously and I think I need to work hard. With my background, I think I should get somewhere in the future … Because I study in the palace school so I also study almost for free. I pay very little and I get everything from the King … After I work in Royal Thai Army I found that most of them [also] work very little. Because I think we have too many people in the Army at that time. Many jobs, but how do you say? Government procedure is quite slow … I found that I should resign from the Army to work in something else that would teach me the world.

Waradom concluded his story with telling of his ambition to set up a world-class business in fire prevention. His means of achieving this takes us beyond Thai regulatory character to the influence of globalization on that character.

From the narrative above, the interpenetrative elements of patriarchalism are clearly expressed. Privilege comes from your position in the hierarchy, in this case a relationship to the Royal Family. It is not to be squandered, but to be used to benefit ordinary Thai people as well as for the maintenance of your own position and that of your family. Whilst at one time this could be achieved through service in the Army, times had moved on and business was now a more viable means of service. The element that is perhaps unusual in the story from the outline in Chapter 4 is the achievement of his sister, rising to the position of judge, which is certainly not a subordinate role. The inspiration of his mother as a spur to his achievements (Mulder, 2000) is perhaps more typical.

Waradom was not alone in enjoying the benefits of patronage. A key bureaucrat had also enjoyed the benefit of patronage, this time from the Dean of his university, who promised jobs to all the members of his class of 15 students. The initial prospects appeared dim:

> ... when I was studying in public health school I have a choice, whether I would like to be in environmental sanitation or occupational health specialist or nutritionist or a health educator. So, I decided to go to occupational health. At that time, could you imagine, there was no vacancy for a job. I can see that after graduation no-one would hire me for that position. I just took a chance. I went into that area without knowing what the future is going to be. I remember the Dean of the school, he came to our class because our class is only 15 people and he said, 'Well, don't worry, I will guarantee to get a job for all of you'!

The Dean succeeded, with many achieving powerful positions within the bureaucracy and academia. Academia, alongside the monarchy and the military, has considerable status, in keeping with the Thai ideals of a teacher or *ajan*. Academia also had considerable flexibility, with many academics taking on other roles either within business or the NGO sector. Dr Voravidh, a prominent academic advocate for workers, explained:

> [As] professors in Thailand we have more flexibility. You take care of your teachings and some of your research but apart from that you can manage your time. So you can get two Thai professors, one can go on to become a consultant to the business firm, or you get others who choose to work with the labourers or the NGOs. So we are this type, you know, more volunteer work.

In performing his volunteer work, Voravidh had some entrée to the bureaucracy, a means of influence that was missing for some other NGOs. This access resulted from both being of a 'similar status' and also sharing a common experience as a student. This then provided the opportunity to push for change:

> In Thailand we [academics] have a link. The link [to the bureaucracy] is through the academics also because the [relationship between] NGOs and the bureaucrats sometimes

it is very difficult, so you need a link because the bureaucrats they will feel [comfortable] ... So the academics are a link. That's why we link to OHS; we link to academics with Dr Chaiyuth or with others. We find good bureaucrats that [way].

There was then an opportunity to work through personal relationships to push for change. Dr Voravidh saw the essence of personal relationships as a contrast to, and on occasion more effective than, a legalistic approach. Relationships emphasized flexibility and appreciation of the role of the other person. It also acknowledged that authority lay in the person, rather than the law:

Yeah. Here the relationship is more or less personal rather than legal, although you have legal ... Personal relationship is, in Thailand [important] ... and we use it also, you know, there is a flexibility in our interaction. It can be used in a negative side ... [but also] positive, like with Kader. If you were to work alone, I don't think you could achieve this much. But we have worked [together], we have been connecting with the politicians through personal connections ... In a Thai society I think this kind of personal [connection] ... it can be created. I think we are more or less homogenous society with the Buddhist [base] ... this [leads to] a kind of tolerance ... [and means] sometimes you can negotiate. It depends on, you can interact or, you know ... I cannot explain it, but sometimes I just feel it. It may be ... I don't know. That's how we work, you know.

Military rule provided for others the means to establish the beginnings of a health and safety structure within the bureaucracy, without political interference. The National Institute for Working Conditions and Environment (NICE) was one of the government departments that was responsible for health and safety, and was set up during a period of military rule. Dr Chaiyuth, a senior bureaucrat, alluded to the lack of politicking as providing the opportunity for bureaucrats to set up the NICE, the government institution with the greatest expertise in health and safety. Asked about the motivation behind NICE's establishment, Dr Chaiyuth responded:

In fact it went back to 1979. At that time Thailand ... we set up our system ... We – the government, the employers, the workers ... we saw that it was time for a change. At that time ... safety and health was not well established and also we have many problems, accidents, occupational diseases, we don't have any organization to deal with this matter ... In a sense there were no politicians ... Well, we were under military government for many years, but I think the initiative came from government officials. The Department of Labour ... the civil service at that time ... they initiated it.

The common goal and the freedom to act were important for a focus on public service. The sense was that politics was tainted by corruption and could get in the way, whilst military rule allowed for greater progress. Dr Chaiyuth was also complimentary about the administration of Anand Panyarachun, the Prime Minister set up by the military junta in a transitional administration in 1992. The personal qualities of Anand, as well as his clear authority, meant that reform was rapid during his administration. Many laws were passed, including the *Factories Act, Hazardous Substances Act* and the *Public Health Act*. In the opinion of Dr Chaiyuth, Anand Panyarachun was an ideal prime minister: '... Very energetic!

Very good man. He became PM two times … yes, we would like to have a PM like that. He had a good vision, and clean.' Dr Chaiyuth's enthusiasm, however, was not shared by Dr Voravidh, whose view was more aligned with literature in the area (see Pasuk and Baker, 1995, pp. 355–61). Efficiency did not necessarily result in a good outcome and Anand's connection to an authoritarian regime meant that for activists a key element, democratic accountability, was lacking:

> No, I don't agree; I think he was efficient in a way, but he was nominated from an authoritarian state … he was nominated by the military to become the Prime Minister. So he could … during his time a lot of legislation came out, good ones but also many bad ones as well … Yes, he was efficient, but you cannot link him with this [OHS reform], because most of this legislation came out because of the social movement in occupational health and safety.

For Dr Voravidh then, the process and inclusion of ordinary people in setting up a health and safety regime was critical to its success. Efficiency did not equate with effectiveness. Whilst both Dr Chaiyuth and Dr Voravidh saw the importance of networks to getting things done, for Dr Voravidh, the ultimate goal was a shift in social norms away from the elite, to a greater level of democracy.

As we shall see below, though, both efficiency and effectiveness suffer when patriarchalism takes on a strategic hue. It is perhaps for this reason that Dr Chaiyuth, a senior bureaucrat, had considerable sympathy for an administration under which legislative change occurred within a reasonable frame of time, even if democracy was circumscribed in the process. Without political interference, those within the bureaucracy who saw the need for change could accomplish something.

Before turning to strategy and patriarchalism, the interpenetrative quality of patriarchy and business needs to be mentioned. Whilst a patriarchal sense of obligation was most often expressed in the form of the King and Queen, educational establishments and the bureaucracy, some conceded benevolent paternalism was present in some businesses. In the words of one informant, 'There are a few kind owners. We have a few kind owner[s], you know!' This paternalism was seen in both small businesses as well as large. Siam Cement was one of the first businesses to try and educate workers about health and safety in the 1960s. Tom Kanathat Chantrsiri,[18] who had since then moved into the area of fire prevention, was involved in this education, through his work making documentaries:

> Long story. When I graduate very long time ago, 20–30 years ago, I was the scriptwriter for the TV, the documentary TV programme. One day the big company, cement company, asked me to make one documentary … [to] make five programmes on safety, teach them how to wear the hard hat, helmet, goggles, ear muffs … I was quite interested, because 30 years ago in Thailand nobody was interested in wearing a hard hat to get into the construction area.

---

[18]   Kanathat was known within the NGO community as 'Uncle Tom'. In the text he is referred to as Kanathat, in keeping with the reference to all other Thai participants in the research who are by convention referred to by their first name.

The local ILO representative also felt business could play a positive role; he argued that it was not from callousness, but lack of knowledge, and in the case of small business a lack of time, that injury and sickness arose. Employers were basically concerned about their workers:

> ... they are concerned with safety and health. Because these days a lot of news arrived in the newspapers ... some explosive accident and many employers arrested and workers killed. Employers understand ... I found many employers, they are basically nice people, but the point is they don't know how to improve the safety health and they are very busy small businesses too. They are very hard working. To be fair, many people tend to blame employers. Of course, there are several employers to be blamed, but in my experience, the majority of them they are concerned with safety health. But, they're not very active, but they are concerned. They want to do something if they can, but they don't know how to do [it].

Patriarchal authority under conditions of interpenetration would then seem to provide some opportunities for safety improvement. Better education of those in leadership positions, and the support of benevolent individuals in positions of power who could influence others by their example, would seem to provide a good starting point. However, an emphasis on paternalism and education as a solution to injury and disease in the workplace needs to consider how the strategic patriarchalism within Thai regulatory character is expressed.

Patriarchalism and Strategy

Under conditions of strategy, the emphasis on patriarchy changes from an ethos of care and responsibility to a strategy of improving status and extending control. Whilst the interpenetrative emphasis, as in Waradom's story, is on the way that status frees the individual to do more in the public sphere, a strategic frame sees status as both an end in itself and a means for extending control. There are several examples from the data where status can be the central purpose of an institution or activity. Education, for example, becomes a means to achieve status, not as a means to further learning and knowledge in the community. To be in a position of high status means that it is necessary to obtain the right status symbols. Tertiary educational qualifications, a prerequisite for advancement within the bureaucracy, could act more as a status symbol, allowing extension of personal control rather than the learning itself improving the quality of the work done. Dr Voravidh understood this dynamic:

> It's a way to get that status into the country ... 'I work for the bureaucracy; I have a PhD from England; I'm important' ... The position ... That's why there is a government mentality here ... It is history, because to get status in Thailand in the past, you needed a government position. When you get that government position you are in the hierarchy, that means you can at least command people; the bureaucrats in the countryside are powerful figures ...

The status achieved by the qualification was more important than the content of the educational programme. Relevant educational qualifications might be important for inclusion in the decision making process, but status level determined the seriousness with which your ideas would be received. Being in a position of high status meant dispensing wisdom. Having status meant that your ideas must be expressed and acknowledged. Waradom commented: 'Like the big guy, they don't know much about safety. But, by their position they have to come to the meeting and give some ideas.' These ideas would not necessarily be helpful. Kanathat spoke of the fire safety area: ' ... Thai people don't know ... even the high-ranking ones ... they don't know how to evacuate. If you are sitting in the big office and the fire alarm go[es] off, 'What is that sound for?,' they will say. This is not to say that relevant expertise was never present; it was. However, when relevant experts were present on committees they were often in less influential positions. The National Safety Council (NSC) expressed how policy reform committee members were chosen, using the expression, 'We choose by power', and then continued:

> Most of the members of the committee are high-ranking officers ... we have a specialist from outside ... It seems like we have committees but in practice it depends on chairman ... because by our regulations the chairman of all committees [is the Prime Minister] he knows what's happening.

'Big' people in positions of high status would network with others of a similar status, but in a different sphere. Bureaucratic elites network with the military and business leaders. During the research, it became clear that many businesses had members of the military or high-ranking police on their boards. This was seen as essential to the smooth running of the business in the local area. The impact on occupational health and safety by having the military and police on a company's board was argued by some to be negligible, whilst for others the involvement of the police in business, particularly if they owned the business, was problematic, since their presence combined with their status would discourage safety inspections. The local representative of the AFL-CIO stated:

> What you have [on these sites] is, you usually have the husband and the wife both working there; you have the four-year-old kid running around without any supervision. The owner of that building is a police captain, so there's no way that any sort of labour inspector is going to go in there and cause a problem ... it would be a very unsafe work site. In fact, I saw people on one site, when they were taking down the scaffolding on the side of the building, they were basically hanging in the air.

The relationships between people of high status within the military, bureaucracy, politics and business played a key role in what happened, or did not happen. For activists, the connections that CP had with the government were also important in explaining the outcomes of Kader. Jaded, a representative of the NGO Friends of Women, stated, 'Remember, CP is very, very happy with its connections in the government ... they have spent a lot of money to get into that relationship.' The role of the military, however, had declined since 1992 and with it their influence on reform. Instead it was the interests of the politicians and bureaucratic heads that were most evident in reform outcomes. Jaded continued:

There is a connection between the military and the government, but after 1992 the role of the military started to decrease ... the government officials and the politicians have some contact, they're all in together, they have got some kind of deal. So you get something, I get something ... If the politicians, the MPs, whatever, or the cabinet approves the budget for the worker, then they [the bureaucrats] get the money.

The research suggested prestige was shifting not only away from the military but also the bureaucracy, towards business and politics. Nonetheless, the strategic manner in which status was used was the same: status was important for the purpose of influence, not a job well done, as Dr Voravidh explained:

Right now they [the bureaucrats] tended to be superseded, as the economy grows the status shifts to the businessman ... It is changing, but it [the bureaucracy] still has power and prestige. That means also businessman will depend on them ... they tend to depend on each other, but both are getting more and more influential because they get into politics. Right now also you get the bureaucrats, [when] they retire they go into politics ... also you get many bureaucrats going into politics straight away. So politics in Thailand, you talk about the bureaucracy, they are in fact the same. Democracy in Thailand is not a real democracy, because people go into that because they want the status.

Status was valued then both for its own sake and because it provided a means of control. The presence of regulations that threatened this control had to be neutralized. This had a direct impact on how health and safety law could be enforced. One such reform proposed following Kader was regulatory reform to allow workers in genuine fear of their safety to stop working until an inspector cleared the worksite as safe. In the draft Occupational Health and Safety Bill drawn up by NICE, the right to stop work was discussed, but was seen as too radical a step for Thailand to follow, as Dr Chaiyuth explained:

... we also thought that we could put in [to the bill] that the workers can stop working, if they feel that they are frightened about hazardous conditions until and unless the inspector came to the workplace and says 'Right, OK, you can continue working.' ... But many people said at that time that this is too soon to bring this into Thailand.

This need to control could result in repressive tactics by those in authority. Activists gave examples during specific political regimes of the use of violence and government incitement of violence as a means for justifying repression. They insisted, though, that this was the exception in Thailand, not the rule. Jaded argued with respect to Chuan Leekpai:[19]

We have the people's demonstration, they [the government] use violence ... there tends to be a third hand, ... in some case it is the police who cause the people to be violent. [Q: Is it normal?] No! Others listen to poor people but Chuan Leekpai doesn't listen ... Some governments did use violence against the poor, the people. But Chuan Leekpai

---

[19]   Prime Minister during the period of field research.

uses it more, you know, more than everyone. He himself doesn't listen to the labour movement at all, poor people, labour people.

Those in authority were also concerned to control the amount of information coming out of investigations into disasters, in particular the Royal Jomtien Fire, which occurred in 1997. Again, here, repressive tactics could be used, such as imprisonment of those with critical information about how the fire started. A fire NGO representative spoke of control by 'big men':

> ... When the police came to that hotel, the first question they asked people around and the hotel staff was, 'Who saw what happened?' So six, four or five guys said, 'Yes! I did.' OK, they said, you come to the police station ... and, you know, they are in the jail until now. They made a case against them ... to keep them in jail ... I don't know [the reason] exactly, but for this case something like this. If you go to ask about the event nobody will tell you ... what really happened. Because they are scared. If I talk, if I tell that *farang* [foreigner], that Australian person, they will get arrested. So, they say they don't know exactly what happened ... Because they are afraid if you then go to high-ranking police ... there is fear from the Thai people.

Most often, though, control was not expressed in a repressive manner. It was more by a process of exclusion of genuine input from workers, which made activists feel that the system was not democratic. Jaded stated, 'The Ministry of Labour, they like to control things; they like to have the power over workers.' This was a wearing process, as he explained: 'So it's hard for the worker to participate in a lot of activity, right? It's just power in the hands of the government agencies and it takes time for us.'

A useful example of the rigidity of status and need for control as a barrier to reform and effective health and safety enforcement was provided by the way the inspectorate worked. Those in senior positions within the regulatory authority had considerable control over subordinates. The inspector, as a lower level bureaucrat, then, had little independent authority. To enforce OHS provisions, in particular the new prohibition notices, they needed their departmental manager's approval, as Chaiyuth explained:

> ... the inspector himself does not have independent power; he cannot say, well, 'Stop this.' Before he says this, he has to consult the boss, and when the boss says, 'OK,' probably he might need his [boss's] handwriting: 'You have my approval,' but that has not yet happened [laugh], so I think – I would really like to see something happen there ...

This needs to be contrasted with much Western OHS law, such as in Australia, where inspectors have considerable independent power, and where obstruction of an inspector attracts high penalties (Johnstone, 1997). Nonetheless, Thai inspectors were required to have a university degree for their position. Dr Chaiyuth argued that education was critical to their ability to communicate on the same level with businesspeople:

> From my understanding, I think a certain level of education, I think, is important. You see, otherwise, when you get to the workplace, you cannot communicate with them, you don't speak their language, sometimes, because your level of education is so low ... you are not respected because you don't speak their language, you don't know what to ask to bring the issues for discussion and so on ...

Education was seen as important. Despite this, however, inspectors had little authority, suggesting that educational achievement was at least in part about signalling the status of the inspector, rather than about how well they were able to communicate or enforce government regulations.

The need for elite bureaucratic control extended beyond departmental employees to professionals. A good example here is doctors who were involved in the compensation scheme. One of the key health and safety concerns expressed in the data by activists involved industrial disease. As was explained in Chapter 4, a compensation fund existed to which workers who are made sick or injured at work had access, provided their company had paid into the fund. In cases of injury where there were eye-witnesses, payment from the fund was forthcoming, although awareness of entitlements remained low. In the case of disease, however, there was considerable difficulty in proving that an illness or chronic injury was caused by work. This meant that access to compensation was seriously limited. Again, the qualification of the doctor in the area of occupational injury or disease was not the major issue, but whose control they were under. Voravidh explained:

> ... when calamities happen like this kind of factory fire, or factory explosion ... people could get compensated with no question, but when it comes to the occupational disease, or disease related to illness, then it is very questionable. [Those] who verify whether the workers are sick or not because of work, [are] doctors supported by the workmen's compensation fund ... The people on the compensation committee are doctors appointed by the workers' medical compensation fund. There are eighteen doctors, but no-one has a degree in occupational disease medicine ... There is another doctor who is qualified, and she works with the Workers' Compensation Board, Dr Oraporan, but the board doesn't accept [her judgement] ... We have to use the court, the labour court, to resolve this conflict ... right now there are about 40 cases that went into the court ... there's a conflict there. So it's still in court. It has been fighting for almost five years now. It's a long story ... very complicated.

Tripartite bodies themselves were also a means to retain control. Tripartite committees – the inclusion of worker representatives, government and industry bodies – are the internationally accepted manner for inclusion of worker perspectives. However, within a Thai context, tripartism was transformed from a body of negotiation to one that maintained the status quo. Tripartite committees often proved an unhelpful forum for change. Part of the reason for this was the fragmentation of both union and employer representatives within Thailand, with the result that tripartite committees were seen as a means to control labour. Voravidh explained:

The government [bill] is more of a traditional tripartite [form], because the tripartite way in Thailand is used to control the labour ... tripartite is used in Thailand in a way that fragmented the unions because we have this nine national centres for labour[20] and we have the 10 employers' associations. It is very fragmented.

Tripartite models were described as a 'prison framework', since when activists made proposals, the first response from government was, 'Ah, you have to get agreement from the other side,' to discuss it according to the tripartite process. Bundit from the Arom Pongpangan Foundation, a key labour NGO, explained how control was further extended through limiting the numbers of worker and business representatives that could be present on a committee or at a conference, as well as careful selection of the type of person chosen to be a representative:

The people participating in this conference are the government officials or, you know, civil servants, just only one worker, right, one labour leader ... one from the employer, one from the employee ... all the rest are from government ... When the government choose the people they choose the one who is very compromising and not representative. Very weak or not well known; they cannot make a decision. Weak person.

The most compelling example of tripartite control came from the senior government bureaucrat, who described tripartite control over the inspector and their authority to place a prohibition notice[21] on a piece of equipment, prohibition notices being one of the new initiatives of the government put in place after Kader. The process that inspectors had to adhere to in order to place a notice on an area of work emphasizes both the hierarchist nature of the regulatory framework and the way tripartite control worked. In order to place a notice on a piece of equipment banning its use because of some hazard, inspectors first had to get permission from the director of their department. In most other regimes, inspectors have the independent authority to use prohibition notices as they see fit. However, the director was not the only source of control on the inspector; they also were under the control of the tripartite committee through a process of appeal and review. In the Thai system, if an inspector's judgement was found to be in error by the tripartite committee, the inspector was personally liable for the loss of revenue of the business. Chaiyuth explained:

... with the new Act, the Labour Protection Act, we have [a] section saying the inspector has the power to stop operations, [so] we now have prohibition notices ... [However] we have not yet really implemented the Act.[22] So far I haven't heard of anyone who has

---

20   According to Bundit (1995) there are in fact 10 national centres for labour.
21   Prohibition notices are a common form of enforcement used by health and safety inspectorates. A prohibition notice placed on an unsafe piece of equipment or an unsafe process compels the employer to act until the hazard has been removed or reduced to the satisfaction of the inspector. No activity can take place in the area affected by the notice until the problem has been rectified.
22   The Act came into force in 1998. This Act, the *Labour Protection Act*, has some health and safety elements. It should not be confused with the two Occupational Health and

stopped the operation. Probably the inspector ... it's very new to them, even though they are also, in my understanding, afraid. If they order the managers to stop a machine, they might damage the business; the inspector has to be responsible. It's a big responsibility, they have to be sure ... The person [inspector] has to be very confident in the safety and health aspect ... I mean, the employer can argue right away to the tripartite body at the ministry. We have an appeal process, and that's immediate. The board has to call a meeting which takes a day or so, a tripartite meeting of 21 members. Right away the tripartite body has to send an expert or group of experts to see the case, whether or not the prohibition order is valid. If [it is] not, they will say, 'OK, stop, finish. You [the employer] don't have to do anything', or they say to the inspector, 'You have to lift it off.' I think it is very new to Thailand. At that time, you see, I still remember when the draft act was in the parliament. It was an argument back and forth between the employers, workers and the government officials whether or not they'll have absolute power to tell a business to stop this ... stop right away ... so at the end [it] came up that when you are going to ask the industry to stop something, you have to be sure that you are correct in ordering that, otherwise you have to pay the consequences. But I think, let's say they ask them to stop for one day or so, and their business has problems, they might bring the inspector to court as well.

Dr Chaiyuth concluded, somewhat ruefully, that the prospect that the inspector might be taken to court to be sued for damages might be one reason why the new clause had not been used: 'That power, it may not be very effective ... That would be one of the reasons that no-one has stopped the operation in the workplace.'

The position of the inspector in the Thai system is a difficult one; there is an expectation and indication of status in terms of educational qualification, but this is not translated into influence or control over the behaviour of business. Inspectors appear to lack any real authority and are stretched in terms of their inspection obligations. Being in this position makes them vulnerable to taking a path of least resistance. This could mean warning workplaces of an impending inspection before their arrival, or of taking a bribe. Bundit explained:

OK ... when there is a safety inspection, right, the inspector gives them advice, comment, suggestions to the management team or the foreman and tell[s] him, 'You need to fix this' but this will take time for them to do this ... It will take a lot of money ... too much money to fix. Sometimes they [managers] say, 'We don't have the money to do that,' and even sometimes they, you know, give a bribe to the inspection official and then the inspector will not come back again because of the corruption, and also they have a lot of inspections to do ...

These sorts of practices then exacerbated the perception that inspectors did not do their job properly and led to calls by some that they be made more accountable for their work. Waradom, for example, argued that if inspectors failed in their duty they should be directly responsible for the outcome, to the extent of being put in jail, 'They cannot do things wrong. They have to [get it right] because this is the

---

Safety Bills described in Chapter 4, which would have consolidated all OHS regulation under the one Act.

law ... if the building [after inspection] has a problem you will not have a licence any more ... you [the inspector] will go to jail.'

Here the emphasis on accountability of the inspector has the potential to lead to a vicious cycle. Waradom's call is understandable within the Thai context, where untoward public influence has played such a negative role (Tamada, 1991). However, the emphasis on accountability of those low in the hierarchy is problematic. The inspectors are in an invidious position. They have little authority and when they do challenge the business owner or manager, they risk being sued for loss of earnings. Expediency means they warn factory owners and even take bribes. To make inspectors more accountable, Thai regulatory character emphasized punishment of inspectors for inappropriate behaviour as a means of improving the quality of inspections. However, if inspectors were to be made accountable in this manner, without being given more authority over business owners to enforce regulations, then the net result may be that they simply demand higher bribes for the increased risk of businesses circumventing regulations.

It is important to recognize that there were different sources of authority, each vying for control. The mechanisms employed by the bureaucracy to maintain or extend control did not have a single source. Strategic patriarchalism within the Thai regulatory sphere is not singular; rather, in the case of workplace safety, it was split between several departments. An apparently logical question for this research was, 'What was the response of the Thai government to Kader?' In reality, however, the split nature of patriarchal authority meant that this question was, to a considerable extent, meaningless. The regional representative of the AFL-CIO put it in the following way:

> At the top level there are some people who say, 'OK, this is the Government policy', but you get down below the Cabinet and things like that and there is no Government. It's like this ministry, in each ministry the ministry has a different view from the other ministry, and they don't communicate with each other. And within this ministry there is this department and this department and they don't communicate with each other. Everything is oriented towards the individual sector and it sort of builds up. So when you say, 'The Government', I would say ... my first question to you is, 'But what part of the Government?' And then you'd figure out what is the interest of that part of the Government at that given time.

This problem of the independence of different government departments was reflected in many of the interviews undertaken for this research. It was not a problem peculiar to health and safety. Speaking of the fire prevention area, Waradom commented: '... In the past I told you each Thai organization works by their own ideas, they don't co-operate.... So we have about three organizations working at the same thing.' Dr Chaiyuth spoke at length about the problem of overlap and the complications this led to, such as the different sets of inspectors, for example, that each business had to respond to. Each department also had a range of responsibilities, not only occupational health and safety:

> In Thailand, I think we will still have to struggle for a long time, because we have so many Acts, as you said; we have the *Factories Act*, the *Hazardous Material Act*, we

have the *Labour Protection Act* [LPA], we have the *Building Code*, we have the *Mineral Resource Act*, which each have elements of safety and health ... At the moment, firstly, we have many Acts that have overlapping in terms of power, and, for example, the *Factory Act* [and] the LPA, they are overlapping here. When you have overlapping you have two sets of officials ... Overlapping in terms of their area. When you are talking *Factory Act* you're not only talking safety and health, its something else, licensing and so on. And the coverage, the *Factory Act*, they will say, well, I will look after the industry, the factory that employs 7 workers or more and 13 horsepower of the machine. In the LPA, we say we cover work safety or enterprise; we call it by a different name than the Ministry of Industry; they call [it] factory and define it differently, but our Act will say [it is] an establishment or enterprise. So we say enterprise or establishment that employ one worker or more, that's different. But when you come to safety or health, in the past, if you go some years back, some of the provisions are different.

Dr Chaiyuth, though, was confident that this could change. He spoke of a recent memorandum of understanding (MOU) between two departments with substantial responsibilities in the health and safety area. His optimism lay in the common interest the two departments had. Whilst the Ministry of Industry had greater powers in terms of shutting down industry, his department, the Department of Labour, had a greater number of officers. Through co-operation, they both had something to gain:

> But recently, the two departments sign the MOU so we will work together, so that happens now. So Ministry of Labour and Ministry of Industry [MOI], we will consult with each other ... we decided to work together now ... In the future I can see that we will even share our power. At the moment, the MOI, they have more power; they can shut down the whole workplace. They lift [remove] the licence and they [the business] are finished. We don't [have a licensing regime]; we can the stop the certain area or the certain machine only ... But they [the DOI] have only a handful of officials; they have, I think, not more than 60 or 70 people at the central [agency]. [Q: Smaller than yours?] Yes, at the central office here. Of course they have industrial works office, they are called Office of Industry in the province. They are doing a number of things there, not only safety and health but other things: licensing, promotion and many other things ... But at the central office, they have 60 or 70. For us in Bangkok we have 100 to 150 safety and health officers, we have three divisions here. And in the provinces we have 75 officers around ... 76 around the country. In each office they might have 8 to 30 officers working there. So that means they don't have enough manpower to deal with the subject, safety and health.

In Dr Chaiyuth's view, a strategic combination of resources, then, could lead to substantial change. Greater powers of the one agency, the DOI, could be combined with greater resources on the ground of the Ministry of Labour. Others were less sanguine about the possibilities of change within multiple bureaucracies competing for resources and prestige. Enforcement was a means to an end, an end that included reducing the status of another person in the public eye. The AFL-CIO representative gave the example of the arrest of a nephew of a major political rival for the then-Prime Minister Chuan Leekpai as responsible for the explosion of an LPG tanker in the centre of the city:

Immediately after this came up, who was the first person they arrested? They arrested the nephew of Taksin Shinawatra, who is the guy who was probably one of the strongest contenders for the Prime Ministership in the next election ... I mean, basically, what you do [with enforcement] is you take advantage, to use it for a political strikeout against one of your opponents ...

Patriarchalism, the importance of the person in positions of authority, and the importance of status was then central to understanding Thai regulatory character. This, though, had two dimensions, interpenetrative and strategic. Interpenetrative patriarchal authority was premised on service and benevolence and was woven into the fabric of how members of the Thai elite view themselves. Certainly, it provided some opportunities for change and improvement in safety. Those from the elite, including academics, who chose to champion change had access to bureaucratic and political elites that were denied to others. The emphasis on personal relationships could also further reform. For some bureaucrats too, control over reform and freedom from political interference could be viewed positively, as long as you had the right person at the helm. For others, though, it was the absolute nature of patriarchal control that lay at the root of the problem, since without public accountability reforms were unlikely to be effective. Indeed, the interviews revealed many examples of control under strategic patriarchal authority that undermined reform. The status that assisted change could also be used as a means to render reform ineffective. Committees where status rather than expertise dominated were one example given. The strategic nature of patriarchal control could be expressed in a repressive manner, with imprisonment (either of witnesses or of political opponents) being one such tactic. Nonetheless, a more usual form of control was corporatist, of developing relationships with like-minded others and excluding those who demanded more radical change. This included tripartite arrangements structured so as to extend control, and whilst debate could be forthright, the outcome rarely challenged the power of those in authority. This was critically the case with enforcement, where intricate rules of responsibility meant that enforcement through a prohibition notice was more likely to result in a lawsuit against the inspector, rather than an improvement in safety. Control, though, was not vested in a singular line of authority, since a critical problem for Thai health and safety lay in the divided nature of control, with multiple bureaucracies responsible for health and safety outcomes. Attempts were being made by bureaucracies to communicate more effectively, but characteristic responses to a challenge of status of one bureaucracy by another suggest that genuine collaboration still has a considerable way to go.

Self-reliance

Patriarchal forms of authority did not exist in a vacuum. They were complemented by a social order that valued knowledge, understanding and acceptance of the social hierarchy. Where leaders were benevolent, this could produce beneficial change; however, where this was not the case, those lower in the hierarchy were very vulnerable. They could not turn to rules, since authority lay in those who made the rules; instead they relied on the norms of reciprocity within patriarchal authority.

Self-reliance and Interpenetration

Under conditions of interpenetration, those in authority had a responsibility to provide the means for self-reliance, to act as patrons. That is, they were expected to act in a way that protected those under their patronage. When this failed, they were expected to restore conditions so that those same individuals could once again be self-reliant. In the case of Kader, there was a real sense that compensation should be paid, since the ability of the family to be self-reliant had been damaged and needed restoration. Monetary compensation was clearly a part of this equation that led to a groundswell of support for the Kader victims in their pursuit of justice in the form of compensation. However, once compensation was paid, there was a feeling of closure, since people were in a position to be self-reliant once more. The company's responsibility was discharged. Jaded from the Friends of Women NGO explained how this worked:

> After the fighting they [Kader] come out to say, 'OK, we will pay more money.' When they pay the money, they make the worker, family of the injured people, happy with the amount of money, because they pay more than the government, and then they need to talk, the owner and the workers talk together: 'OK, after you take this money, you're happy; so do not sue us, take us to court; you are happy.' Make everything finish, right? Take the money and finish.

Self-reliance under conditions of patriarchy is a complex achievement. On the one hand, it was argued that within Thailand there is an expectation that those in positions of authority will be benevolent and help ordinary people. Kanathat explained, 'Thailand is very different; this [expectation] is very deep in the culture. Thai people ... what we call *survive*. If you have no money and you are jobless, you can go to the temple, to the *wat*, and ask for the monk, 'Please give me something to eat.' On the other hand, self-reliance meant living in the moment, since the future was beyond your control. Survival and even thriving in a patriarchal system requires living for today and taking pleasure in the small gains won. This optimism was well illustrated by Channa, a PhD student researcher at Thammasat University:

> The people, they say, 'We can survive.' they have some hope. They think maybe tomorrow will be better; that is the Thai thinking style; they never feel hopeless. Last weekend, I went to one province [where] they are taking their vegetables to the market from their field. I saw them packing up and putting them in their pick-up. They went away and 20 minutes [later] they came back very happy, and I ask what happened. 'We got one baht higher than usual.' Just one baht! It is nothing, [you can] just use it for the public phone [but you] cannot buy anything. I estimate they got about 50 baht higher from their produce than last week, and they are so happy. They are so happy with their happy. I asked if they think they can survive next month, or [in] six months time. They still have hope: 'We have land, we have food to eat, so we survive.' That's all.

This ability to live in the moment was at the core of self-reliance. Dr Voravidh explained: 'The Thai mentality, it is more ... when it happens, it happens ... you cannot get back to the past.' It involved first surviving and when possible thriving, even if only for the short term, as Channa's observation illustrates. On an everyday level this meant that relationships worked well, even if the long-term implications were not good. Phil Robertson, the AFL-CIO representative, stated, 'I don't know ... you see in Thailand, you seem to be fine, with them everything's all right, even if in fact you're not ...' This ability to live in the moment was highly valued, since it meant that you could keep moving forward:

> People like being Thai. Being Thai is a good thing. I mean, there's a lot of injustice in the system ... there's been systems developed where injustices are mitigated or explained away so that you don't have specific conflicts. See, if you had the sort of disparities and injustices that exist in this system in other systems, where people were much more militant and wouldn't take it, I think you'd have a lot more conflict. Here, everything [is] sort of 'smooth it over ... move it forward'.

Self-reliance within a characteristic frame of reference needs to be distinguished from self-awareness or self-sufficiency. Self-awareness and self-sufficiency holds within it a conception of individual control over the future; self-reliance does not. Further, living within a patriarchal regime means awareness of risk may itself be dangerous, including risk to the self. Awareness brings with it responsibility to mitigate the hazard. But, just as in the case above of the government safety inspectors at risk of a lawsuit if they attempted to reduce a safety hazard, it may well be difficult, or even impossible, to mitigate that risk without incurring the wrath of those in authority. The safest course of action then is to remain ignorant or naïve. If you remain ignorant, there is the possibility that those in positions of authority will avert the danger from before you, since their awareness and their position means that they are responsible. If you become aware of it, you will then be expected to take responsibility for your own safety, something you may not be in a position to do. This response of 'self-reliant ignorance' can be understood as entirely rational from the perspective of the patriarchy/self-reliance nexus, where the need for clear roles and responsibilities is critical. This, then, becomes institutionalized through explanations of Thai culture as being fatalistic.[23] The National Safety Council argued:

---

[23] A pertinent illustration of this dynamic is a comparison of the process of crossing a busy street at an intersection, in Bangkok and in Australia. In Australia, the convention would be for the pedestrian to look the driver in the eye to ensure that the pedestrian is seen, if they want to indicate their presence when crossing the road. The driver will then be obliged to acknowledge the pedestrian and stop to let them cross. In Bangkok, the opposite logic flows. If the pedestrian who wishes to cross the street makes eye contact with one driver coming towards them, the pedestrian will then be expected to get out of the way, since they have signalled their awareness of the danger. Awareness means responsibility, even if this is difficult or even impossible, since getting out of the way of one car may put the pedestrian in the path of another. This is certainly the case if eye contact is made in the middle of a busy street. This is not, however, acknowledged. The driver will keep moving ahead into the path of the pedestrian. On the other hand if a

... the problem is in the general public. Thai people, we think about when you have an accident that happen you cannot help it ... In Thai, the culture, our culture is when you have something bad happen ... we talk about fate ... like when something happen to you like car accident, then it is your star, ... Sometime they think that that happened is their bad luck [karma] for their lives.

The perception that 'accidents happen' and were not something that could be avoided was evident in certain workplaces, where there was an acceptance that a number of workers would be killed each year. Phil Robertson of the AFL-CIO recalled:

I was over on an industrial area ... about four or five months ago and was sitting in a meeting of a bunch of unions and they were all discussing their problems and one of them was a metal-working factory where a worker had been electrocuted the week before. You know, and they said, 'Well, usually, there's one or two people who die in that factory every year' ... You know, there was a sort of a built-in attrition rate, you know, and they probably even put aside a little bit of budget and said, 'OK, well, you got a "dead worker" budget.'

The long-term impact of disasters in improving safety conditions then also became influenced by the short-term dictates of self-reliance. At the time of the disaster there would be considerable public interest, but it would tend to be short-lived. Bundit explained: 'Thai society tends to pay a lot of attention at the time that this happened and then they tend to forget it. People forget it.' In addition, there was always the next disaster to divert attention. During the first field trip, an explosion at a factory in Chiang Mai had captured public attention, as had the Taiwanese earthquake in which a number of Thais lost their lives. Somyot Pruksakasemsuk, a union activist with the Chemical Workers Union Alliance, summed up the almost routine quality of disasters and their aftermath, 'There will be another disaster, another explosion, another seminar again.'

The difference between workplaces, then, falls back onto the particular owner or general manager. The AFL-CIO representative continued:

... there probably are some [employers] that probably react differently. The question becomes a little bit of local leadership of the company, and responsibility. Everything becomes much more personality-based. You know ... 'What does the owner think? What does the General Manager think?' ... it's more like personality drives things.

The emphasis on personality or benevolence of a particular management complements a focus on the status differences between management and worker, as

---

pedestrian puts their head down and strides into the middle of the street, studiously ignoring any acknowledgement of danger, the driver will then have the responsibility to get out of the way. In this example, it is the awareness by the potentially injured party that brings danger, not the presence of danger itself. Ignorance in the expectation that someone else will take responsibility for averting danger is, in this case, a logical response.

Bundit explained: 'Management tend to think that the worker is lower ... like a hierarchy, so they don't have a lot of opportunity ... because of this.' This then flowed on to how effective worker representation could be, since there was no assumption that workers had the right to know to what dangers they were exposed. Bundit commented: '... the union team doesn't have the right to know what's going on, and doesn't have the right to talk with the inspector in the process of that.' Somyot described how it was up to management to allow inspections by workers to occur, and even if they found something unsafe, they had no powers until the inspector arrived:

> ... if management allow you [safety committee] to inspect [then you can]. But government does not recognize the authority of those people who are on the committee ... they say only government inspectors can tell you the authority to say this is right or wrong in the workplace.[24]

Those who were persistent in drawing the attention of management to dangers would be under pressure to leave the job. Somyot explained how paying troublemakers to leave the workplace was a way to restore a smooth-running workplace:

> Money is given to him and he's finished. No objection. The excuse of the company is that it is to get the new worker. Only compensation that has been responsible [Q: So as long as they give you the money, they can get rid of you?] Right.

Many of the interviewees commented on the low level of unionization in Thailand, and how this made implementation of legislation, like the safety committee requirement for workplaces of over 50 workers, difficult to enforce, or when a committee did exist, for it to be effective. Jaded reported:

> Most factories don't have the trade union. So when you've got them about, OK. Some owner, they try to form a safety and health committee. OK, but only some of them. But most of the owner, they don't follow this law.

Dr Chaiyuth, a government bureaucrat, concurred, adding that activists were also weak and did not feature highly in political considerations of working conditions:

> You see the worker's group who you met, they are very small group and it's like their voice is not loud enough for the politicians in different parties to understand and do something for safety and health ... They are rather weak.

The lack of worker representation meant that the government schemes that did exist could be side-stepped. Dr Chaiyuth commented on the combination of low unionization and the perceived 'lack of interest' in the worker about whether the employer reported the injury or not:

---

[24] As we have seen above, not even the inspectors have much authority.

There are only a handful of trade unions. In Thailand we have 9 million people; only 300,000 are unionized. So that is why [there is little reporting]. The worker doesn't care much in the factory whether or not the employer reported or not, unless we come to see them and keep asking questions. Then they say something, then we say, 'Well, you lied to us.' I mean, the company should do something, but very seldom do you get that.

Self-reliance, or in the terms of safety, 'lack of awareness', then had a very real presence and influences safety outcomes. But it was certainly not stupidity or simply a lack of knowledge per se. Further, it was not irrational, rather a worldview that allowed a focus on the immediate realities of day-to-day life. Historically, it has been the best assurance for survival, and may also allow life to be enjoyable.

But in an era of rapid industrialization it has a very real downside, since for many workers, illness and injury ends their working life – and their capacity to survive. Others paid the ultimate price and lost their lives. As Somyot pithily summarized the situation, 'Today there is two choice for the workers. One is accident or die; the second one unemployed.' The priority of Thai workers was that the job came first; the reality of losing a job is more pressing than the danger of injury or death. A focus on the immediate environment, rather than taking a long-term view which may or may not eventuate, seemed a much more sensible choice. Self-reliance within an interpenetrative sphere where there is an expectation of patriarchal benevolence according to social norms brings with it a causal connection between awareness and danger.

For a health and safety regime that relies on responsibility and awareness of both employer and employee, this presents major problems. In policy terms, though, the complex relationship between patriarchy and self-reliance was simplified and reduced into the need to raise awareness of workers through education. The National Safety Council stated, 'The main problem is awareness of the people.' Kanathat emphasized the need to change perceptions of where help would be found:

Thai people think that if you [are] in the dangerous situation, maybe police, fire brigade will come to help you. They think all the time that people outside will come to help you. This is the wrong thing; this is a misunderstanding of life.

The hope for some was in education of the young, since amongst the current adult population educational levels were described as 'very low'. In this way it was hoped that eventually awareness would filter through the society as a whole. Waradom commented:

I would like to have the lesson in the kids' school, the kids' courses. To let them understand about fire safety. And when they grow up they know, and then they'll have ... sort of ... an understanding of this area. If they become the building owner or become the big people in government, they'll pay much more attention in this area.

The National Safety Council was working with the Department of Education to change the school curriculum to include fire prevention training, so the young would be able to teach the old:

> We think about education in the school, and how we try to have curriculum to set up the prevention ... We think that the young generation should be better than the old generation; they [the old generation] cannot change their attitude; they cannot change their ideas.

However, education alone did not break the nexus between awareness and danger. Indeed the form education took could reinforce hierarchy and difference in status that implicitly strengthened the link between being aware and being in danger. The content of an education programme may be about safety measures, but the implicit message reinforced the social order and the importance of place. The AFL-CIO representative put it in the following way:

> It's traditional, you know. The big people speak and the little people listen ... I mean, even training techniques. We're basically revamping our training techniques from what I found when I came in. I found training that our Institute was sponsoring where it was ... opening ceremony ... one hour speech ... 15 minute questions ... coffee ... one hour speech ... 15 minute questions ... coffee ... one hour speech ... 15 minute questions ... lunch ...

Education alone, particularly if the style reinforced the need to temper awareness of dangers to health with the far more immediate dangers of losing the patronage of an employer (i.e. losing your job), is unlikely to bring with it radical change.

The government investment strategy also reinforced the concern of self-reliant workers on the need for a job first. Most interviewees spoke of the government's emphasis on investment above all else. It was clearly a priority, irrespective of the safety standards that came with it, as Waradom explained:

> The money [comes] first, the benefits from the business first; so most of the local people don't want to invest in the safety area. Thailand goes so fast in the past, ... we accept a lot of investment, a lot of technique, everything, without safety.

This emphasis on investment complemented workers' primary concern with minimum wages. Khun Bundit from the Arom Pongpangan Foundation argued that most of the conflict between workers and government was not about safety, but rather about pay. The lack of attention to safety meant that all investment was welcome, rather than sorting out whether the investment would have a negative effect on health. Somyot argued that for government, economic growth was most highly valued: 'The government attitude is yes, we need economic growth; health and safety after. We have to compromise, we have to come down in standard.' However, for activists, it didn't matter how much investment came, the time never came to shift attention to broader concerns such as safety. Somyot continued: 'It's never the "right time" ... the appropriate time coming.'

The consequence of this was that most informants commented on the low priority on safety by government. Some recognized that change took time, but felt that the emphasis was not there. Waradom commented: 'It's a normal thing [for government to take a long time]. And also maybe they have many things to do. This is low priority, something like that.' This was despite the Government's official Eighth Development Plan having as one of its aims the reduction of accidents. When asked about the presence of safety in the plan, Dr Chaiyuth responded, 'They do say something on that, but I don't feel a really strong emphasis from the politicians to push this issue that much.' He went on to give an example of what he saw as indicative of this lack of emphasis.

> I think, for example, if you are going to inspect the workplace, if you tell them ahead of time and they know you are coming, they ... normally don't wear any masks, but for that particular day they will all wear masks.

Self-reliance within an interpenetrative frame is a complex achievement. It requires survival and thriving within the norms and expectations of patriarchal authority. There are expectations (see Woodiwis, 1998) that could bring with it demands of those in authority, such as the demand for compensation. However, the shift to prevention inherent in a robust health and safety regime was much more difficult. This was because self-reliance could best be achieved when the responsibility of those in authority was unequivocal, that is, by signalling that you are not aware of the risk in the environment. Awareness of risk by workers brings with it the possibility that they would be seen to be responsible for avoiding that danger, even if avoidance was in reality impossible. As long as there was no awareness, there could be no expectation of taking responsibility. When something happened, there was recourse to notions of fate and karma to explain the event. For safety and fire prevention this was particularly unhelpful; however, the response tended to be to emphasize the need to raise awareness, without recognition that there was a real benefit in self-reliant forms of not knowing. Further, education could re-emphasize the difference in status by the form it took and so reinforce the connection between awareness, responsibility and danger. Interpenetrative self-reliance was particularly vulnerable under strategic forms of patriarchal authority, since the government philosophy had a clear priority of the need for investment first, not safety. In this environment, being safe is to take a gamble, albeit one in which the odds are better than the gamble of losing a job.

Self-reliance and Strategy

Self-reliance under interpenetration means acceptance of both the social hierarchy and of one's social position within that hierarchy. Under conditions of strategy, however, institutions are not only accepted but are seen as critical in the effort to improve one's status. Using the skills of self-reliance learnt from within Thai society, strategists take a gamble on the long-term. Advancement involves building networks with others whose interests coincide with yours. Amongst interviewees this was most often discussed in light of politics, where building networks with others whose interests were aligned with yours was essential, since politics was an expensive game. The NSC explained, '… if you want to be an MP, you must spend money. To be a Member in Parliament, to be an MP … not cheap.' In the conversation that followed in this interview, the NSC spoke of how relationships were central to getting the necessary money. When asked if this was considered corruption, the NSC answered, 'That's the democracy, yeah?' For activists, democracy in Thailand was more about the politicians' interest, not about a process that gave the population as a whole a stake in the society. Dr Voravidh explained the sport-like quality of Thai politics:

> From our experience [of] the formal politics in Thailand, I think there are a lot of problems. You could see that from the formal politics, not only in Bangkok, but when you go into the countryside, it tends to divide people into groups, factions; like you belong to this political party, and this political party either define themselves by giving shirts with the political party names, and then you know. Rather that being helpful in democratizing Thailand, it tends to get people into factions and fight, you know. To get into the local politics you fight not for the principal, [but the status]. And this kind of formal politics, it gets stuck, it becomes institutionalized.

Unions could also provide the framework for individual strategy and gain. Union leadership provided the means to work with government officials for individual gain. Activists were quick to point out that not all unions were the same. For meaningful change it was important to work with unions that had a genuine interest in the workers, as Jaded explained:

> … there are many kinds of trade union. It can be a good one, bad one, other ones working for the government, or have a good deal with the government or the owner. But what I consider is a good trade union is like what we call the KunYan at the industry group level, because this level is much more active than the other level. Sometimes even some leader at the level of the labour congress … there are some of them … they're corrupt. What I consider good is the groups at the industrial zone, it's better.

Others spoke of the relationship between the union leader and the employer. The corrupt nature of this relationship was given by the AFL-CIO representative as a reason why, in one firm, the safety committee set up in the wake of reforms after Kader did not work:

> It's a place that's got a 20 per cent union, the committee doesn't work, there's suspicions that the union President at that time … I think he's now been replaced … he was basically in the pocket of the employer …

It is not possible, then, to associate strategic self-reliance with any one type of organization, since all were vulnerable.

This is further illustrated by the reality that NGOs themselves were not exempt from a strategic orientation towards self-interest. This worked at two levels: the level of the organization itself, and the level of the individual. For example, businesses could set up their own NGO, a support organization for workers. Activists such as Jaded viewed this with scepticism as a means to improve their image: 'They [companies] have the NGO themselves, set it up by themselves to build up an image.' Companies could also donate money to NGO groups. Whilst on one hand this could be seen as positive, even benevolent, without real change in the working conditions of those who donated their money, Jaded argued that such donations were seen as strategic, rather than any attempt to make substantial change:

> A lot [of companies provide] support for NGOs, they give them money to say 'OK, we care about this issue', to make them look better [and] make us feel like they are a good organization. It's just image. What we want is international organizations taking care of the rights of the worker, you know, to not take advantage of the worker. What they do now is talking, dealing or giving money to an academic group or NGO; it's not a real solution. The real solution is thinking or caring about the human rights or labour rights.

There was also a problem in the recruitment of volunteers for some NGOs. NGOs had to work hard at being clean organizations, particularly when there was some financial incentive given by a third party for the work the NGO and the volunteer was doing. This was a constant challenge for a Fire and Rescue NGO in which Kanathat was involved:

> I want the clean volunteer. You understand. Some say [they are a] volunteer, but it's funny money, it's not clean. I don't like that way. Many rescue volunteer this way. They stop the car in the dark corner of the street and when the car crash, go take the patient to the hospital; they will select the hospital to get the commission, like 10 per cent, so if that case pay 30,000 [baht] they will get 3000 baht. But today he want 30,000 baht, he say this case is cheap! [the injury] is really bad, [so he'll] run over that body to get more money. [Q: They will kill the person?] Sometimes.

This sort of behaviour from a wide range of groups meant that members of the Thai public were keen to hold individuals responsible for misbehaviour. As in the case of corrupt inspectors described above, there was strong public support for finding the responsible individual, and isolating and punishing their behaviour. This sentiment can clearly be seen in the finding of guilt against Viroj Yusak and his 10-year sentence. However, strategic self-reliance meant that this, too, could be used for the purposes of getting ahead. It was too easy to find a scapegoat and for that person to take the blame. Jaded told of the actions against the engineer of a building project in which the building collapsed, killing many people. Once the scapegoat had been punished, interest in the case waned:

> He was the scapegoat ... since they got the scapegoat maybe it's less interesting for the media. So maybe the media pays less attention to this case ... The owner paid him, bribed him to say, 'I'm the one who did that.' It might be just a scapegoat; maybe he didn't do that.

Scapegoating did not only involve people. This essence of scapegoating is to isolate a single element for blame whilst allowing the system to remain intact. So, isolating a single redeemable 'cause' was a way to 'solve' the problem. Phil Robertson from the AFL-CIO, and the research's interpreter Roong Poomipug recounted a story of an LPG explosion in the middle of Bangkok that incinerated many in the vicinity. Both argued that the investigation deflected the blame so that the regulatory structure remained the same. Real change did not occur:

> What happened was a truck carrying liquid LPG in two big tanks swerved to miss a *tuk-tuk*,[25] hit a telephone pole and cracked open a couple of LPG containers. There was a spark and there was a huge traffic jam and there were about forty cars with all their passengers [that] were incinerated at this traffic light ... And what was the solution to that? The solution was that we shouldn't allow deliveries of LPG to occur during traffic hours. It wasn't discussed how the load was tied in or any thing like that; it was that the substance was in the wrong place at the wrong time. But at that time ... that accident happened at one o'clock at night! So, it's a scapegoat.

The reason for such behaviour was that it was clearly difficult to blame people in positions of power, so blame would tend to become attached to the weakest, but not necessarily the most responsible party, or on a supposed cause that would not disrupt traditional routines. As we have seen in Kader, the worker who was blamed for starting the fire was imprisoned. When blame was attached to powerful people, it was unlikely to stay for long. As highlighted in Chapter 4, the two directors of Kader were charged, but found not guilty. Scapegoating was closely allied to deflecting blame. Where important organizations were involved, deflection was an important skill. In the cases of powerful organizations, like the police, there were other ways in which blame would be deflected, by blaming resources, or the lack of skills of their members. The National Safety Council argued:

> When the Social Welfare criticize the police, that ignore the problem like law enforcement in an accident, they [the police] must say it is because they have no university [education] and they have limited staff, limited manpower.

These problems of individual misbehaviour and scapegoating were openly canvassed and discussed in the media. Thailand has a vigorous media, but this created further difficulties for developing a rigorous safety regime as a result of the understandable public cynicism in government policies and practices that led to a disengagement from the issue, even when the policies were a step in the right direction. Reforms followed Kader; the growth in the number of employers required to contribute to the compensation fund was one example of a positive step, one which had the potential to improve outcomes for injured workers, particularly those employed by small business. However, the management of the fund and the reality of its growing surplus described in Chapter 4 added to the cynicism and made employers and employees reluctant to commit to more schemes. Phil Roberston argued:

> This [compensation] fund has a huge surplus, and what it does, it creates a great deal of cynicism about anybody who contributes to these type of funds. It's very difficult to

---

[25]   A three-wheeled taxi.

persuade workers that they should contribute more to Social Security funds for unemployment.

Self-reliance, then, is the complementary element to patriarchalism. Under conditions of interpenetration it involves an acceptance of hierarchy along with the expectations of assistance that form the obligations that attach to patriarchal authority. Compensation for Kader had to be fought for, but there was public support for the campaign because it resonated with obligations that the company had towards the workers. However, self-reliance under patriarchal authority means understanding that if you are lower down in the hierarchy you cannot change things. Survival (or more) means that living in the moment is critical to well-being. This creates enormous challenges for health and safety reform that require a very different worldview and an emphasis on long-term strategies. Whilst there was an understanding by many that awareness of safety was lacking and attempts were being made to raise awareness, its connection to patriarchy was less well recognized. The value of self-reliance, with its short-term focus as a way of surviving within patriarchal forms of authority, was largely ignored.

The very real skills required to become self-reliant also allowed considerable innovation under conditions of strategy. Here, resourcefulness was used to advance in the hierarchy – but not to change it. Politics became a game of strategy in which the population were pawns, not actors. But it was not politics alone that could form the basis of strategy. Unions and NGOs were also arenas in which advancement through the hierarchy and self-advancement was possible. The focus on the individual meant that deflecting blame and scapegoating were important qualities. The purpose of this activity was to allow the basic structure to remain, whilst deflecting criticism. The way this worked was spoken about quite openly. However, the cynicism that resulted meant that getting commitment to policies that had the potential to be a genuine step forward was made more difficult.

Phil Robertson encapsulated well the depth of change that was required for safety to become a prominent concern:

> ... there needs to be a system ... right, there has to be a sort of proactive planning system, a proactive system, where there has to be actual change in the way people think about these things. That's what you're talking about. You're talking about attitudinal change. You're talking about talking to people about, 'You as worker have a right to have a say in issues of health and safety in your factory. It's not entirely up to the owner; even if he says it is.' A big change. I mean, that's what we're about.

Conclusion

This chapter has outlined the dominant relationship within Thai regulatory character, that between patriarchy and self-reliance. This relationship could emphasize Thai values of benevolence and reciprocation, or strategy and control. Interpenetrative patriarchal authority, where present, provided some opportunities for change and improvement in safety, at least to the extent of reforming regulations. For those bureaucrats coming from this perspective, their control over reform independent from 'political interference' was seen as positive, since politics was 'tainted' by strategic machinations of dubious motivation. More could be achieved without such interference. Further, those activists from the elite who chose to champion change had access to levels of the bureaucratic and political hierarchy denied to others. Where they met a sympathetic ear, their reform demands were taken seriously, assisted by the characteristic emphasis on the importance of personal relationships.

In contrast, the chapter has revealed many examples of control under strategic patriarchal authority that undermined reform. The emphasis on elite status could stymie reform effectiveness. For example, policy recommendations emanating from some committees could reflect principally the opinions of high-status members rather than those with relevant expertise in OHS. Further, strategic patriarchal control could be expressed in a repressive manner, with imprisonment (either of witnesses to a disaster, or of political opponents) occasionally used to silence dissent. A more usual form of patriarchal control, however, was corporatist (Cooney *et al.*, 2002), that is, developing relationships with key groups of like-minded others and excluding those who demanded more radical change. This included tripartite arrangements structured to maintain control, with access to tripartite committees manipulated by government (Bundit, 1995). Whilst debate on these tripartite committees could be forthright, the outcome rarely challenged the status quo in a meaningful way. The clearest example of this from the chapter is the way OHS enforcement was subject to tripartite oversight, with the effect that an OHS inspector placing a prohibition notice on a dangerous machine could face a lawsuit from the business owner for lost production time, should the inspector's judgement be considered overzealous by that committee. Critically, the emphasis on control and status within the bureaucracy meant that OHS responsibilities were divided amongst multiple bureaucracies. This created gaps, redundancy and overlap in regulatory responsibilities, a situation that has proved endemic within the Thai bureaucracy (ADPC, 1994).

Self-reliance needed to be seen in relation to patriarchy. Under conditions of interpenetration it was experienced as living in the moment, whilst cultivating relationships and patronage. Certain expectations arose out of the relationship – such that compensation was considered the morally right response of the company. However, self-reliance did not have an easy relationship with safety awareness. Self-reliance relied on people in positions of power shielding others from risk. Taking on awareness meant accepting responsibility – even when that responsibility could not be discharged.

Within the areas of both safety and fire prevention, regulatory authorities recognized the need to raise awareness, but did not want to do so at the expense of undermining patriarchalism. Their response tended to emphasize the need to raise awareness through education campaigns. Such policies did not acknowledge, however, the relationship of self-reliance to patriarchalism or the advantages for workers in self-reliant forms of 'not knowing'. Further, education programmes themselves could re-emphasize the status differences and thus the need for self-reliance by the form it took. Highly stylized seminars where 'experts' lectured and others sat quietly and listened reinforced the reality of the status quo and the importance of self-reliance. The content of these seminars on the need for self-awareness was undermined by their form. Interpenetrative self-reliance was particularly vulnerable under strategic forms of patriarchal authority, where any pretence of obligation was lost. Here, the government philosophy of 'investment first' left little room for a priority on safety. In this environment, assuming that work is safe is to take a gamble, albeit one in which the odds are better than the gamble of losing a job.

Under strategic forms of self-reliance, the skills acquired in achieving self-reliance were used to avoid blame and to advance up the status hierarchy. Deflecting blame and scapegoating, such as using prosecutions used to stymie political opponents, were necessary qualities in strategic advancement. The strategies employed transformed others into pawns or tools for advancement and were found not only within politics or the bureaucracy, but also within unions and NGOs. NGOs and unions agitating for safety improvements needed to be aware of these possibilities to ensure the ongoing integrity of campaigns and operations. The way this worked was spoken about quite openly; however, the cynicism in the general population generated as a result of such strategies meant that getting public commitment to policies that actually had the potential to be a genuine step forward, such as moves towards a comprehensive compensation scheme, was made more difficult.

Chapter 6

Regulatory Character and Response: Protest and Law Reform

This chapter explores the relationship between norms and laws through an analysis of the impact of activism, both on regulatory character and law reform, following Kader. The first half of the chapter explores the activist vision of reform, in particular how it emphasized collectivism or egalitarianism in Hoods' (1998) schema. Activists argued that reforming law itself was not their only challenge; rather, workplace norms needed to be transformed so that individual workers and ordinary people could engage with that law to have their needs met. Thus, their protest was tactical and deliberate, aimed at bringing about structural change in both laws and norms. In short, regulatory character as a whole needed to change. The fate of these protests and the negotiations was complex, with the demands of the protesters shaped by the interests of the bureaucracy. Largely, however, the data revealed the resilience of the traditional patriarchal character of law within regulatory character, with little concession towards either the independent authority of law or the ability of individuals or groups to assert their legal rights through the courts. Enforcement, too, was shaped by the predominant emphasis on patriarchalism and self-reliance within traditional Thai regulatory character, with change associated often with 'good bosses' (a patriarchal model) rather than using the safety regulations themselves. Regulatory techniques put in place after Kader could be viewed as superficial, useful to convince outsiders of the advanced state of regulatory standards in Thailand, yet with less impact on the ground than might be suggested by their presence. The Thai expression, *pak chee roy nah*,[26] or 'it looks good but it tastes the same', captured the reality of this aspect of reform.

Activism and the Response to Kader

Activism in the wake of Kader was about changing the patriarchal/self-reliance dynamic. It was about a transformation in the 'right order of things' and working in a way that was antithetical to traditional Thai regulatory character in both its interpenetrative and strategic hue. From a traditional conception, interpenetration within Thai regulatory character was imbued with the accepted social order and working for the public good within that order, where 'big' people worked for the public good, and 'little' people responded by living in the moment and surviving, even thriving. Strategy within the norms of patriarchy and self-reliance involved

---

[26] Literally, 'coriander on ordinary fare', or 'coriander on the rice'.

using the system to change individual fortunes, but not the social order. Strategic action was understood as using the hierarchical structure for self-advancement and as such signified if not immorality, then amorality. In contrast, the protests and demands of the groups that formed after Kader were motivated by a desire to engage everyone in negotiation, not only those at the top. In doing so, the methods of the activists moved away from accepted patriarchal forms of social order to an order where those at the bottom were central to the process. There were costs to those involved, since the deliberate strategizing of the activists was viewed with suspicion by some commentators, wary of the deliberate tactics of campaigners, tactics more often associated with manipulative self or narrow group interest.

Initially, the Kader fire sent a shockwave through all levels of society and clearly provided a graphic illustration of the need for change. There was openness in the social structure created by the fire (Quarantelli, 1993) as much by the fact that an event like this was possible as it was about the magnitude of the harm that occurred. Change was needed; if this fire could happen, then even worse things were possible, as Dr Chaiyuth described: 'You see, once it happened, the people said, "Well, it could be even worse." [It was] a shock to all agencies; we never thought that kind of incident could happen.' This realization that something must change was an opportunity for activists to push for reform. Bundit explained, 'Sad to say, when the bad accident happen we use this as a case to educate people, to make people aware of the risk.' It was the animus driving the campaign for long-term change, not only for Arom Pongpangan, but also the Friends of Women, as Jaded explained:

> What our organization is trying to do is to get those people impacted directly and from their families to keep it alive, to make it long-term. Maybe it's not necessary for themselves [to see the importance of safety] but for where it might happen again, to make [people] have more vision. So when they get together they have more power to negotiate by collective bargaining with the owner.

The campaign then, used the fire to precipitate a regulatory 'crisis', so that substantial reform could follow. The disaster and the demand for compensation provided an opportunity for activists and victims to work together to change expectations of the 'normal' way things happened in a workplace. The experience of negotiation saw victim expectations change through the course of negotiation about the level of compensation a company was required to pay:

> They [the victims and their families] like it [working together]. When they talk with the owner, the owner will say, 'OK, now we give you this amount of money.' And they say 'OK, if you're [the workers] happy, you take this,' but if they say 'No, we aren't,' then they give you [more and say] 'OK, if you take this higher amount of money to the [rest of the] workers then, OK, if you're [all] happy with this money then don't have any protests, don't fight more, don't sue us,' and so on.

Thus, it was not only the money, but also the *process* of getting the money that was critical. Compensation was not 'charity' or an indication of benevolence, but the first step in a change of the norms of the employment relationship. The employment relationship also sat within a broader context, which activists saw as also needing to move away from expectations of patriarchalism and benevolence (see also Schmidt, 2002).

An early challenge in the post-disaster period was to prevent the campaign and the event being used by politicians and other groups simply to bolster their own legitimacy. In the view of activists, in the wake of the disaster some groups simply came in to further their own interests, not to create a groundswell for change that would see improvement in the long term. Voravidh explained the difference between patriarchal assistance and that which was based on a collectivist model that went beyond the short term:

> But we find when disasters happen, politician will go, ministry will go, everybody will go and then put the Band-Aid, you know? So I call it a showpiece. The even don't help the villagers to organize or negotiate. That's why we have to go. They said 'We'll come as a charity' ... it's easy to do that. But we think that doesn't help much. So the people have to learn by themselves, the victims, they have to rely on themselves, organize and set up for the negotiations. It's not really hard, I think, only a little bit. They can do that once they know. The problem is that the people, they don't know.

Somyot concurred: 'To see the way of Thai government, the Thai NGO working – its like a charity. To ask for compensation but not see that in the real thought of the government.' The result of this 'charitable' activity, requesting assistance but not radical reform, was that the status quo of patriarchal authority depending on the self-reliance of workers was restored. It was this that activists saw at the root of the problem.

Using compensation as a tool to push for widespread change, though, was a two-edged sword, since if the effort stopped at compensation alone, the underlying paradigm of society could remain untouched. As highlighted in Chapter 5, the need to pay compensation could be accommodated within traditional Thai regulatory character, within a framework of benevolence. However, the aim for activists was different. It was to raise awareness so that compensation was the beginning point for greater change. In the long term, the concern was not only about money for specific victims. It was about establishing the principles of change, a benchmark that could be built on. Jaded saw the beginning of this process after Kader:

> They [the victims and their families] started to realize the money is not the point here. Because if they [the company] give out easily, it's because they don't want those workers to sue them ... what we get from Kader is the highest standard of compensation, [more] than the regular compensation, it's not just, 'you lost your life and get nothing.' Those people who died, their families making sure their compensation is good, makes it better for the people in the next one, you know, the next case.

This way of working, to protest around a specific interest in order to challenge the status quo, was not new to Thailand. As was clear in Chapter 3, Thailand has a long history of protest, most notably the protests against military rule in the 1960s and 1970s. The way the Kader campaign resonated with this history was reinforced through the interviews. Voravidh stated, 'Now [former protesters] are in control of some of the bureaucracy, especially in the Ministry of Public Health … people in these organizations are very strong.' There were bureaucracies, like the Ministry of Public Health, that were seeking to work collaboratively with the activist NGOs to create different ways for government to intervene in ordinary people's lives. Change was not exclusive to groups working outside the bureaucracy.

Yet, more needed to happen. New groups were formed in the wake of the Kader Fire and were brought in to increase the momentum for change. The key to success was to draw on aspects of Thai culture that resonated with local people and then use this to raise issues and push for change. For example, one group specifically was concerned with paying respects to those who had died, and then using this to make sure that the deaths were not in vain; as Jaded explained:

> … This group of people and NGO form like a party, what you call … a memory party for those people who died in the fire. Also the family of the deceased from the Kader fire, they all came here at May 10 to make merit for those who died … That's not just only they're saying that they're dead, they also try to talk about the problems that have been found. We've been trying to emphasize this … what happened, last year, what happened two years ago, and what happened last year and what's going to happen [in the future]. So we tell them, tell the public … tell the public that this is what we are trying to do to solve this problem. A lot of people lost their lives because of the fire; we don't want them to just lose their life and get nothing back from that.

These new groups could then work together with groups that predated the Kader fire. This included more than just unions. Dr Voravidh argued that the weakness of the unions in some areas meant that protest had to draw from a broad base: 'You have to use NGOs, academics and others; it has to be very broad. That's the movement here.' Kader was not the origin of labour protest aimed to improve workplace safety, but acted as a catalyst. Many of the strongest groups did not form specifically after Kader, rather they coalesced around Kader and used it as a platform to renew the push for change, as Jaded described:

> After Kader fire, NGOs, academics and the labour movement worked together to form a committee, safety and health campaigning committee. This involved trade union, labour movement, NGOs, academics – also workers from Bisnosis support group; they organize themselves like a victim group to campaign against the government for a change of policy … The original group [that constituted the CCHSW] started before the Kader fire, two years before Kader.

Each of these groups shared a common goal: to change the basic rules by which people were assisted. Jaded continued:

> Some NGOs are working specifically with sub-contractors, some deal with the construction workers; there are all different ones. But they are all labour NGOs. Arom Pompangan, community organizations like Dr Voravidh, Dr Oraporan … if you get a variety of those people, those organizations come to help to solve the problem together.

A central element of the campaigns was the involvement by those who were injured or who were made sick by their work. It was this element that Dr Voravidh felt could keep the impetus going from the fire:

> ... if you are not sick, you don't know [what can happen]. You don't think that you will be sick. You don't know what is the sickness. When you ask the workers of the council of the occupational patients network, 'Why are you sick?' And they say they are sick, they cannot be cured. Why can't they be cured? They are to live with that sickness for life. These people who are not sick, they don't feel [the same], like they don't know what is sickness. That's why we try to involve the sick as representatives. It is different from the workers who are not sick; they don't have the same interest.

So, although Kader formed a focal point for the campaign, it was not an end in itself. Indeed, the number of disasters in Thailand had formed a chain of events that activists such as Voravidh tried to use to push for change through bringing together the common elements in each disaster, 'with this grass roots case-by-case approach we are trying to develop [the] common things that you could see ... You can do a lot if you build up cases.' The purpose was more than health and safety, more than labour law or labour rights. It involved a change in the paradigm of society.

An interesting element in the strategy for change was that rural groups featured heavily. This was not so much by their direct support, but rather in the use of their 'modus operandi', and in the breadth of their vision. Dr Voravidh argued that the rural community had a lot to teach urban activists in general, and workers in particular:

> ... the rural community are more aware of the need for democracy than the workers. Because they are quite open, you know the society, while if you talk about the workers in Thailand, their society is very limited, within the four walls, so when they think of democracy they will only think of labour rights, labour law. So we are trying to break this kind of thinking by picking up occupational health and safety as a social issue, to link the workers with the community. We are working along this line.

The rural community had become quite sophisticated in its protest strategy. The most prominent rural protest group, the Assembly of the Poor, had achieved a number of victories in its push for greater political recognition of its plight, suffering that resulted directly from government policies. The group was a network of rural groups, each with a particular grievance against the government. They joined together for the purposes of increasing the numbers pushing for change. Phil Robertson explained how the assembly worked:

> The Assembly of the Poor is best understocd as a gang tackle. The way they operate is, it's a very expansive coalition and you have this long list of demands. The Government can discuss any of the demands they want when the Assembly of the Poor comes in. They're given the demands, every demand is on it, and the Government picks and chooses which one they want to talk about. Sometimes one group goes in and says, 'These are our demands.' But the idea is that you try to get as many people to try to tackle the Government as possible at the same time. [Q: You'll get something out of it?]

> Yeah. The idea is ... Well, sometimes you go in there and you don't get something on your agenda, but somebody else might have got it ... they have a big mobilization ... It's not an assembly; it's a network.

The Assembly of the Poor was not universally popular. Part of the reason for this was that their protest could be more effective at bringing about change than the official political process. There were some who argued that if they were this successful, it must mean that there was something untoward going on; the NSC, for example, argued that the Assembly was not a neutral platform to further the interests of the group, rather it must be being run for individual gain; that there was 'some important person in the group, they're not impartial'. Dr Tassannee from Thamassat University argued that the Assembly deflected attention from the official political process and this was not helpful:

> They are an interest group; they don't set up a political party to assist the people in their political issue ... They get together and they demonstrate to get something for their benefit, because they know their rights more than before. If they need something, they group together and go in front of the parliament and try to negotiate with the government. But if they are not big enough it is useless, [since] the bigger one is the winner, like the Assembly of the Poor. You ask me what is the best way to get things done? This is the quicker way ... our government is not in a good situation at the moment ... I think the way of passing things in the bill process is better by democratic process, not just [protest] in front of the parliament. It means they [the government] can't do anything that satisfies both sides.

However, for others it was not just the outcome that was important, but also the capacity of movements like the Assembly of the Poor to reinvigorate the democratic process, both by influencing law and, critically, in terms of regulatory character, by changing the relationship between ordinary individuals and the law. 'Know[ing] their rights more than before', meant drawing on laws directly, not working through benevolent leaders, nor assuming that the law was for show and not a mechanism for ordinary people to use. Ultimately, if there were to be a change in the life of Thai workers, it would have to involve a different form of democratic process, and a changed regulatory character based on a more egalitarian model of society. This vision was to be realized through experience of the trauma of successive disasters and by the involvement of victims and their communities in changing the agenda of government. Each event, then, brought with it a different dimension and a new opportunity to bring in more people. Voravidh explained the process in a recent campaign where pollution from a factory was poisoning not only workers, but those in the local community:

> ... we have the case of the cobalt 60 where the OHS issues extend beyond the factory where it reaches the community. So in this case we have tried to link the community with the workers and that's what we are working towards ... We have a database on OHS on each of the cases and identify what are the problems and what are the solutions proposed by the grass-roots people. We then try to put [that] to the government, and learn from the limitations. Try to see this from our experience. So we are building this; it is hard work!

The process of change, then, was more than just the outcome. Voravidh argued that the richness of working together was invaluable. It is in this context that the value of the proposed Occupational Health and Safety Institute in the original bill was best understood, that is as a framework that encouraged a different process in developing health and safety practice, rather than simply a regulatory framework that required a compliance with a particular safety standard, as Voravidh explained:

> ... in setting up an institute, our purpose is to link in labour participation. But when we look at labour we work through those [victims groups] who think about safety ... [Those who are well] they don't feel or they don't detect the same rights as those who are sick, you know. Workers who are sick themselves and [who] have also organized themselves to a sort of an association [need to be involved]. So we wanted to bring all these social actors into play in this institute. It shouldn't be research only, but it should also go into prevention. The institute that is set up will be focussed on empowerment. The workers, the sick, the academics will work together with others.

For the activists involved, the shift in focus from compensation to prevention required a change in the structure of occupational health and safety regulation. There needed to be a break with the old patriarchal model. This led to the concept of a five-partite institute, which grew out of their experience in campaigning, and their lack of satisfaction with the tripartite framework. The institute provided an opportunity for a real partnership with government, not simply a change in health and safety law or 'more of the same'. Voravidh continued:

> ... this body [the institute] will build up on cases, you know and then these cases will provide the input for the legislation. We developed this from our practical experience [and] arrived at the concept of the institute. We developed it [further] through our interaction with the government. We have been unsatisfied with the tripartite body, that's why we have moved to this five-party [structure] where there is real representation.

This ideal was far-reaching, and required a sustained level of protest. This, in turn, required resources for the long term. A disaster could bring with it much-needed funds to keep a campaign going, but after they were spent, then time had to be diverted to fundraising and away from campaigning. The process was time consuming. Jaded explained the nature of the problem:

> ... one of the important problems is about the funds, the money, the lack of money. When we start to do it [a campaign] we have the money but at some time the money is gone and then we need to consider about this fundraising. The second problem is everything takes time. We cannot change everything ...

Further, while the vision of social change was far reaching, the campaign had to retain a pragmatic core that could resonate with worker needs. This meant providing ongoing information about health and safety standards and worker's rights. Both Jaded and Bundit saw this as central. Jaded described their role:

... what we can do is, we try and give them more knowledge, educate them about their rights, what they need to know, what are their rights, what is the poison, what is dangerous in the workplace, to try to educate them to know what kind of rights that they have in the working place ...

Sometimes the level of technical knowledge required in building up a democratic structure based on health and safety, though, was beyond the resources of the activist groups. One of the early casualties of the Kader campaign was a telephone hotline set up to inform workers about the dangers within their workplaces. There was a real demand for the services of the hotline, but there was not the technical expertise from the activist side. Voravidh explained:

Yes, [the request for information from workers was] very specific. And that's why we found out that when we set up this kind of [telephone] centre, conceptually it was very good because we wanted to try to build up the advice on health safety by the NGOs working closely with the workers ... But we found that we had a limitation and so we couldn't operate ... We have no capacity to do that ... The NGOs, they organize the workers, but when it comes to more specific knowledge, especially when it concerns occupational health and safety, it is difficult.

Activism then, involved a learning process with a view to changing the nature of the democratic process. Whilst it began with compensation, it moved to health and safety, with an understanding in each campaign that the purpose was to build a different political and democratic process. It moved away from the assumptions that lay behind traditional views of patriarchy and self-reliance and so had to challenge the assumptions of both interpenetrative and strategic forms of this relationship. It was not a matter of leaders benevolently taking care of people, nor did it assume that working strategically was in itself immoral. Indeed, for the Assembly of the Poor their tactics were central not only to their effectiveness but because they also resonated with their village traditions. For the campaigners after the Kader fire, the challenges to create a more egalitarian ethos were considerable. The vehicle to change regulatory character included initiatives aimed at responding in a practical manner to the needs of workers and the broader community. This could involve skills that the activists did not necessarily have, such as practical expertise on health and safety.

A second, and potentially more difficult, problem was that the change needed went beyond a change in the hierarchist nature of government and authority, to the norms of everyday social relationships, in particular those between men and women. Again, compensation illustrates this point well. Whilst the compensation paid after Kader had bought real relief for some victims, there were ongoing problems. This was shown in the Kader case through follow-up studies and reports on the Kader victims and their families, mentioned in Chapter 4. A detailed study by the Arom Pongpangan Foundation (Napaporn, 1997) showed how compensation alone could not ameliorate structural problems. For those with little long-term income, repairs to houses and medical treatment soon consumed compensation money paid to family members. But economic issues alone were not the only source of problems. Critically, this report highlighted a number of cases where the effectiveness of the compensation payout was lost largely as a result of entrenched gender inequality. In particular, the report found that cultural practices allowing men to avoid responsibility for dependants further victimized children and mothers of victims. For example, one woman had been left with sole responsibility for her granddaughter, who had been less than four months old when she was left without a mother. The grandmother, in poor health and earning at best 60 baht (US $1.50)[27] a day from weaving flower garlands, worried constantly about the fate of her granddaughter if she died or became too ill to care for her. The father, having used some of the compensation payout on a new motorbike for his work as a motorcycle taximan, had moved away and taken a new wife. He had subsequently stopped contributing to his daughter's support, claiming that he could not afford to. Another woman, who had lost two daughters in the fire, was left with responsibility for a young grandson. Her own husband had left her for his minor wife, taking some of the compensation money. Further, her deceased daughter's unregistered husband, the father of her grandson, was in receipt of the boy's education scholarship payments. He remarried within 100 days of his wife's death, and did not pass on the education payments to the grandmother for his son. The case histories also highlighted the ability of the husband or father of the victim to squander the compensation money on highly risky business ventures or simply high levels of consumption.

Thai society brings with it radically different outcomes for men and women. This was evident in the aftermath of Kader through the disparate outcomes for women who had been affected. This meant that the activist worldview and campaign strategy through the fight for compensation and safety necessarily was required to challenge not only the relationship between government and the people, but also the accepted relationship between men and women.

Competing Visions and the Law Reform Process

The challenge for activists in the wake of Kader was ultimately twofold: firstly to change perceptions of democratic process as a model for egalitarianism, not paternalism, and secondly, to have their vision institutionalized in legal reform. In this section, the challenge for activists in the law reform process is reviewed. How law reform occurred, what was achieved and what demands failed gives a unique insight into the impact of regulatory character on legal change. Traditional conceptions of the relationship between norms and laws were challenged by the activist vision of what norms should underpin law and how law should relate to norms. On one level, activists were optimistic about the potential for change, as the government appeared willing to entertain the need for reform. Somyot commented, 'At least the government has interest to do something.' However, tension remained between the activists and government vision of 'appropriate' law reform, about whether the law would support the egalitarian values of the activists or reinforce the hierarchist philosophy of the bureaucracy. Here the letter and wording of the

---

27   About a third of the basic wage.

law was critical, since subtle changes could lend weight to one vision over the other.

Nowhere is this clearer than the battle for the OHS institute. As was clear from Chapter 5, the importance of bureaucracy and control over health and safety policy and enforcement was acute. Traditional forms of safety regulation centre on the patriarchal/self-reliance nexus, where control is vested in leaders who carry personal authority. Activists felt that the structure of health and safety that had resulted from this regulatory character lay at the heart of the problem. Changing the rules governing health and safety, and through these reforms, the process of ensuring safety, was central to institutionalizing a different notion of the public good. Voravidh explained:

> We were looking after Kader and we felt that this kind of problem is linked to the structure [of the system]. It's a structural problem, because health and safety is in the hand of the government, so we wanted [to reform] that in order to prevent such kinds of thing from happening.

Legislative reform to change the health and safety framework to share power and resources with workers and communities, an egalitarian vision, then, was central to the model proposed by the activists. As was described in Chapter 4, to push for this change, the two major activist groups joined, and together they were invited to work with the Ministry of Labour and Social Welfare (MLSW) to draft a new health and safety bill. At first, the activists seemed to be able to convince the Ministry of the need for substantial change. After six months of negotiation, a bill was agreed upon that included the five-partite institute and a rationalization of the complex health and safety regulatory structure into a simpler, more effective form. But, after initial agreement, the Ministry reneged, and rewrote the bill back to a model that both retained government control and, most importantly, kept control of the compensation fund away from the proposed institute. Voravidh explained:

> So we drafted for about six or seven months until we got the bill, and then the bill was supposed to pass from the labour ministry to the Cabinet. But then the labour ministry changed the model of the institute in the bill from an independent body thing to sort of a government department ... They [the government] wanted to create a new institute, but the difference is that they wanted it to be a governmental agency ... also they don't want the workmen's compensation fund to be transferred to the new institute.

This produced a stalemate, since the activists could not agree to the government model that would simply be absorbed into the same hierarchist regulatory structure, with a role that was circumscribed to ensure it did not impinge on the authority of existing government departments. Voravidh continued:

> We say we cannot [agree with the government model] ... Because it [the new institute] should be more of a comprehensive approach from prevention to compensation, to rehabilitation. If you want to do that then you should have the workman's compensation fund inside this institute. We don't want [the institute] to be just educational or training, they wanted it to be just that. But we said no, we cannot have this in our concept of the institute ... such kind of an institution is not to be a technical one. It should have a

social, grounded perspective. That's why we integrated also the academics or NGOs into the institute. These positions will be elected by the council, while the others [the tripartite representatives] will come through the normal election process ... [so] the government, they have a problem. They said they have two bills, they cannot pass two bills. They have to pass one.

The result was a stalemate, since the MLSW vision of the institute was very different. The Ministry's model of the institute was that, as an education and research institution, it should be an additional element to occupational health and safety regulation, not a reformation, and one that would have no regulatory authority as such. Critically, it would not be given control of the compensation fund. From the Ministry perspective, the compensation fund was working adequately within its current structure under the Ministry of Industry. Dr Chaiyuth argued there was no reason to change:

> You see, the NGO and the workers, they are proposing the independent body, which would comprise two things: compensation, and safety and health. But at the moment our ministry feel that probably we should do it without compensation; we should establish a new independent safety and health [body, with] no compensation. The workmen's compensation is in the social security office. They [the social security office] thought as well, what they are doing is OK, nothing wrong, why don't you let us continue doing that?

The government model of the institute allowed a continuation of a regulatory framework that accommodated a patriarchal model of control. The institute would be an addition to the existing regulatory structure. It is interesting that the previous reports on the Thai response to disasters had found that new 'disaster' centres within the bureaucracy were a common response (ADPC, 1994),[28] so this proposal by the Ministry did not set any new precedent. As an addition to existing bodies, the Ministry vision of the institute could accommodate the disparate demands of departments for resources and status within the bureaucracy.

In contrast, activists saw a role for radical reform of the bureaucracy to bring the focus back to health and safety by rationalizing bureaucracies. For them, the government model would simply compound existing problems. Bundit argued:

> The departments from each ministry with health and safety responsibility should come together, to make the separate institution. These departments in the different ministries, they are redundant, there is too much overlap, it compounds the problem. Like, some people just ignore some part [of the problem], Ministry of Labour would like to do this, Ministry of Health would like to do that, Ministry of Science another thing. If it could be all together, when we put it in one institution, maybe some department or one [of] those ministries need to be closed.

---

[28] The pattern continued in the wake of the financial collapse in 1997 where budget cuts fell more heavily on programmes, rather than cutting the number of personnel in the bureaucracy.

Bundit recognized that this was a major change and 'might be a problem for government'. However, when the demand for a new institute was at its peak, support for an independent institute came from an unexpected source. An historic division between political and bureaucratic interests led to political support for the proposed institute, which breathed life into the insitute as an independent authority. This support for an independent institute, rather than one headed by a government bureaucrat, emerged because politicians saw it as a way of reducing the power of the bureaucracy. Bundit explained the way negotiations had proceeded:

> Each department section of the government, says, 'I am the main group' to take care, say [of] compensation, or so on … people are concerned about their power and the belief of what they can get [out of reform]. Maybe the benefit comes in the money, but maybe it is sufficient for their power interests … At the beginning the high-ranking bureaucratic official would like to set up another department so they can have that position in that institution. But because the government would like to limit the bureaucrats' power, they decide to develop the idea of the institution as independent [body], rather than have a department and have the bureaucrat come to be the top guy of that department.

It was this division between the politicians and the bureaucracy that enabled the initial bill to progress as far as it did. Ultimately, though, the stalemate between the two bills remained.

There was one final avenue open to activists to break the impasse. This was to use provisions of a new constitution to force debate on the original bill the activists had drawn up with the MLSW. This 1997 constitution, set up in the wake of the 1992 coup, provides for direct public input into the legislative process – a decidedly egalitarian shift. The constitution stated that if there was sufficient public support for a bill, it had to be debated by the Assembly, and not held up by the cabinet. All that was required was 50,000 signatures on a petition. Dr Voravidh described how this provision provided the activists with a glimmer of hope that they could achieve major reform:

> So [after the bill was replaced] we went and got 50,000 names [to support the bill]. That's according to the new constitution. If you have 50,000 names you can use this along with the bill and pass this through to the Assembly … They have to pass it. They do not pass it through the cabinet; they have to go [directly] to the Assembly and then hand it in to them.

However, although the constitution existed at the time of the signature campaign, it did not specify the form of signature that would be accepted to force the government's hand. Although the activists asked for clarification, detail was not forthcoming before the campaign to get the signatures had ended. The campaign was difficult and took time, since care was taken to make sure that those supporting the bill understood what they were signing. Voravidh explained: 'People asked, "What is the institute?" and you take a long time to explain before you convince people to sign. But we got 50,000 people to sign in one year.'

But the lack of guidelines on what constituted a 'legitimate' signature was eventually the undoing of the signature campaign. The guidelines introduced by the government stipulating what was needed went beyond what the activists had obtained. Voravidh described how the new requirements made a successful signature campaign difficult, if not impossible, since some of the identification material required meant that workers had to return to their birthplace to obtain a copy of their house registration form:

> When we came [with] the petition, three weeks later the clause [about identification documents] came out. The clause came up and said that along with this signature, 'we [i.e. the government] need two things: one photocopy of your ID card, one is a photocopy of your house registration.' And then that's why I wrote to the *Nation* newspaper: 'We have completed this; you asked us to produce the two things. Are you plucking something from the air? Because if we're going to the factories, workers are not even from Bangkok. How can we get their house registration form? Or we ask them to send from home? It's impossible.' ... If you want to do this in the countryside then we [need to] get the photo matching, to ask the villagers to go to the town to get that photocopied ... So that's the problem.

The timing of the government releasing their guidelines on the new constitution was appalling for activists. Voravidh argued that part of the reasons the signature campaign took the time it did of was because activists wanted to make sure people understood what they were signing:

> But then we want to show that the people who signed, they signed it and they understand what they signed. So we want to show that there is some legitimacy in the signatures, that everyone supported the institute ... At least to be clear that it's the last thing, the framework of the institute ... but really, we were just too slow. So we were too slow. Three weeks too slow ... [but] I wanted to tell the workers it was legitimate [because] then we can push the right [form of institute] across. You understand?

The government and the bureaucracy saw the issue differently. For them, there was a need to make sure the signatures were legitimate. Dr Chaiyuth presented the government's case:

> ... we have a new constitution and the subordinate laws have not yet been finalized. When the new regulation was put out, [the 50,000 signatures] didn't comply with that, they have to take it back again ... I cannot blame the government, because the government had nothing to do with that. But I know our NGOs were complaining about that. I think it was normal, unexpected.

The net effect of the reform process, then, was that those elements that could be accommodated within traditional regulatory character were integrated into reform. Radical change, such as the five-partie model, languished despite the new constitution that contained an egalitarian mechanism that the OHS regulation lacked.

It is important to understand, however, that it was not only the activists that had difficulty in the reform process. Those pushing for more moderate change also faced challenges. Dr Chaiyuth explained the opposition those within the bureaucracy faced when they pushed for improvements. One of his examples related to the need for safety officer training. The requirement for safety officers in companies had predated the Kader disaster but the need for improved training was an issue highlighted by the fire. Getting improvement meant a protracted process of negotiation with employers and government:

> When that draft for safety officer training was being discussed, many employers they would like to scrap the bill. They went to the politicians and said, 'That bill will cost us a lot of money.' But they did not succeed at the end, you see; that regulation was passed ... The Minister of Interior at that time gave his support. We were under the Minister of the Interior ... I think our boss, my boss went to see the Permanent Secretary of the Ministry of the Interior and convinced him to submit it to the Minister concerned. But I think before that, I think the board, the legal advisory committee, we had three or four rounds of discussions. They said 'Well, it is too much, for industry. How could you people put this thing up this way?' ... We were the ones who came up with text, programme, textbook and so on. It was a hard time for us; everyone kept blaming us: 'Well, you are the ones, you are the problem; you create a problem for us; we have to spend a lot of money.' It takes a lot of money to send someone for a month for training ... the industry has to release a man for the month, pay the salary for no production at the workplace, and pay for training as well.

The common goal of safety reform meant that progressive bureaucrats and activists would occasionally work together, despite the differences in their vision. This was important for bureaucrats since they did not have the same level of knowledge on the ground as the NGOs. In turn, the NGOs needed bureaucratic support to give effect to their demands. Nonetheless, NGOs valued their distance from authority because sometimes it was necessary to have demonstrations to put pressure on government. Voravidh explained:

> We try to show that bureaucrats ... they cannot do everything because they lack first ... they don't have information ... So we have a force there, we have ideas. We have information. The Ministry, they lack that ... that's why they depend on us. We know that. So right now they are open. We interact with them. But this doesn't mean that sometimes we don't have to put pressure on them. We have to organize a demonstration or something like that, to get something done. Because when you have a demonstration it turns it into a public issue, we need the press, to get the public awareness. Then from this we can get debate going on to that. So we work like that.

Overall, there was considerable resistance to change, whether that change was of a radical or a more reformist nature. In either case, successful reform had to negotiate with the governmental and bureaucratic structure, replete with the assumptions underlying patriarchalism and self-reliance.

There are many points at which this resistance was experienced. Dr Chaiyuth explained the tortuous nature of the law reform process, each stage of which was susceptible to inertia and political pressure:

> In fact, when you come up with a draft bill, the draft bill has to go through a process, a long process. For example, from our department, when we have finished drafting the bill, then it [is] submitted to the ministry; the ministry, they have two other committees to look at the draft, and they have the right to suggest for change. They have to bring it

back with their suggestions; if we agree, we will change it; if we don't, we just put it back to discuss with them. After that we have to submit it to the cabinet. The cabinet will send it to the state council; the state council, they are comprised of all lawyers there. The senior lawyers, they have wide experience, they will look at it section by section and if they see, 'Well, this is overlapping with the other bill,' they will make a note of that and send that to the cabinet to fix it, and they will send it back to us, and we will have to fix it. Or discuss it with the related agency to settle it out, before we send it back …

Regulations as well as legislation had to go through the full drafting process described by Dr Chaiyuth above. Because of this, the subordinate legislative mechanism of ministerial notification was often used as a way to get through specific regulatory techniques. But while such a process was quicker, there was no way that such notifications could be considered a radical change of direction. Bundit described the change thus far as 'insignificant', since the context of reform that did occur was unchanged.

For major change, the legislative process was the only way. Thus, slowing down this process was a way to stall change. Many interviewees spoke of the slow rate of legislative reform. Chaiyuth reflected on the process:

I think it is too long. We are currently revising the old regulations. I am afraid that these new regulations will take about 10, 11, 12 years. Too long, I don't like that! … I think that is the process has been too fixed … For each step that you have to go through it takes a long time … I am afraid that, for example, the fire protection regulations, when they go to the cabinet and state council it might take another six months. If something [in the regulations] has to be fixed, if they say this section it overlaps with the Building Code, we have to bring it back and discuss it. It goes back and forth … it will take another six months, one year. I don't know how long it will take, the 11 to 12 regulations, the draft regulations we are working on. So for the time being we have to use the old ones, which are outdated already.

The length of the process was extended; not merely the process of checking, but because of pressure from various interest groups set to lose from the outcome. The NSC described how there was always a way to explain the delay as necessary, as responsible government, but the reality could be different:

Like, if you want to amend the regulation in the building, for the Building Code to have a higher standard … it means that you must spend more and more. And so their supporters, they say, 'No, no, we cannot do that.' They try to slow down … Because they have many ways to sow doubt on the benefits of reform. Set up the working group … [laughing]. So the media, forget it! That issue is not interesting.

There could also be a resistance to public scrutiny, particularly from some politicians with dubious networks. The NSC continued: 'They [the politicians] don't show this to the public because then they cannot do that. The politicians that are not true to the public influence some things so we don't want to touch them.' Kanathat said of the fire protection legislation, 'It's just like an oak tree: the change is very slow. A hundred years before it will come, and it's too slow for me.' Reforms in many areas were in process, but when asked if they were enacted, often the answer was 'not yet law'. This included the requirement for a safety engineer in buildings, reform in fire prevention, as well as the development of dedicated health and safety legislation.

The first battle then, was for law reform. Law reform could be initiated through protest activity, or from the bureaucracy. In each case it was difficult to achieve. Change that was achieved tended to be reform that allowed for the maintenance of traditional regulatory character, that is, norms surrounding patriarchalism and self-reliance. Law reform has to be seen as a process of engagement with dominant forms of regulatory character, not just as a beginning point for regulatory change. Further, there were casualties from the negotiation process: those within the bureaucracy who had become associated with radical change could find themselves moved aside. Dr Voravidh described one such event: 'We negotiate, we took him [one bureaucrat] to the outside community, then he became isolated from the [other] bureaucrats, and he lost his place.'

Nonetheless, change was greatest where public protest could be generated. Sometimes this could mean that protest sidestepped the Thai legal and political system entirely, as was the case when compensation was paid directly by Kader itself. The constitution had enhanced this potential for protest to bring change. Indeed, in terms of the legal framework itself, it is arguable that the most radical reform in the health and safety arena was that associated with constitutional change, not in health and safety law. This constitutional change had the possibility of changing regulatory character by allowing direct input from the general public; the possibility of public demand forcing parliament directly to discuss a bill is a radical shift towards a more egalitarian ethic. But this left areas that were not amenable to public protest, which includes much of the area of building law and fire prevention, languishing in the bowels of the bureaucracy and government. Those areas less amenable to public protest, like building standards, could safely be left to languish.

Formalism and the Implementation of Law

Despite the difficulties of law reform described above, activists felt that the changes that had occurred had the potential to improve safety. But law on the books was one thing; implementation another. Here then, the focus of regulatory character switches from the patriarchal–self-reliance nexus to the dimension of grid or authority. Implementation or effectiveness of law depends upon its authority independent from patriarchal power. Chapter 3 argued that within Thai regulatory character the authority of the law was weak; the data supported this. Activists argued that the law was not the real problem; rather, the law was empty of authority. It existed, but nothing changed, as Voravidh explained:

> We feel that we have good law but there's no implementation. That's the problem ... I think, yes, it's reasonable. Yeah, it's reasonable, the law. Because there's been a lot of campaigns and intervention, so the laws in Thailand were quite satisfying but ... [for

example] after the Kader, the government has required that the Health and Safety Committee should be set up in the factory ... it's only the form, you know, but the content is yet to be decided. The problem is that if you want participation of the worker in Health and Safety you cannot [do so], because the workers are not trained on health and safety. So we find that education on health and safety is lacking. But there is a law there ... it has to be set up and they have to set up, but how it functions, I think that's another thing. But we have this committee, there's an obligation by the law that we should have [it], but I don't think it functions.

Somyot was more graphic in his description. In his words the law was:

... artificial. They set up a committee but they have no right to do anything, so it's like a puppet. See, you just sit down in the meeting, half of them are the management, half of them are worker representatives and in many cases they are not the real representatives, or they don't know anything [about] how to take charge.

In this way the law was able to be seen to be there, but without changing the power structure of the workplace so that it could really be effective. Somyot continued:

The health and safety committee in the workplace, they have no time to investigate the health and safety. They're just complaining committee. Or some consultation committee on health and safety issues in the workplace.

Without broader structural change and egalitarian orientation, most activists felt the law was not effective. This did not mean that there was no implementation, but that the initiative would be devoid of content. Yet at the same time there could be agreement that this was working well. In reality, the law would be enacted, but not used. It remained external to the way the factory or workplace functioned. The traditional authority structure of the person, not the rule, would be seen as more effective. Phil Robertson explained further:

You see, Thailand is sort of ... you seem to be fine with them, everything's all right, even if in fact you're not. In fact the problem is shown in occupational safety and health. You're supposed to set up, for instance, a health and safety committee. In most of these factories, the first thing they [the regulator] does if there's a problem, they'll come in and say, 'You need to set up a health and safety committee.' But you know, no-one understands what a health and safety committee is ... What you have, OK, [is a system where] health and safety problems can go over there and you can deal with it informally in the factory.

The bureaucracy was, not surprisingly, more optimistic about the reforms. For them, though, a major challenge was the strategies used by business to avoid the new regulatory requirements:

I think it's [the safety committee] working well in some of the industries. Some still playing games with us. In the sense that, well, they have appointed the safety committee members, but they don't call a meeting. In our regulations we say that you have to call a meeting every month; some they don't. Sometimes when our inspector goes out, when we ask for a record, they find they have not convened a meeting. They [the inspectors] will immediately put a fine on them. We have to report it to the office, and the office will look at how much fine will be given, what type of violation, is it serious or moderate or not very serious. The maximum of the fine is 200,000 baht.[29]

Yet having a meeting and making substantial change was not the same thing. NGO groups also argued that businesses were adept at finding their way around the letter of the law. For example, under the Ministerial Directive, companies with under 50 employees would not need to create a health and safety committee. Companies with large seasonal fluctuations in employee numbers would use the smaller number to justify their lack of a committee. At a longan factory in Chiang Mai, one where a devastating explosion killed all its workers, there were large fluctuations from 43 to over 250 in the harvesting season. Yet no committee existed in either the on-season or the off-season. This was not peculiar to health and safety law, however, but rather a way of running a business in spite of the law. Jaded argued:

> Most of the owners, they have illegal workers, you know, like Chiang Mai, illegal girls. For the Labour Law, they don't follow Labour Law. In Chiang Mai also, you know, they don't follow the Labour Law, they don't follow anything.

Health and safety law did exist, but was not able to make substantial inroads into Thai regulatory character. This characteristic of the law as existing, but dysfunctional, was well understood by the Thais, with the expression '*pak chee roy nah*' ('it looks good but it tastes the same') often used to describe the process of reform. Here the appearance of taking safety seriously was what was most important. It might involve a law being in place and a ritual associated with compliance with the law, but the actual change in safety standards was lacking. Phil Roberston explained:

> There's a problem [that occurs] … then there's effort to resolve the problem or do enough to make it look as if the problem's being resolved … and then the whole thing fades away until another accident occurs. You get a situation where … it's the whole concept of *pak chee roy nah*, which is … making something look good … you know … making it appear as if progress has been done. For instance, … a classic *pak chee roy nah* is putting a little sprig of coriander on the top of the food. *Pak chee* is the sprig of coriander, *roy* is 'put on top' … floating on top of the *nah* is like a … so what you have is … you want to do just enough to make it look good. A classic case of *pak chee roy nah* is the Institution of National Health and Safety Day on May 10, where every year there is a Government festival or exhibition. The NGOs stage their counter-exhibition in March somewhere or do something like that, a bunch of speeches get said, and that passes for progress …

There were a number of ways in which *pak chee roy nah* was seen to work. It could apply to training, for example. Many of those interviewed mentioned the importance of education, of training to improving the safety regime. However, Dr Chaiyuth expressed some frustration with the ritualistic nature of training that never seemed to get anywhere:

---

[29] US $5,200.

Training, system training. It doesn't mean that we are not providing [it], we do provide many training [sessions] – too many! But it's not as expert as I would like it to be. You see we provide so many training [sessions], we keep calling the inspectors from the country for certain training, three days, four days, send them back and bring them back again, but no evaluation, no follow-up, you see. So what have you given them?

The nature of *pak chee roy nah* was to make everything look like it was working from the outside. It was appearances that were important, that the law existed and the training took place, but not whether the process actually functions to improve hazard reduction or compliance. A good example was in the area of fire prevention and the installation of a fire prevention system in a building: the fire alarms, fire panel, smoke detectors and sprinklers that spring to life in the event of a fire and extinguish the flames that spread and lead to loss of life. Waradom explained how this worked in Thailand:

Mostly we put in heat detectors; it's all wrong. Because the price of heat and smoke detector [is] about three or four times different. Yeah, about three or four times different. So the owners try to avoid big budget. At the same time, the designer doesn't understand correctly about the standard of equipment, so they help together to put [in] the cheaper [system], and it didn't work, that fire alarm system … By putting in a not-so-good system, you're not breaking Thai law, you're just abiding by Thai regulations …

The focus on appearances as opposed to function was clearly a critical problem in the area of fire safety. Fire safety systems are not used often, but when they are, they need to work first time, without error. But with the emphasis on appearance, the need for the system to function was lost. Other systems would be fixed, because the outcome was immediate, but the fire protection system would languish without testing or maintenance. Waradom continued:

… we still lack of some maintenance programme. About 90 per cent; nobody maintains the product really well. Because people in the building maintenance system [work to reduce visible problems], when the lights are out, you know that they are out; when the air-conditioning is not cold, you know they're not cold. But when the fire come, didn't work. Nobody knows. It just leaks all the time.

Occasionally, there were accreditation systems put in place for checking the equipment. However, this did not necessarily solve the problem of *pak chee roy nah* if the checking process itself was one that emphasized form, or ritual, over function. Lack of knowledge by those assigned to check the equipment would mean that critical errors would be missed. Kanathat spoke of 'Thai style' accreditation: accreditation where everything would appear to be in place, but it may be the wrong style of extinguisher in the wrong place, or a heat detector rather than a smoke detector. To the untrained eye, all would appear well, but the system would not work in an emergency.

Yet experts existed. Both Kanathat and Waradom were experts in the field of fire prevention, and their expertise would be drawn on. However the number of experts appeared small, particularly when compared with the need for such skills. Further, experts could themselves be *pak chee roy nah*: they could give the appearance that everything was well by their presence but would have no authority. Bundit spoke of the role of 'the office of the expert' within the safety bureaucracy:

> This man is in a position, he is like in the centre of information, he is very useful for Ministry of Labour to send for the government when they need to go out to the labour groups or NGOs or whatever. They can say, 'So-and-so said was this!' so he is the expert! But he doesn't have the power to make the decision ...

It might be expected that such a system would fall down when actual demands were placed upon it. Indeed, investigations into a number of the fires, including that at the Royal Jomtien, revealed the presence of fire safety equipment, but also that it failed to operate. Disasters were one area where the problems in the system would become known. However, the day-to-day events, the small fires and the individual accidents, could be masked by the system, or by a particular interpretation put on statistics. For example, a fall in absolute numbers of occupational injuries (but not the rate) in the years following the financial crisis in 1997 was claimed as an improvement in health and safety. Somyot explained:

> ... in terms of numbers, it is reduced. The government declare if you see the statistics ... They compare from last years. Declining, is to reduce the number of people ... One year they reported three hundred thousand people. But it has no meaning.

The laws could exist, then, but it was the form, not the function, that was emphasized. Indeed, for many, the number of laws was itself a problem. Both from within government and outside, the number of regulations were seen as a problem. Somyot argued that he '... cannot solve any problems, because there are so many regulations by the government'. The National Safety Council concurred:

> They are never-ending! You know in Thailand right now, the number of regulations never end ... more than a hundred of [them] ... are still compulsory ... In Thailand the government tried a revolution [i.e. a major reform] for all the law and regulations but they give up.

The safety laws and associated policies, then, lacked urgency. The fact of the law was disconnected from its function. Without a strong sense of the purpose of law being to improve safety, the law would be co-opted for an alternative purpose. In this way the problems for safety associated with strategic patriarchalism would resurface. There were problems of inertia, for example as explained by Somyot:

> The problem is, the government programme, it's ...like ... a very slow process, to solve the problem. You see, one problem is, we rely on the government. You submit some complaint letter in your province. The province will send this matter to the central office, the file get there, go to investigator, wait some time before that, there's some action ... So this is no way out.

The lack of structural change and continued lack of co-ordination by government departments would prevent action being taken to improve problems, even when they were clearly brought to the bureaucracy's attention. Somyot described one situation of an unsafe building in which workers were destined to lose either their income or their health:

We got the government to inspect the building. Then the government said the building is unsafe. That's all ... No action ... They said because it's a different department [responsible] – not the Labour Department. The Building Department, something like this, it belongs to another ministry. So we go to the Building Department or the Thai Construction Inspector to see the standard [of] the building. They're like a district level; we go to district level and ask them to investigate. They have the standard. Then they said this building is unsafe, they just said, 'This is unsafe.' So, the only response was to say 'OK, you workers, you can repair it. There, you 50 per cent workers [left], you can go home if you don't want to work in this building.' The workers after then receive 50 per cent of their wages for two weeks. They decide they cannot live on this, because the wage is really low for them already. So the problem is not solved ... but trade union go to the department and then the government send the experts. They're going to check. Then the experts said, 'This is unsafe.' Now, who is the authority who can change the situation? ... We are still fighting [about] who will be responsible. Labour Department said, 'No, it's not my job to see the building department.' Then the Building Department said that their part is finished ... It could be the government health and safety institution should be the one responsible. Should be ... You see, they [the workers] are not in a very strong place to say 'Stop working first, and change the building, or repair the building' ... There are too many regulations for them. And this is the most terrible system in the world.

The importance of status would then resurface as critical to the effectiveness of some reforms following disasters, exemplified by reforms following the Royal Jomtien fire. It was decided following this hotel fire that fire safety responsibilities should be moved away from the police force to a dedicated unit within the Bangkok Municipal Authority. Unlike some other initiatives that went through a full legislative review, this involved only a change of Ministerial Directive, and so the legal change was relatively quick. The reform was put in place but as it was given effect, the problem of lack of expertise within the BMA arose, as Kanathat explained:

With the ministerial directive we transferred the duty of fire safety from the police to the fire brigade in the BMA, the Bangkok Municipal Authority. The duty has been transferred, but not completely, because in the BMA nobody knows how to do it, to be the fireman. They have the new regulation to transfer expertise, but it's not working. Not perfect.

However, this lack of knowledge was not simply a problem of lack of training, rather it was one of status. Expertise did exist, but within the police. Those with relevant expertise were unwilling to move from the police, which had more prestige than the Bangkok Municipal Authority. Existing expertise was lost in this shift and it was necessary to start training people from the beginning:

Yes there is a new department, the fire brigade of the BMA ... Just started, about five years ago. But they cannot transfer all the trained police, all of them that were from the police fire brigade because the police have a ranking [status] they don't want to transfer themselves to the BMA. That's why altogether we have around 2800 fireman, from the police fire brigade they transferred only 200. That means they have to train new fireman.

Giving authority to laws that were set up after disasters, then, was a complex exercise. Firstly, the purpose of the law could be focussed on the fact of its existence alone, as *pak chee roy nah*. As such it remained ineffective. It could initiate practices, such as safety committees and Safety Days, but the challenge was always to get these beyond the level of ritual. Certainly, there was prompting by unions, NGOs and inspectors to give the regulations some weight. However, traditional means of creating inertia, those discussed above and in Chapter 5 under strategic patriarchy, such as the emphasis on form not function and the struggle for resources without taking on extra responsibility, were a constant battle to changing regulatory norms. Where there was a disjunction between regulatory character and regulatory technique the law remained a ritual, with corrupt practices such as bribing inspectors able to feed off the contradiction between law and 'normal' practice.

Further, laws associated with safety, compensation and fire prevention could provide new avenues for the advancement of status or material gain. The emerging area of fire prevention training provides considerable insight into the challenges of creating a regulatory framework where fire prevention remains central, and where practices with questionable relevance to fire prevention are minimized. Historically, much fire prevention training in Thailand has been undertaken by NGOs who have provided a low-cost accessible means for disseminating information in the community. But, as concern about fire prevention grew, so too did the opportunity for creating businesses in the area. From the perspective of some NGOs the involvement of a business model was unwelcome:

> They [new businesses] want to open an institute or a school or whatever, but they charged too much for the poor Thai people. I try to do this through social welfare, but that group try to make the benefit from the poor people to make their business ... Their school is very expensive! If they charge you for the basic fire training, [for] one day they will charge 30,000 baht; it's very high. Even for business or regular people ... they go to the company in their place, it's very expensive ...

But there was an added complication. The fire prevention NGOs' concern was that those who wanted to start a business would try to lock out any other fire prevention agency from the process. They would try to do this through ensuring that training through the businesses would be made compulsory for business registration, thus discrediting the training given by the fire NGOs. One NGO representative was very concerned as he related the following story about an emerging businessman in the area of fire safety:

> ... [One businessman] tried to make the [fire prevention] school through the Bangkok Municipal Authority [to create a monopoly]. But, I already give free education to the people. But that group try to kick me out ... everybody out! He will say he will make a business service to the big company. He was talking to the high-ranking people here to

issue the law [that said], 'If no training with [this business] you will arrest or fine them.' This is not good ...

The NGO conceded that maybe for some sectors of Thai industry a fire prevention business was viable, but not for the majority of the Thai public and certainly not in the schools and community areas:

> If you charge the big company for training, all right, no problem, but if the factory is nearly dead because it has no money to pay salaries, this is murder! I am afraid of this. I'm sorry ... business is not bad, everybody have to do the business. But what I['m] talking [about] ... if you use the people's tax and you make a lot of money, I think it is not good, not fair ... [Maybe] a fire organization can charge a business to finance free services to those who cannot afford it. But not to do all the business ... Nowadays many people want to pay me, but I don't want to do this thing like a business. This thing should be social welfare. For every country, you have a government, you have a fire brigade, don't you? And they go out to schools, it's free, don't they? But over here, all the government [they want to] charge the people for the business; come on! ... They are telling lies, they are not telling the truth. What I say is, why don't the government and the people help in the basic facility for the people first, before you think [of going to] the next job?

From the observations above it is clear that the political pressures associated with setting up a regulatory framework can be intense, particularly where private financial gain and social status is involved. In the example above, NGOs felt they were being sidelined to make way for business. But the final outcome was far from settled:

> My style is the voluntary style. The businessman cannot scare me! ... I started fire prevention with the hotel; a hotel is a big business [and] has the money to pay. Then, they [the new fire prevention businesses] go to the hotel, so I don't go. I go to the community; nobody follow me to kick me out. I go to the school; nobody comes to the school because [they have] no money. I start this young fire fighter group ...

However, even the move of the NGO to the community areas did not stop the battle for the ear of the government:

> ... Now they [the fire prevention companies] accuse me and say I bring the children together to make the business, they say! But the government look at me and say 'No, we don't worry about this NGO!' ... My way is to work with local community ... What I think it means, everybody have to try to improve [the fire situation] ... [but] don't let the businessman, no. I mean, some people who is not clean, come to take advantage to our society. I worry about this ... I worry about the group of people, who use the fire safety law to make money. I don't like that.

As economists from Marx (1976) to Stigler (1975) and Kolko (1963, 1965) have long recognized, regulation creates winners and losers. Regulations define who may enter the marketplace, not only in terms of the business sector being regulated, but also, as in the case above, of who may assist business and the community to comply with their regulatory responsibilities. In the narrative above, businesses in the regulation compliance industry were not categorized as good or bad. However, the NGO was adamant that there needed to be recognition of the ability of business to pay for their regulatory compliance, since the primary concern of government and regulations themselves should be the reduction of harm, in this case from fire. In a twist to the usual rent seeking/regulation narrative, here it was the regulation business that was cast in the 'evil' role and the commercial business in the 'good'. But neither can the narrative above be used simply as an example of regulatory capture in the economic sense, that is, regulations used to capture the market for private gain, since the NGOs' concern was not to forgo fire prevention training altogether, rather to create a regulatory form that was appropriate, and affordable, to the context.

What is clear, then, is that implementation of law and regulation in a manner that improves safety is difficult and prone to failure. Laws, regulations and ministerial directives exist in a complex relationship with underlying regulatory character that places a low priority on formal rules, but a high priority on status and hierarchy. Further, the nascent regulation industry itself can be used strategically to improve status or for material gain.

Conclusion

This chapter explored the nature of law reform after Kader, with a particular focus on the authority of law, independent from its author. In the first part of the chapter, the analysis showed how regulations and their reform exhibited the underlying tension between traditional Thai regulatory character, with its emphasis on patriarchy and self-reliance, and activist demands for a more egalitarian approach. The narratives in the chapter illustrated that this shift to an egalitarian ideal was not new, but related to the long history of protest within Thailand that brought together a diverse range of people who, to varying degrees, saw the need for Thai regulatory character to change. In the aftermath of Kader it was not charity that was needed, but a change in regulatory structure so that the voices of workers, particularly those with illness and injury, could be heard. For activists, the process of change was as important as the result, as merely imposing a regulatory scheme seemed likely to result in more *pak chee roy nah*. Until both a new process was institutionalized and a new regulatory structure put in place, activists argued, reform would not lead to substantial change. The contest between these two visions of the ideal regulatory framework, patriarchal and egalitarian, was played out through the reform process. Activists saw the five-partite model of a new occupational health and safety institute as central to changing traditional regulatory character, as it held the greatest promise in combating the emphasis on status for its own sake, the heavy-handed nature of control through tripartite committees and bureaucratic hierarchies and the fragmented nature of safety regulation, all a constant drag on substantive change. However, their vision failed to come to realization. The bureaucracy's vision for the institute promoted in its stead failed to tackle the deep-seated problems of regulatory overlap and bureaucratic control. Despite activists using all their skills, as well as clauses in the new constitution to further their demands, substantial reform languished. Reform that did occur was incorporated into the existing traditional character.

Regulatory reform could not be viewed as separate from regulatory implementation. Regulatory effectiveness emanating from law reform following disasters required the rule itself to carry weight. The independent authority of law in Thai health and safety regulation remained weak. Once reform occurred, conflict around reform was displaced to the level of implementation. Here, even when regulatory techniques were available and could be drawn upon, ritual could replace substance. There were several ways in which regulatory reform remained little more than *pak chee roy nah*. Critical replacements could be made in the way regulatory compliance was achieved, for example using cheap ineffective fire safety systems that looked good but did little, complex standards could be translated literally word for word, but not understood. Statistics could be misused to illustrate progress where there was none. Finally, reforms could be moulded to suit status needs. Critically, the data showed that safety regulation itself was not immune from this process, regulation could not be considered uncritically as a 'public good' without analysis of both its content and the manner of its implementation.

Chapter 7

Globalization, Self-reliance and Global Rationalism

In the aftermath of Kader, globalization influenced how regulatory character developed over time, but these effects were in turn mediated by that character. In this chapter, the first two questions posed in Chapter 2 are answered, namely: how did economic pressures and the push towards individualism affect regulatory reform after Kader? Secondly, how did global rationalism – the plethora of rules circulating the global stage – find their way into the Thai context? What was revealed by the research was that the dynamics generated by globalization worked through separate aspects of regulatory character: the emphasis on individualism within the economic reforms intersected with the self-reliance within regulatory character, whereas global rationalism, the generation and dissemination of international rules was drawn into the Thai context through formalism, a dynamic working at the opposite 'end' of regulatory character. The economic reforms that aimed to promote a competitive international market fed into the self-reliance within Thai regulatory character demanding greater resilience. But this in turn re-emphasized the links between self-reliance and patronage such that networks and local contacts were more, not less important. At the same time, a plethora of internationally generated rules and standards found their way into Thai law, those aimed both to institutionalize the global market and to introduce into Thailand a range of global safety standards. What was critical to ongoing change, however, was how these rules were viewed and how they intersected with the local context.

Free Trade and Self-reliance

The connection between self-reliance and globalization worked in two separate ways. The first of these was the link between self-reliance and competitiveness as global economic pressures meant that being competitive was the pre-eminent means of getting and keeping investment. The rapid economic development coupled with the Asian financial collapse reinforced this need to remain competitive and to stay ahead. In terms of regulatory character, competition complemented strategic forms of self-reliance in the acceptance of the status quo, in this case abiding by rules of competition, and the emphasis on creative use of the symbols of the market to demonstrate competitiveness and forward thinking. If this meant reducing wages, for example in rural areas, then this was undertaken. If this meant using safety as a competitive edge, through promoting company codes of conduct, then this also would be considered.

The second link between global economic pressures and self-reliance was the intersection between the demands for flexibility by the global market and interpenetrative self-reliance. The need to cope with uncertainty was familiar to Thai workers as it reiterated the need for living day-to-day, but also finding support from patriarchal figures or patrons. Whilst policies supporting economic globalization see one of its benefits as reducing the opportunity for 'corruption', the emphasis of these policies on self-reliance may have a critical role in maintaining conditions under which informal 'corrupt' sources of financial support thrive.

For Thailand, the current wave of economic globalization began with the inflow of investment, much of it from Japan in the 1980s. Increased costs associated with production in Japan and the West, including regulatory compliance costs in areas such as health and safety, meant Japanese companies searched elsewhere for production facilities (Pasuk and Baker 1998, pp. 33–8). Rapid industrialization and social change followed, with the speed of change outstripping coping strategies, as Phil Robertson explained:

> ... Japanese capital goes from nothing in 1985/86, to over two billion US dollars in 1987 in direct or indirect investment ... [the money] poured in because they just shifted production ... What we're talking about is an incredible acceleration in industrialization here fuelled by foreign direct investment, largely coming from Japan, where technology, production, industry raced way ahead of the knowledge level of both owners and the workers – and the government.

The government largely welcomed this massive increase in investment. Retaining it, though, was harder since Thailand itself was now under challenge from countries, particularly China, where wages were much lower. The bureaucracy was well aware of this. Dr Chaiyuth argued: '... when you look at the level of the wages, we are higher than China, than Indonesia; you see we cannot compete with them. They have so many people there. In China, they are making only $40 US a month, a third of our wages.' For activists, this meant that globalization forced poor conditions on workers since, activists argued, '... because of globalisation we cannot say no to the company'.

The increased connection between Thailand and the international economy opened up both the possibility of massive investment and the frightening prospect of rapid disinvestment that engendered a feeling of lack of control. The Asian financial crisis of 1997–1998 reinforced, in dramatic detail, the implication of close ties to international investment trends and sentiment. Dr Voravidh described how the crisis affected many small and medium-sized businesses:

> One thing [that occurred] was the failure of the SME [small and medium enterprises], because of the credit line being cut and plus the high interest rate. When we [at the University] went into this – the interest rate was very high, because according to the IMF we were lucky to keep the money ... [so] they [the government] upped the inflation, they wanted to stabilize [the economy]. So, with this high interest rate and credit cuts, a lot of factories, the SMEs, have been affected. Many closed down ... We

also have a sort of a belt-tightening [that] led to a lot of break down on the domestic market.

A further response by government was to decentralize wage levels, further weakening the involvement of labour, as Voravidh explained: '... now they have even decentralized the wage setting system from a centralized tripartite system, to the provincial level ... each province would decide on the wage differently'. For many, the crisis meant formal employment was no longer an option. They ended up with informal street vending work; but with few buyers, life was difficult. Voravidh continued '... the people who [lost out] ... they're out of job, they have to go into the small commerce. They also can sell things ... but there's no money [to buy]. So a lot of problem ... that's why there's no inflation finally, because nobody is buying anything ....'

In terms of safety regulation, the impact of the economic crisis was complex and ultimately tied into finding the 'right' market signals both to justify compliance or non-compliance, or to find a creative way to combine market and safety success. For business, the impact for some was clearly great, as Voravidh highlighted, yet not all were equally affected. The downturn also provided an acceptable motive for not spending money on safety initiatives. The emphasis on investment first meant that safety standards were not a priority; Jaded argued that the crisis could then be used as another excuse to push standards down:

> After the crisis ... some owners of the factory tried to take advantage of that ... they said, 'It's a good chance for us to take advantage of our own workers by reducing their wage, give less compensation, less welfare.' Even like some protection in the working place, like equipment to protect the worker, owners said, 'We can't afford it; you use the old ones ... You cannot buy a new one because we don't have the money.' Even if they didn't get a real impact from the crisis they use it as an excuse. For the workers themselves, they are working in a hell environment; it's a really bad environment, working environment. They have no protection for their health and safety.

For those within the bureaucracy, the impact of the crisis on their ability to regulate was mixed. Some argued that the downturn provided some means to reflect on the need for improved safety. Waradom argued in the area of fire prevention '[in] the economic crisis, people have to sit and think a lot'. For him, the crisis meant there was time to plan and get things right. Certainly, there was a time where inspections were cut back, for fear of even greater economic collapse. Dr Chaiyuth spoke about inspections during the crisis:

> I remember at the very beginning when the crisis came to Thailand in 1997, the inspections [were affected]. We went out less than normal, because the industry ... they are dying, we just ... we would like to give them some time so they can think about where to get the money ... that sort of thing, but we do visit them and talk to them, [to ask] 'Can we help you?' ... We were afraid of too many people to be laid off at that time. In fact, they did lay off almost a million [workers]. But now it is come back to normal.

However, there were deeper lessons learnt both from the rapidity of economic development and the subsequent crisis experience. Firstly, that the enormous size of the job of inspection swamped the capability of the government inspectors. Dr Chaiyuth argued that this meant there needed to be lateral thinking about how safety standards were going to be improved, given the capacity of the inspectors:

> ... we cannot expand our activities, just holding. I don't think this is the right way. Unless in the near future we come up with a new innovation, a new way of getting the work done ... If you cannot increase the number of inspector, how can you enforce the law? Only 400 to 500 people to deal with 400,000 enterprises; there is no way [it can work] ... The small business, we rarely do inspections on those. For the enterprises that employ less than 10, even 20, you may say we are not able to go there ... At the moment we are blamed: 'Well, your people, you don't enforce the law; do what you are supposed to do.' So what do we do? We have to find a way out, a new innovation, which innovation should be implemented? Should be adopted?

Secondly, there was a real fear of another round of massive disinvestment and transfer of money and jobs to cheaper places of production. The financial crisis had left a legacy of vulnerability. The date 2005 loomed as the next date whereby chaos might result from disinvestment. The anticipated expiry of the Multi-Fibre Agreement[30] in 1 January 2005 means that historic quotas placed by Northern importers on textile and clothing exports from developing nations on a country-by-country basis were all removed. On expiry of the agreement, Thailand expected it could lose much investment in these industries, as Chaiyuth explained:

> WTO says by January 1, 2005 there will be no barriers in terms of tax barriers, so by that time this standard will be required; social responsibility, workers rights, human rights standards will come and then the small firms will [go to the wall]. Not only the suppliers' [standards are important] but suppliers' contractors; ... if this company has a contractor and subcontractor and so on, all those on the line have to follow the same standard ...

These two elements left the regulator with the experience of being caught in the middle of contradictory forces. Something had to be done in terms of safety reform, but not at the expense of scaring away capital. 'Innovative' regulation solutions were desperately needed, but they had to resolve an impossible dilemma. Chaiyuth continued:

> ... at the moment we don't know what to do. If we keep going the same way we have been doing, we cannot accomplish anything ... The public says, 'You have to do something'; the government also, 'You have to do something.' [Q: But you mustn't scare away capital?] Right, that's right [laughs] ...

---

[30] An agreement allocating quotas for textile and clothing production. It is not clear at the time this book went to press in mid 2005 what the impact of the actual phaseout had been (MacDonald and Vollrath, 2005), however unions within Thailand have reported layoffs and declining conditions (Pravit, 2005).

Not only did regulation need to solve the impossible, but Chaiyuth explained how it also needed to do so in the absence of strong support by politicians, or sustained protest by workers:

> Another thing, in Thailand our politicians, they are not aware of the importance of safety and health. Also ... our Thai workers, in Thailand we have 9 million formal workers, but it is only handful who you met who are pushing [for change] ... We have so many [political] parties, and safety and health is not the issue that they would like.

In light of this, Thai regulators felt they needed to work with the market to build a competitive advantage. Using human rights as a competitive advantage was one such scenario being envisaged. Self-regulation would enable a blending of the public and private good. Fear of capital flight, then, had led to looking to new regulatory forms as a means of attracting and keeping foreign investment. These schemes had to go beyond a 'command and control' regulatory framework because of lack of resources, and were a potentially innovative solution to ensuring free trade is associated with increased standards.

The scheme most commonly referred to in Thailand was SA 8000 accreditation, the MNC code of Social Accountability International (SAI). SAI is a North American based network of international NGOs that has developed the social accountability code, along the lines of the ISO set of standards, with the aim of promoting ethical production. Many companies also have self-regulatory strategies to raise standards – 'codes of conduct' – that their own factories and their suppliers must adhere to. Initiatives, both those initiated by NGOs (such as SAI), and by companies themselves, are seen as a fundamentally 'pragmatic' response to the realities of free trade. It is argued that it is the MNCs, not governments, that hold power, so it is the MNCs that must be cajoled/forced/encouraged to act responsibly, primarily by consumers and NGO groups. Dr Chaiyuth explained using the example of Nike, a company with its own code:

> ... the company here in Thailand is under pressure from the buyer from abroad; for example, Nike is an American brand; they have suppliers here in Thailand to do the work for them. So Nike, because of the world pressure, pressures them [the suppliers], who violate human rights or the workers rights in developing countries. So when Nike come to Thailand and hire the supplier to do the work for them, they will say, 'OK, when you produce our product, please comply with this set of standards.' Nike has given them a set of standards to follow; in that standard it includes safety and health, no child labour, no forced labour, working hours limited, working hours compensation, the salary, the wages, and disciplinary action, discrimination, that sort of thing have to be complied with ... So, in fact, the supplier here, they have to do [it], to be a good guy to follow the standard of Nike.

However, there were clearly limits to this new approach of combining the market and safety. Elsewhere in the interview, Chaiyuth expressed reservations at the ability of this means of regulation to make a substantial difference across the board. In response to whether human rights could be an effective marketing tool for Thailand, to retain business, Chaiyuth responded somewhat doubtfully, 'Well, I think we certainly hope so, but at the end I think the businessman will think about the cost. The same shirt can produce at different cost, you see.'

Further difficulties were also apparent. Under whichever model of corporate code, initiatives the companies missed from this agenda are the smaller to medium-sized enterprises that form the bulk of the local economy. Such companies lack the resources to implement schemes such as SA 8000, and many have no relationship with high-profile MNCs. Without bringing the state along with it, codes such as SA 8000 could only ever be limited in scope. Further, the emphasis on large business and increased standards threatens the viability of the small business. Indeed, on expiry of the MFA in 2005, and the subsequent uptake of codes as a means of maintaining market share, it was anticipated that many small and medium-sized employers would disappear.

The dynamism of the market, too, was problematic. Globalized economic production meant that companies could move to less visible rural regions, or to China where costs were lower. Kader had taken advantage of both, moving to regional areas as well as establishing factories in China. The potential for rigorous NGO oversight in these areas was weaker. Further, if there were improvements of standards globally, including in China, in line with the aim of social responsibility initiatives, Thailand would only retain temporary leadership in this area. This had formed the basis of some discussions between NICE and Nike described by Chaiyuth:

> We did discuss this with Nike representation. They say that, well, they see Thailand have good opportunity to lead the way, and we should quickly [capitalize on it], yes. To get a reputation and also improve our business a little bit, upgrade it … our product to a higher level.

The idea was that Thailand would eventually leave some industries entirely:

> The product [must change], we must not just produce cheap clothing. We have to go to a different level … the man said so [exactly] he said, 'Well, you should step up gradually, you see, because you cannot compete any more with China and Indonesia.' … We have at the moment three industries: apparel, shoes and toys. These are sunset industries. Shoes: some have already moved to China because our minimum wage is too high … After these three we move to electronics, frozen food, canned food, you name it! … maybe jewellery?

Further, the type of industry may make a considerable difference to the effectiveness of 'consumer advocacy' based regulatory regimes. Because of the need for activist consumerism, these initiatives seem most likely to change the practices of not only large, high-profile companies but also those in vulnerable industries. In the case of toys, vulnerability is experienced because of the nature of the end product. Consumers may have heightened sensitivity to buying toys and high-profile sports goods that have been produced at the expense of worker safety, but this may not translate to other products. Products such as plastic buckets, brass appliances for doors, or any host of other goods, are unlikely to capture public attention to the same degree. Consumer taboos, not the degree of hazard, may dictate where these regimes meet their greatest success.

The proliferation in the number of codes also creates problems. SA 8000 is only one of an increasing array of corporate codes of conduct. The Ethical Trade Initiative is another UK equivalent that attempts to get MNCs to take their responsibilities seriously; the Fair Labour Association yet another. There are also industry initiatives. Specific to the toy industry is the development of a Toy Industry Code of Conduct by labour NGOs. The toy industry has also developed its own industry code. The Australian Toy Association, for example, has an extensive code covering health and safety, child labour and labour rights issues within their members' manufacturing plants, both in Australia and overseas. Whilst diverse, all such initiatives rely on companies seeing it as in their own interest to sign up to the code and prove their 'good corporate citizenship' credentials. Finally, there are individual company codes. Companies such as Nike rely on their own corporate code of conduct. These initiatives may be interchangeable from a consumer point of view; a company may be able to switch from one code to another, less rigorous, code with little impact on product sales.

Critically, these audit systems have no role for the government. They are a private affair, a fully privatized, market-based system of regulation. The only role for government is promotion of the scheme, since even enforcement is undertaken by private auditors and the state is bypassed:

> Nike will hire Pricewaterhouse [to inspect] ... Some companies, they are under SA 8000, social accountability 8000, so if that standard is required the SGS,[31] DNV,[32] BVQI,[33] TUV[34] from Germany, which have offices in Bangkok, they will come to do the auditing. So third-party auditors will come ... We [government inspectors] have nothing to do with that, because the buyer would accept only the third-party auditing. They don't accept the others. They don't accept the government inspectors' inspection.

The reason that private auditors are used is that government inspectors and inspections are to convince Northern customers that labour standards are acceptable. As a result a new auditing industry has blossomed, with large accounting firms diversifying and expanding to take advantage of the growth in auditing in this area. Yet, there is little evidence that the private audits are themselves comprehensive and effective (see, for example, O'Rourke, 2000). Scant information is released on the content of audits, the enforcement of these codes, or the outcome of any disciplinary action taken. With industry-based codes and company codes, most audit reports on compliance levels are private. There are exceptions; Mattel, for example, initiated an independent monitoring initiative, MIMCO, with audit reports available on its website. Yet even here there are

---

[31] All of these are international accreditation and auditing companies, such as SGS (Thailand) Ltd.
[32] Det Norske Veritas.
[33] Bureau Veritas Quality International.
[34] Technischer Überwachungsverein.

problems with worker representation. A report on auditing by MIMCO makes the following observation:

> ... in the MIMCO report factory life is reduced to percentage points, graphs and charts. In fact, we were continually struck by the invisibility of workers in the entire code of conduct process. They fail to feature at every step, from formulation, through implementation and publication. Despite claims from TNCs that workers matter, they do not seem to play a role worthy of their status – as the lifeblood of manufacturing (Frost and Wong, 2001, p. 4).

Codes were primarily designed for a Northern audience, and the language used, of charts and figures, was a scientific bureaucratic language. AMRC, an NGO in Hong Kong, took a particular interest in codes, and emphasized this aspect of the code phenomenon. There were some benefits to this, however. AMRC had found that codes could bring some change, particularly if the change could be easily enumerated and checked (for example, increasing the number of toilets), but there were problems in other areas where falsification was easy. Doctored time cards and memorized answers by workers were common, and although some auditors knew the tricks, without evidence and with limited time, they felt little could be done. Further, the audit process created resentment. Workers complained to AMRC of being given more work (in terms of memorizing codes and the 'right' answers) and being told to smile, and local managers were resentful of being made to 'prove' their worth to foreigners. Codes could be intrusive and heavy-handed. In some sense, codes were felt as a new form of colonialism – an unwelcome intrusion by meddling outsiders. The link between economic globalization and global rationalism is evident here, a theme developed more fully in the latter part of the chapter.

In addition to the promotion of codes of conduct, a second response of the bureaucracy to their dilemma of resolving the tension between regulation and the market was to emphasize self-awareness as a solution to safety, a pattern familiar from Chapter 5. As that chapter showed, regulatory initiatives were often designed to raise 'self-awareness', to educate workers about hazards so they could take appropriate action. Here, international examples could be drawn on for support. A number of organizations and regulatory agencies mentioned one event that crystallized for them the need for education and self-awareness. This was a dramatic escape of an American woman and her daughter from a burning hotel, The Royal Jomtien in Pattaya, a fire in which many people, including a number of managers of the Electricity Generating Authority of Thailand (EGAT), perished. The woman used her fire awareness education to block smoke coming into her room and used bedding to enable her and her daughter to climb to the roof of the hotel, where they were rescued by helicopter. This woman became a role model for bureaucrats and others on the need to for the Thai public to increase their fire-safety awareness. The National Safety Council was one such organization that drew strength from this example to bolster education:

> We think hard. Like it happened in Jomtien, they had a foreigner from the United States ... they can save their life [the mother and the daughter]. In that case, we try to explain

to them [Thai people] ... how they can save the lives. We try to give as an example for the people. They are studying it, in their workplace.

One of the fire engineers who had inspected the Jomtien hotel after the fire also commented on her escape, which was captured on videotape:

If you saw the investigation videotape from Royal Jomtien, you saw American lady escape from the building. [They climbed to the roof. She knew what to do.] I went to her room and inspect everything. Actually, I went through the whole building and I found that if people stay in the room they were safe. They could have saved their lives. There were dead bodies all over in the corridor, in the escape stair ... And I talked to my friends, the foreigner friends, they said, 'Oh, when they were very little, they study in school, then they can say the first step, second step, third step of fire safety.' They know everything to save their life. That lady did that, so she saved her life and her kid's life through education in the past. Very easy, they just put the towel at the door and then just stay and tell people that you are here, that's all.

As argued in Chapter 5, the focus on the need to build self-awareness and responsibility alongside self-reliance could mean that those in positions of power could efface the critical connection between self-reliance and patriarchal forms of authority. Examples such as that of the 'American lady' could be used selectively to highlight the need to augment self-reliance with self-awareness, but not the need for political or bureaucratic reform. Bureaucratic emphasis could then be drawn towards the need for education and raising awareness, independently from tackling its connection to patriarchal authority.

From the perspective of workers, globalization simply re-emphasized the need for self-reliance, a condition that was very familiar. Government promises to resolve a situation were often seen to be empty. Ultimately, each individual, each family, had to make the most of what they had, doing anything to survive, even with income below the minimum wage. Jaded argued:

Officially, 162 baht (US $4 per day) is what the government says is the minimum wage. But a lot of people since the crisis ... a lot of people get laid off from their companies and they start a new job with a small company ... they even get less because the company is in some kind of illegal thing on the black market. But, they still need to survive. They won't kill themselves; they won't commit suicide because they have been poor all their lives. They need to struggle through it. It doesn't matter whether they get 160 or 130, they still need to go on living. They're OK. If they get this much, 'I eat this; if I get less, I eat less,' something like this. But this is just short-term.

In some sense, the economic changes brought about by globalization were incorporated in a manner that fitted a familiar condition – the need for self-reliance. Again, as was shown in Chapter 5, self-reliance was coupled with the need to think in the short term, since the long term was unpredictable. Planning for the long term was not necessarily rational, since with the pace of change and the unpredictability of work, taking life a day at a time made more sense. But, Jaded argued, this has long-term effects:

> But the long ... long-term problem is education for their kids. Some need to get out ... need to quit the school, need to quit studying to come to start working and making money themselves, because if the parent doesn't make as much as before, so you [the child] need to help yourself by coming and work for yourself.

Emphasizing the success of surviving another day, particularly within an interpenetrative frame, could mean that life could be enjoyed in the moment, one comment being, 'Our people don't think. Our people are optimists.' Thai people say, 'Never mind, tomorrow is better.' But, this method of coping with uncertainty by focussing on short-term survival could exacerbate problems associated with global change since there was no measure of what 'better' might be in the context of global change. A comment from a university academic exemplified this idea of globalization as an external force exploiting the innocence of Thai people:

> They are very innocent, the people from the rural [areas]; they think other people will think like they think. So it is easy to be cheated. We must prepare. It is very easy that the bad thing will happen to our Thai people. In the provinces, prostitutes come from other countries ... from Russia ... come to Pattaya to sell sex here ... This is the effect of the globalization. Russian prostitutes come because of the economic crisis in Russia, illegally. The world is very small now, so the bad things come to our house. And if our house did not prepare our people, they will easily adjust themselves to foreign culture, they do not know what is good or bad, it is just the foreign culture. They just think this is good. This is our problem.

This emphasis on self-reliance had an uneven impact on women, as self-reliance and dependability were the ultimate domain of women (see Chapter 3 above). It should be remembered that the long-term coping in the aftermath of Kader fell disproportionately on women. It is their responsibility to cope with whatever vagaries life serves up.

The ideological underpinning of economic globalization and its link to self-reliance was well illustrated with the constraints placed on the Thai government in terms of what they could or could not do to help people cope with the economic uncertainties associated with the global market. Direct economic assistance by government to workers was considered unwise, since it sent out the 'wrong market signals'. Rather, it was necessary to emphasize the need for flexibility and creativity in generating income. Somyot argued that global policies saw social safety nets, even those that had been long planned, as unwise and so had to be postponed since they could undercut the motivation of the workers to work:

> They [the ADB] said it will take four years for us to be ready for the social security unemployment. Then ADB said, 'This is not the right time ... This is not the right time to give social security. People might be lazy.' Something like this. And also the tendency worldwide that other countries reduce this kind of benefits. So it's not suitable for Thailand at the moment ...

It was not surprising, then, that many activists were adamant that the sole function of global institutions such as the IMF and World Bank was to maintain an economic system in which workers were destined to lose. In this system, providing government support and maintaining a strong government regulatory presence was harder. The conditions that allowed for strong regulation and substantial enforcement were being undercut, through demands such as privatization. Phil Robertson argued:

> ... there's a lot of organizations that could do a lot more to talk about enforcement and issues like that. The World Bank and the ADB are very good at telling people to privatize things, but they don't tell people to enforce laws.

As a consequence, the lesson for workers was that they had to survive without the assistance of government – in other words to be more self-reliant.

This emphasis on self-reliance, though, needed to be seen in context. Globalization acted to re-emphasize the importance of individual coping strategies, yet within Thailand 'managing' remained largely tied to a patriarchal frame of reference, as Phil Robertson explained:

> You just have an incredible sort of rocket rise here where everything changed except the mentalities of the economic elites ... a lot of it is Thai-Chinese which makes it even more clannish and more unlikely to bring in external assistance and professional help. It's all very much family.

Certainly, global financial institutions have viewed the closeness of these relationships as an indication of corruption or a 'capture economy', economies where powerful, 'incumbent' businesses shape government polices to suit their own interests (Hellman, Jones and Kaufmann, 2000). Combating corruption, then, is seen by these institutions as an essential component to successful economic development (World Bank Annual Report, 1998). The emphasis on 'good governance', the development of adequate regulatory controls on business and government behaviour, is increasingly seen as an essential corollary to development (Higgott, 2000; Jayasuriya, 2001). As Jayasuriya (2001) points out, however, definitions of corruption and the need for 'good governance' solutions bring with them predetermined ideas of how governance is to proceed. Governance strategies are tied to economic liberalism, the promotion of the 'free market' where economic activity is free from political 'interference'. In Hood's (1998) terms, the ideological orientation is individualistic. Politics, with its emphasis on networks and connections, is seen almost by definition as corrupt (Higgott, 2000). Little attempt is made to draw a distinction between patriarchalism and corruption (Mulder, 2000), or to appreciate the nature of patriarchalism and corruption in the private sector (see Pasuk, Sungsidh and Nualnoi, 1998). Indeed, corruption is seen primarily as a misuse of public funds. Policies that emanate from within a market philosophy draw a dichotomy between the market as 'free' (and uncorrupted) and politics as problematic and corrupt. Policies such as privatization are then seen as a good way to cut through problems of corruption since privatized systems allow for greater accountability through the market. Certainly, in the Thai context, the demand for the health and safety standard to be audited by a privatized company, not government, was one example of this policy at work.

Yet, for activists, there was a sense in which globalization exacerbated both corruption and the worst excesses of patriarchalism, as rapid investment provided new avenues for gaining power and wealth. Foreign investors, as Voravidh explained, needed connections within Thailand if they were going to succeed:

> And if you look, I can tell you that in a great many investments you cannot succeed as investor coming into Thailand now; you need many political connections. In investment in every project you can see the military profit, you can see investor coming in, you can see they are also are cashed up by the political parties, as well as the military.

The distinction made in corruption-combating programmes between market as good, and politics as bad does not necessarily hold. As studies in Thailand show, the connection between the public and private sectors in Thailand is blurred (Pasuk and Baker, 1995; Hewison, 1989; Suehiro, 1989). Simply privatizing a government industry or service does not ensure it is 'clean', since corrupt relationships and abuse of power can simply transfer from the public to the private sphere. Whilst there is some recognition of this at a policy level within the World Bank (see Hellman, Jones and Kaufmann, 2000), the technocratic approach to 'solving' problems of corruption remains blind to the centrality of political contests and political visions to the nature of a 'good society'.

Further, the emphasis on the market and individualism as the solution was received within Thai regulatory character as a need for self-reliance and with it the need for patronage. The market is unpredictable and fickle; the Asian financial crisis was stark evidence of this. Relationships bring with them certain obligations and were preferred by many Thais as sources of support. The need then was to find a local patron who will help you solve everyday problems. Research evidence from Thailand (Tamada, 1991; Pasuk and Sungsidh, 1994; Pasuk and Baker 1995) suggests that local patrons or *jao pho* are strengthened both by their ability to control certain 'private' industries and also their popularity in meeting local people's needs, the same needs that the government appears unwilling or unable to meet.

In labelling patriarchal relationships themselves as corrupt, whilst at the same time emphasizing self-reliance through the market, global policies themselves may have a critical role to play in sustaining the conditions under which 'black markets' in both goods and services thrive. Within an economic perspective, self-reliance is a quality divorced from its relationship to the broader social structure. Thai regulatory character links self-reliance to patriarchalism, in a relationship that brings at least some reciprocal obligations. However, global economic policies that severed this link freed economic elites from traditional constraints. This could have the effect of making workers more, not less, vulnerable.

Global Rationalism

Much of the emphasis on economic restructuring was on the need to replace patriarchal authority with more 'accountable' forms of authority, namely, the market and market rules. Thus, the separation of self-reliance from patriarchy within the individualistic ideal of economic reform had a related impact whereby the basis for authority in the international arena shifted to rules, in particular rules that entrenched the market and market mechanisms within local communities. Global rationalism, the process whereby ideals and philosophies were translated into rules and procedures, was best exemplified by rules governing the market. The growing use of consultants and accountancy firms to ascertain the viability of reform and the way restructuring should take place was one example of the increased emphasis on market rules commented on by activists. These firms could be viewed as the 'new rationalizers', bringing with them a new system of authority based on what 'the market' demanded. Somyot recounted:

> They [the IMF] said the government must be reformed ... labour law reform. They make a restructuring. Reform/restructuring, the same. So they employ one company, private company called Brooker company. It's a research company. So, this company has come up with the idea to restructuring ... need to cut lower wages. First, only cost of living considerations to be included in wage increases – not economic growth.

Economic restructuring was at the forefront of change, with consultancy firms and global institutions entrenching market ideologies through identifying what policies were consistent with global competitiveness and which were not. Consultants were a catalyst of global rationalism aimed at institutionalizing economic reform by linking global policy (from the IMF, ADB and World Bank) to local policy.

This 'stage-setting' by consultants and others then encouraged other formally rational[35] rule-based systems that embodied the ideals of the market to be popularized as a signal of aggressive competitiveness and high standards. A prominent example of this was the International Organization for Standardization (ISO) set of standards aimed at assuring the quality of the product or service. The ISO is an international standard-setting organization that has developed rapidly from an institution primarily concerned with ensuring parity in engineering standards, to one encompassing a broader and broader range of concerns centred on market relationships of supplier and customer. One of its most successful standards has been the set of standards for guaranteeing the quality of a product or service. Adherence to the ISO family of standards for quality (in particular ISO 9001 and ISO 9002) became synonymous with signalling enthusiasm and acceptance of international trade. ISO compliance was then seen as a way of 'legitimating' Thai business – and important for attracting investment. Lists of newly accredited companies appeared regularly in local newspapers and heralded that yet more Thai businesses could compete with the best in the world.

These quality standards were seen by the bureaucracy as critical to the long-term interests of the Thai economy, as a statement about the international marketability and quality of the product or service. The National Safety Council argued, 'The consumer products, because we produce our goods to export, they must have the ISO standards.' As new ISO standards were developed they were also included as necessary to signal competitiveness. The National Safety Council

---

[35] In the Weberian sense of rules, not individuals and relationships, having the authority.

continued: '... So many, many, right now you see increasingly you need [more], Thai company now need ISO 18000.'[36] The progressive growth in the use of standards was one example where regulation could be argued to be 'ratcheting up' (Fung, O'Rourke and Sabel, 2001; Meidinger, 2002) as companies were becoming accredited in a range of areas. Whether accreditation to an increased array of standards is an accurate indication of actual improvement was unclear, since accreditation was primarily a way of Thai-based companies signalling their credentials to the market, as Phil Robertson explained:

> It [accreditation] brings in a system like, 'Here's your system. Adopt it and you're ISO-compliant.' ... They say, 'Ah well, we'll do this to get the inspection certificate and we'll have a little sort of special announcement booklet in the *Bangkok Post* ... It's like – like wild-fire. I mean, this is the perfect appeal. I mean, you know, 'OK, we pass this test, and we're world class.' So, it's like, 'OK, all we need to do is get into the huddle. Everybody needs to get into the huddle.' It's like cramming for an exam.

The priority for adoption of these standards is clear: the code enables a company to compete. Whether this particular standard translated into better working conditions, in addition to its central purpose of guaranteed quality of product, was not clear. There were some who argued that these codes, concerned with the quality of the product, would increase standards overall, since the environment of the worker influenced the quality of production. Also, ISO standards generally were certainly more prominent than codes specifically related to worker welfare, such as SA 8000, and so had the potential to produce more widespread change if effective in improving working conditions. However, others were less sure that ISO standards improved the working environment, or simply added more pressure for workers. Jaded argued:

> The ISO is like the tools to fight the competition. [It] makes the export more high quality for the outsider. It can happen in the big businesses and maybe the medium, but the small ones, it's difficult to get them. Most of them can try to get ISO 9002 but they try to use ISO as a tool to get more business ... In some factory, they try to force the worker, try to work harder to get this standard, but for the worker themselves, they are not sure, is this going to be better?

High quality products then did not necessarily result from safe workplaces. Bundit described the focus in the electronics industry:

> Like in some businesses, like the electronic business, or making computer part, something like that, when you go there you will notice that it is very clean, you know, all the workers have the masks, have the safety suit or whatever ... only the masks they issue are not for protecting the labourer, but is protecting the chip, because of the moisture.

---

[36] ISO 18000, the Safety Management System Standard, had been abandoned by the ISO due to its encroachment on the preserve of the ILO (see below). It is not clear whether what was meant here was the ISO 14000 system series pertaining to environmental management systems.

Global rationalism, then, was most aggressive in areas consistent with competitive market philosophies. But this was not the only form it took. Other rule-based systems that had an explicit safety focus were also extending their influence. The Asian Disaster Preparedness Centre (ADPC), based in Bangkok, was one organization that was committed to the dissemination of international standards in the area of disaster prevention and mitigation. ADPC was a regional NGO that worked with both government and UN bodies to assist those in the region reduce the impact of disasters. As such, the dissemination of international standards and principles through education of local communities was an important part of their work. The APELL[37] set of principles was one set of standards the ADPC was interested in promoting. These standards grew out of a series of disasters in Europe, most notably Flixborough in the United Kingdom in 1974 and Seveso in Norway in 1976, and aimed to increase emergency preparedness at the local level. ADPC was keen to take on the role of dissemination of APELL within Asia:

> Everything which we have done before fits in well to the APELL network. They're formalising that and hopefully this leads to a more aggressive pursuit of the subject ... So we are on the verge of signing an MOU with UNEP to be their regional collaborating centre, a kind of partner to promote and support the adoption of APELL in Asia.

The emphasis on safety here has a technical rather than political emphasis. The focus is on planning and procedure. Such processes emanate from the elite through the bureaucracy down to the community. Much of the planning in this area involved the National Economic and Social Development Board of Thailand that then drew on international expertise in this area. Mr Rego of the ADPC explained:

> Within Thailand itself there is an ongoing project between the NESDB, the National Economic and Social Development Board, this is like the Planning Commission of Thailand. They have a collaborative project with GTZ[38] and that is to strengthen the regulatory framework or response to regulatory failures.

The dissemination of knowledge about proper safety standards to the bureaucracy of Thailand was not only a central concern for regional bodies, such as the ADPC, but also traditional donor nations to Thailand, such as Japan. Dr Chaiyuth described the process of rationalization in the area of industrial hygiene, where Japanese expertise was drawn on in an attempt to institutionalize certain standards within Thailand. The process could be a lengthy one:

> They [the Japanese] are providing a 5-year project with the NICE at the moment. In fact, I discuss with them 8 or 9 years back – almost 10 years. It was in 1992 or '91 we had a Japanese expert to sit with us for two years and during that time we prepared a project and that project is being implemented now. I discussed with them, you see, I would like to see a technical institution, I think, to upgrade NICE to be able to provide a good facility for hygiene lab, medicine lab, and so on. And also we would like to be a

---

[37]   Awareness and Preparedness for Emergency at the Local Level.
[38]   Gesellschaft für Technische Zusammenarbeit (Society for Technical Co-operation).

technical training centre for our Thai industry; we would like a demonstration centre for anyone to come and see how safety and health in the workplace is working. We even thought about to set up a construction site over there, but it is not yet realized, but at the moment we get only to improve our technical capability at NICE, but I would like to set up a factory or a construction site, but they are not there yet.

Global rationalism could also take different forms with respect to the involvement of national and regional governments. For some rules and standards, such as ISO standards on quality, there was minimal involvement by government. The relationship was between the International Organization for Standardization (ISO) and the company. In other cases, international standards were re-created within Thailand and given effect through the organs of the state. The process of re-creation of globalized standards within Thailand and the Thai legislative framework was common. One example here was NFPA standards, fire safety standards originally developed within the United States but used extensively internationally. These were in the process of being used as the basis for fire prevention standards in Thailand. Their currency within Thailand began with educators coming from the United States and bringing their manuals with them. Waradom recounted his experience at engineering school:

When I studied in engineer school for the last year, I study NFPA course called NEC – National Electrical Course. This course was very old, about twenty years ago, and we made copies, copy, copy, copies and copies. Cannot read anything. You study [these standards] in the school because most of our lecturers came from US, study there and come back to teach our people.

The re-creation of standards within Thailand could relate not only to the content of the rules but also pressure to adopt a particular regulatory framework. In the case of the NFPA this included an independence of the fire institute from government, as Waradom explained: 'We try to run it privately because if it includes or depends [on] government it complicates procedure ... We tried to copy the system from US, like the NFPA, they run by themselves ...'

Codes being developed in Thailand did not necessarily come from one particular model, although they may use one as a basis. A wide range of country standards might be reviewed. Waradom continued to explain this in the case of fire safety:

They [the bureaucracy] also study other standards – Japanese, Chinese. And we summarize the thing that's common to all country that issue the code of standards. Right now it's the beginning stage of this thing. They just finish fire alarm code of standards, the first one.

Despite the appearance of these standards as apolitical and technical, global rationalism could be a highly politicized process at the international level, particularly in the area of labour standards. This occurred when the rationalization of market-based dynamics, through mechanisms such as ISO standards on quality, spread into the domain of international processes and rule development based on a different philosophy. A prominent example here is the conventions and guidelines developed by the ILO. As stated above, the range of ISO standards have extended in scope dramatically, beyond engineering and quality standards. In line with this expansion, there was preliminary discussion about the development of standards for employee health and safety within a safety management standard. Direct involvement in labour standards, however, was contentious. Here, ISO involvement could conflict with other institutions, such as the ILO, with different visions of the regulatory ideal (Trebilock and Howse, 1995).

In the area of health and safety, international initiatives have historically been the preserve of the ILO, which emphasizes the importance of the tripartite framework. ISO standards primarily involve simply customer and supplier. From the perspective of the ILO, ISO standards were deficient because of the lack of union involvement. Research by the ILO confirmed that the content of many industry and NGO codes also had serious deficiencies with respect to the rights of workers to organize and collectively bargain (Diller, 1999). The ILO was then keen to retain the lead in this area and to shape the philosophy in this area of global rule making. This included influence on NGO worker health and safety codes such as SA 8000 described in the previous section. Kawakami, a regional ILO representative, explained:

We have very strong initiative to develop our own international guidelines on the safety management system, separate from the ISO. The ILO has been requested by the trade unions and other constituents to develop international guidelines on OHS management systems. So our people in the headquarters in Geneva, now they are very busy to develop this ... we are going to conduct some regional seminar on OHS management systems, especially the ILO guidelines, inviting our constituents from various countries in Asia ... The ILO is worried because nowadays a lot of consultant companies and private companies, they develop their own standards. They may be good but they use it as a business, use it for their business and it costs a lot, and then there are many different standards in each country. The ILO position is, they had better develop some kind of guideline to integrate all the different standards ... Another important aspect of the ILO's concern is that the involvement of workers [in some codes] is not strong because they developed as a part of the business ... that is why especially the trade union constituents in the ILO, they are worried.

Influencing the form the rules take, as in the example of the ILO above, is clearly an important part of the understanding of global rationalism. In order for the standards, rules and regulations to have meaning, the ILO felt there had to be engagement by workers in their development. For rules to be effective there needed to be active involvement of workers in the development of what constitutes reasonable standards.

Important here to the discussion of global rationalism, then, is not only the content of the rules and the regulatory framework, but how they are developed. The process of global rationalism and the re-creation of international codes as Thai regulatory standards could be experienced by workers as a fait accompli, one in which that they had no part to play either in their development, or in their implementation. As a worker, demanding compliance within a company when the content of the standard is foreign and so to insist on compliance is likely to lead to reprisal. Consequently such standards remain meaningless. Voravidh explained:

> With the code of conduct or the ISO ... it is being imposed, you know, or imported. It tends to kill the process. I think the process is very important. Through the process, the contradictions, the problems, you can solve this, it [the end result] is more firm. If you accept the standard, that means you know the process.

The drafting of rules, codes and regulations, however, is only one part of the problem. As important is the degree to which the rules actually have authority – and can change corporate behaviour. As Riggs (1961) pointed out, the intersection of authority and the law does not have a single dimension. It involves both the power to define the law and the power of the law to influence actual behaviour. The political struggles between the ILO and competing bodies on the proper framework for industry safety codes is one example of the former dimension. Once rules are in place, however, the concern switches to the authority of the rules themselves in changing corporate behaviour.

Compliance with 'foreign' rules can be resented. Resentment of compliance demands was present in companies subject to the codes of conduct discussed above. Each code has its own particular requirements in terms of what constitutes compliance and how and by whom it must be audited, with many relying on accounting firms or companies with particular interest in safety such as DNV or BVQI. These firms are multinationals in their own right, and the market for social and environmental audits is growing. The impact of such codes on standards, however is not clear. For managers, this auditing process could be onerous and unwelcome, yet they were compelled to undertake audits if they wanted to keep their licence with Western MNCs. Workers, too, could find the audit process problematic; it broke their everyday routine, there were 'scripts' to be learnt, answers to be given. With auditors there for only a short time, workers had to know what the reaction of management was to codes. If it were merely a ritualistic process, then, the best solution was to get through the ritual as quickly and painlessly as possible. In short, the proliferation of codes within workplaces was not universally desired by either management or workers. Apo Leong from the Asia Monitor Resource Center explained:

> Each auditor is doing between 2000 and 3000 audits per year, thousands, but they're all confidential ... It is a huge industry that is a money earner. For example in Nike, 62 garment factory managers were targeted. The managers don't like this; there is conflict. 'I'm innocent,' they say. 'I can do this, I will do this to prove that I am a clean manager.' Merchandisers look for a clean company, want [a] clean company, [so the managers] must abide by this rule ... They have to pretend 'I'm happy', and so on. This builds up worker resentment ... It is a top-down approach.

AMRC had received complaints about the code process and the ways companies use to get around their compliance responsibilities. Some auditors are aware of these problems, but without concrete evidence, are unable to rectify problems. Some good could occur, and some longstanding problems could be rectified through the auditing process, but the price was high in terms of disruption to work. Apo continued: 'In a few cases it did help a bit; there was some improvement. In one factory they demanded one toilet for 20 ladies; it didn't happen. But after the code was audited, then the company complied.'

The research did not undertake any systematic analysis into compliance levels within multinational companies, however there was widespread agreement between both NGOs and government bureaucrats that levels of compliance varied between MNCs originating from different countries. Multinationals, particularly those well-known to Western consumers, including Japanese multinationals, were argued to be more aware of their responsibility to abide by the law. Some took their responsibilities, under Thai law at least, seriously. Understanding why this was the case, was complex. Somyot argued that the publicity in the West of poor working conditions was seen as partly responsible for this difference. 'People who are working and supply the produce export[ed] to your country, they have to pay attention to the rights of the workers. So it's quite useful in terms of the pressure to the government, to pay more attention.'

Both those in the bureaucracy and activists argued that consumer and legal pressure meant that Western companies would take more account of local laws. Dr Chaiyuth stressed that it was not the governments of Western nations that were putting the pressure on factories in Thailand, but unions and consumers of those nations. Buyers had to take care who they were buying from:

> It is not their [the national government's] initiative, I think! Because the consumer is in the States, and trade unions in the States who lost their job because they move their plants from the States to developing countries to make the cost lower. So, those are the people who put pressure on them, on Nike, on Reebok, on the other brands that move to Thailand.

But consumer and legal pressure alone was not a full explanation for the differences in standards. Dr Voravidh had made a study of labour management in Japanese and American firms in the mid-1980s. His study had found that Japanese firms tended to have better practices, but the reasons for this remained unclear, as he explained:

> I tried to ... you know ... I made a study, but that was a long time ago, about 15 years ago, between American and Japanese factories, about their labour management. I found the Japanese are better in their labour management. But the reason is not clear ... it may depend on the products, for example ... I found that employment in the Japanese are more stable. When you look at the age of the workers, they tend to keep people of longer age. But, I don't know whether it was a product of ... you know ... the American company was making an electronics circuit for the computer chips, the integrated circuit, but the Japanese, it was electrical. One is export-oriented, the chips were totally exported. One is more a domestic market.

Bundit argued that financial incentives from the Thai government might also help account for the difference in standards. Incentives are provided by the Bureau of Investment (BOI) for multinational companies aimed at encouraging them to invest in certain regions. This meant that their overall costs were low, and they could invest more in compliance:

> The local family businesses, they have a low capital, right, and they don't have any privilege from the BOI to decrease the cost of making a product, like the labour costs to make it low, and the welfare for the workers to make it better. ... But the big companies, especially the international corporations, for example, the Seagate from US, they pay twelve times less than the regular minimum wage in the US ... even they pay twelve times less than their country's level, but it's still more than the local and family business in Thailand. Since it's cheap for them, you know, twelve times cheaper, they can pay more attention to the safety issue.

Whatever the reason, companies that had higher standards could demonstrate to local managers that some attention to safety was compatible with running a successful business. Waradom, when working on a construction project for the American Embassy, had been surprised by the idea that it was possible to build such a building without loss of life. 'They bring their standards with their business,' he commented. On this project, he saw a different way of looking at work, one where safety and success were possible. Waradom saw the effectiveness of international standards and experienced a commitment to making those standards work:

> So at that time I can speak and communicate in English; I study US standards and I build Thai buildings ... The building of US Embassy, I built that. So, I work with really high standards, and this building can stay in the war! ... It's good for me, because when I work there my boss told me he liked me to work for four days to see buildings, to inspect people, [so] the building is in my head [even though] when I work I may not know anything about [written] US standards. When I worked at this time with many people talking about NFPA standards and many things, sometimes I don't know the code, but I know the real building that follow the code. So I have the picture in my head. This helps me.

The connections made at this time meant that he could further his interest in fire safety, and gain some support:

> And also at that time I tell many specialists from US that I like to do my own research about being help people internationally and they help me to arrange the training course in the US about the fire safety. So I got very good connection for the US, and I go to three, four factories and train the product and also work in inspection area.

The level of safety standards within even the best of these companies, however, was lower than in the industrialized nations. It was necessary to reassess what the actual standards were, since, Phil Robertson argued, 'What you are talking about is shifting the whole scale down.' Overall, standards in Thailand were lower, and this meant that workers suffered. Somyot argued:

> Our Thai industry has really come from the advanced country ... and it's moving from one country to another country. They move all their dangerous work to Thailand,

assisted by weak implementation mechanism of the government. So it's very difficult to do anything good for the big or small. Small might be worse. Big company might be better. But, they're same content. Maybe in the small you can see that happening very quickly. For the big company you will die maybe 50 years or get affected, then you already quit from the company.

Further, higher standards were not synonymous with being an international project or a large multinational. Both those from the bureaucracy and activist NGOs argued there was a difference depending on the source of the multinational. This was one such comment from the NSC:

> In my opinion, I think it [safety standards] depends on which country the multinational company is from ... Like in Asia, like Taiwan, Hong Kong ... they're not much concerned about this. Because they invest, they don't want to spend money for the safety, they [only] want to make a profit. But, for the country like United States, I think because they realize about the safety in their country, and so we have here the safety [in US companies] ...

Bundit from Arom Pongpangan made a similar argument: 'The Hong Kong and Taiwan investor tend to take more advantage of the situation, especially the Taiwanese ... Sometimes they escape from the factory – I mean, they just disappear from the factory so the worker doesn't get paid.' Jaded from the Friends of Women concurred: 'The Taiwanese are the worst. A lot of Chinese here come to invest here. They are still better than the Taiwanese.'[39] Activists argued that those companies with the lowest standards would resort to repressive means to ensure control over workers. Jaded recounted some of the tactics used to punish workers:

> Some [companies] video taped the female worker using the toilet, and sometimes they take a worker to sit outside under the sun. Thai people hate the sun – and they just abuse them, to punish them. This worker, it was because she was part of the trade union.

For workers working under these conditions, the authority of any law that existed outside of the company gate was absent. It had little impact on their daily lives. Global rationalism, whether aiming to entrench competitiveness or to improve safety, depended for effect on implementation – implementation that required both state involvement and a commitment by the business concerned for it to be any more than piecemeal.

---

[39] The implications of these comments need to be treated carefully. Firstly, there were some Thai companies, such as Siam Cement, that saw themselves as leaders in the safety field within Thailand. Further, the connection between an MNC's country of origin and bad behaviour needs to be carefully teased out to prevent an unreflective and unhelpful analysis.

Conclusion

The chapter has reviewed the two major ways in which globalization intersects with regulatory character, through self-reliance and formalism, elements at opposite ends of that character. The research showed that the relationship between globalization and self-reliance then was complex. Rapid economic change and the experience of the Asian crisis emphasized the importance of self-reliance. Further, the reality of global competition and the need to retain investment meant new strategies in safety regulation were seen by the bureaucracy as critical since the free trade agenda did not allow for strong command and control regulatory forms within a rapidly industrializing society. Because of this, using consumer pressure as a means for improving safety standards seemed one of the few ways open. Yet it was an uncertain strategy. Indeed the forces that bring with it the potential of raised standards (such as SA 8000 accreditation) also threatened local small and medium enterprises. Further, from a Western perspective, neither Thai business nor Thai government were to be trusted, so development of a state-based regulatory strategy lagged behind. International NGOs bypassed both in order to be seen to be 'untainted' by local standards. Labour codes were audited by non-Thai auditing firms since Thai regulators, also under pressure from politicians and workers, were not trusted by Western consumers.

In response, Thai regulators emphasized the benefits of safety awareness as a means for workers to protect themselves. Education of workers was seen as the way forward. Yet the practical experience of Thai workers coupled with the financial crisis re-emphasized the importance of living in the moment, of working day-to-day. The emphasis on looking to the future, of being self-aware, was viewed warily. Further, policies that might have allowed workers to look to the long-term, such as increased social safety nets, were specifically those policies that were eschewed by global institutions such as the IMF. Social safety nets undermined motivation. Workers were thus pushed to look to patriarchal forms of authority for support. Where these were not found within government, local leaders or *jao pho* could fill real needs to cope with everyday demands. The dilemma was, though, that such relationships, either within or outside government, were labelled by the West as corrupt. Thai workers were allowed neither the support of patriarchal forms of authority, nor the state support provided to those in Western nations.

Global rationalism, as part of the process of globalization, was an important aspect to understanding how regulatory standards developed after Kader. The development of global rules was experienced in the first instance as a process to entrench policies aimed at institutionalizing the free market. It involved international bodies and consultants deciding what rules and procedures should be put in place to keep Thailand competitive. For this to be achieved, authority needed to shift from people in positions of power within Thailand to the rules and laws themselves. This then flowed on to local companies which adopted signals to demonstrate that they were world class, able to satisfy the needs of the customer. ISO standards on quality were particularly useful for this purpose and were embraced with considerable speed and fanfare. The ISO model was based on the primacy of the customer–supplier relationship and as such was ideally suited to being the rules of choice in the global marketplace. However, as the ISO extended its range of standards, it was brought into conflict with other global bodies, such as the ILO, which had a different vision of regulatory development, one that involved unions through the tripartite framework, not only customer and supplier. Bodies such as the ILO were keen to influence the direction of international standards' development so that their tripartite vision was retained. The shift to the authority of the law in the process of rationalization, then, was accompanied by intense interest in the form and content of that regulatory framework. However, the relationship between authority and the law was not singular; it involved not only influence over the content of rules but also the authority of rules to influence actual company behaviour. The need to comply with 'foreign' rules including codes of conduct could create resentment. Compliance also varied between multinationals. There was some indication that MNCs from countries with an active consumer and union movement were more likely to adhere to the standards and regulation developed, albeit to standards lower than those in their home countries. The transfer of knowledge to local Thai management on the importance of compliance and safety standards in those companies with higher standards could follow from this. However, those working in MNCs without such interest were in a difficult position. They could feel alienated not only from the lack of improvement in their working conditions, but also from the process of rule development itself. It was experienced rather as a new form of colonialism: irrelevant or unhelpful.

Chapter 8

Globalization, Sovereignty
and Activism

As Chapter 7 highlighted, the regulatory aftermath of Kader was affected by the twin pressures of global economic reform and global rationalism. The re-establishment of sovereignty, in Mittleman's (1994) terms, was the ultimate reply of the government and bureaucracy to each of these imperatives. It is this reestablishment of sovereignty, and the challenges to that process that form the basis for this chapter. In the wake of Kader the reassertion of Thai political identity involved the re-creation of global rules through the contours of regulatory character, with the attendant emphasis on the importance of hierarchy, status and formalism. Regulatory character influenced what standards were picked up from overseas and how they were translated into the Thai regulatory system. In some cases this was the basis for positive change, however, in others the result was little more than superficial, or *pak chee roy nah*, or even a distortion of the original intent of the standard. Further, however, this response had to be seen as legitimate by both global and local actors: it both had to convince a Northern audience that Thailand was becoming an ethical (whilst also remaining a profitable) place to do business, and signal to a local audience that the reforms were not 'selling out' to a global and imperialist elite.

The work of activists at both national and international level was an important dimension of globalization that contested hegemonic forms of both sovereignty and globalization. Thai protests against development in the form of infrastructure projects, most notably in dam building supported by institutions such as the World Bank and the Asian Development Bank, had built up a viable NGO network within Thailand with which to challenge government and international initiatives. International activists played an important role in assisting local NGOs to influence the way regulatory reform unfolded. A second development was the way protest led to a softening of the stance of some international bodies, such as the World Bank, away from a narrow focus on economic reform as the solution to development, towards a more inclusive vision of the future. In some ways, then, these institutions were moving towards the more inclusive framework of the ILO, and the ILO's work in this area was instructive. The ILO was involved at a range of levels, in both 'top-down' strategies and in those aimed to change behaviour from the ground up. The diverse strategies of the ILO defy neat categorization, yet the chapter highlights how activists viewed them not in a hostile manner, but more as irrelevant. Despite this, the ILO had programmes that, like the egalitarian activist vision of the institute, had the potential to change regulatory character.

Globalization and Sovereignty

It is not enough to look at globalization simply as imposed from the outside of Thailand, either as an economic process or one intrinsically bound up with the development of rules and regulations. The nature of the Thai response to both global economic reform and global rationalism is also part of the process. It is encapsulated in the term 'sovereignty' (Weiss, 1998), the process of making a global social change understandable within the Thai frame of reference.

The importance of taking account of sovereignty was well illustrated in the research on the difficulty well-meaning foreigners had in generating enthusiasm for improvements in safety standards. Difficulties were encountered particularly when the problem of poor standards was perceived as purely technical, with the assumption that when technical expertise was provided, standards would rise. Waradom explained the difficulties the National Fire Protection Association (NFPA) had with one of their first regional representatives for Southeast Asia, whose task it was to convince the Thai elite of the importance of fire safety and fire safety standards and to offer expertise:

> We do not speak the same language; we think differently; we have different behaviour. It's difficult ... this person before, just one person work in Thailand and cover the whole area. He cannot achieve his goal, his objective. So he got to go out from NFPA because he saw technical problems but not the cultural.

Further, it was not simply a matter of resources and effort. Later in the interview, Waradom continued:

> After two years this [NFPA] man didn't accomplish anything. But he work a lot, he worked very hard ... the budget that this man spend was about US $500,000 for two years ...

This was not a problem peculiar to the NFPA. GTZ, the German technical agency, also encountered similar difficulties. Phil Robertson explained:

> As the Germans in GTZ are finding, you can have all the technical people in the world ... You put them together [with the Thai regulator] and they're all trying to get this Occupational Health and Safety Institute going, but they still can't get it because the political will does not exist.

Some argued that the problem of communicating international expertise in a way that could make a substantial difference stemmed from misunderstanding the importance of national pride. The following example from Kanathat illustrated how miscommunication resulted when the need to maintain national pride was misunderstood; it had a detrimental impact on his efforts to raise fire safety awareness. In this story, the President of an international NGO (INGO) wanted to meet the Prime Minister to impress on him the importance of fire safety, and elicit his support for Kanathat's work. The attempt back-fired as the approach taken by the INGO met a face-saving response that did little to assist the local NGO in his work:

... I try to establish this fire association [here in Thailand] ... [but] over here nobody [is] interested in fire safety. So one day I saw an international fire magazine with the President's [of the INGO] face in it. I think maybe she can help me. I fly to the US to see her and I make appointment. I say 'Hi ... my name is Tom[40] and I am from Thailand. I want to see you,' and she say, 'Fine,' so then on that day I explain, shake her hand and say, 'I fly over almost six thousand miles to see you.' After our meeting she understands the situation of fire safety in Thailand ... so I invite her to come here [to raise awareness], and she comes. But, [then] she wants to interview to my Prime Minister! The Prime Minister quite busy, so he gave his Deputy Prime Minister to her and many [other] people. I never had *anyone* coming from the government [before]! Our government is poor, they don't have any money, not much opportunity to give money to some people, like my fire NGO. OK, [this] I understand. But when [the INGO President] asked the Deputy Prime Minister and high-ranking officers if they supported my NGO, they said, 'Yes, we fully support him.' But, the reality is they give nothing. How then can I now ask anything of her international organization? You understand? Because if I say the truth, that I get no support, that will expose that Deputy Prime Minister is telling a lie. This is a big deal, Huh!

Effective regulatory reform, then, involved more than simply 'technical transfer' of global standards, or standards from the industrialized world to the industrializing. In the case above, communication was distorted because of assumptions made by 'outsiders' of how to raise awareness; they misunderstood the need for those in positions of authority, in this case the Deputy Prime Minister, to provide a good impression about Thailand's commitment to fire safety. National pride was on display, and had to be preserved. This should not be seen merely as a preserve of the elite; Kanathat himself also felt issues of pride and identity were important. He felt angry at the way Thailand was viewed by foreigners, 'We need Thai people to stand at the same position as the human being all over the world. I don't like every time I go to foreign airports, the immigration looks down like this to me; I feel shy and angry.' Exposing the government as untruthful and unwilling to help, then, was not an option. The INGO President's visit had seen no additional resources from government, or from the INGO itself, since Kanathat now felt he could no longer ask the INGO for money, as they now assumed that he had been fully resourced by the Thai government.

Effective reform, then, required the transfer of expertise that also appreciated the need to preserve sovereignty. There were initiatives that aimed to bring these two together. Such initiatives were, arguably, bringing Thailand to the fore in OHS improvements. One interesting example of this was the development of the Thai health and safety standard TIS 18001, which drew from the ISO model and was developed for use within Thailand (described in Chapter 4). At one level, this indicated that the Thais were developing leadership in the area of health and safety, ahead of the ISO, which as we have seen above, had decided against developing a health and safety standard. Thailand, in contrast, was well down the track of not only developing the standard, but also promoting it for use by Thai industry. The Thai standards department, TISI, a member of the International Organization for Standardization, had developed the standard. TIS 18001 accreditation was seen as

---

[40]   'Tom' was Kanathat's preferred English name.

a means of demonstrating to international consumers the company's commitment to health and safety. The auditing of the standard was separated and undertaken by another government department, MASCI. The scheme had obtained some support from the IMF, with the understanding that, over time, the auditing would become fully privatized. In this way, the IMF were supporting an innovation consistent with their philosophy, but allowing the Thai government to take the lead. This move to private auditing was consistent with the global shift towards small government, as Chaiyuth explained: 'In Thailand, now they say the government body has to be small. Some of the activities should be privatized, give it away.' TIS 18001 was thus a Thai initiative that drew on international ideas, but was unique, arguably at the 'cutting edge' of health and safety management.

The challenge, though, was to raise the profile of the scheme with both companies and Western consumers. The initial aim was to promote the scheme through the argument that accreditation would improve business success. One Japanese firm had signed up to and had fully implemented the scheme. MASCI reported that the firm was arguing the benefits of the scheme from the perspective of improved productivity of over 100 per cent, as well as improved safety. Initially, getting others to join was a difficult task. At the time of interview, in 2000, 250 companies had indicated some interest in the scheme, but only one was fully accredited.

In order to stimulate greater interest – government regulators, both the Ministry of Industry and NICE – were considering a range of initiatives. The Ministry of Industry was considering making it a part of the licensing requirements of high-risk industries. In addition, NICE was contemplating an incentive scheme similar to schemes in the US, where accredited companies would experience lower levels of government inspection. Chaiyuth explained:

> I think they might read our mind, that if they get TIS 18001 we will not go to their workplace for inspection that often. So, we are thinking if we will make that as the incentive in the future. Probably, the company that has been certified by TIS 18001, they might get exempted from inspection for three years.

Another advantage of the TIS 18001 initiative was the way it was linked into the overall economic and social development of Thailand – as expressed in the Eighth Development Plan. The plan saw as a major initiative the reduction of accidents, and inclusion in the plan a means to raise the profile of the scheme. The development of TIS 18001 was one way of bringing safety standards within a framework that had a Thai identity. The expertise within the bureaucratic machinery that developed Thai policy and regulatory regimes, TISI, was used to frame a Thai safety management system. These overall strategies met with some success, such that three years later over 100 companies were accredited to the scheme.

Sovereignty, though, itself needs to be understood in terms of Thai regulatory character. As evident in Chapter 6, Thai regulatory character can emphasize the importance of the form of laws and regulations for the purpose of convincing an outside audience of their importance, not for actually making inroads into safety improvement. This formalism was evident in the way international standards were taken up within the Thai system. Chapter 6 described the problem of *pak chee roy nah* – it looks good, but does little. The presence of increasing numbers of international standards fitted in well with regulatory character that emphasized form over substance. The assertion of sovereignty in the translation of international standards could then simply be to demonstrate the existence of standards in regulations to show competence, rather than actually to have an effect in reducing fire hazards on the ground. Examples were given of fire standards that would be directly copied from overseas (particularly from the National Fire Prevention Association in the United States). Kanathat explained:

> They [the regulator] have a regulation they copied from the NFPA. Fire Code 100 ... something ... I don't know. They copy, they translated [them] from the NFPA. But just copy 'OK, fire-safety-the-buck-stop-here,' but they don't understand. They don't rewrite for Thailand, they don't know how to do it. No hands-on training. Even the people in the group who issue the regulation, they don't know how to do it.

Some within government recognized this problem. Chaiyuth commented: 'Sometimes we make a mistake, also we just copy! ... We do, sometimes we just copy, but sometimes we put in thought there as well. Because our process, our drafting committee, is tripartite; we discuss a lot there.' Tripartite discussion, however, whilst it might change the content of the standard, may not make the regulations more effective, since as we have seen in Chapter 5, Thai regulatory character could transform tripartite negotiation into corporatist control. Through this discussion, critical elements considered unsuitable for Thailand within the standards could be replaced so they were rendered ineffective. Not surprisingly, Western experts argued that the translation process often meant weakening of the standards. For example, smoke detectors were replaced by cheaper heat protectors, and cheap fire panels were purchased from China or India, panels that lacked proper laboratory testing. Waradom explained what this meant in terms of fire prevention:

> Products from US, mostly they've got UL [Underwriter Laboratory] standards ... And these standards cost a lot to Thai people. When I went to the US, I study in factories and studied standards and fire products. I found that sometimes products cost about 40 or 50 per cent [more] another 50 per cent if UL [accredited] ... OK, so some projects buy the high standard product, but some projects cannot afford to buy high standards product. They just buy something similar ... In Thailand I think we cannot produce some equipment like that, [we buy] Chinese, Indian [one] ... our quality that we make in Thailand is not the same thing as the US. So when we had a fire, mostly it didn't work.

Accreditation processes, also, were referred to as 'Thai Style', shorthand for weak and ineffective. The emphasis was on show, a performance, a ritual to demonstrate compliance, but not one aimed at ensuring that the process actually worked. Kanathat argued that accreditation within Thailand was 'Thai style, but I try to catch the standard and show them.'

The emphasis on form over substance not only hindered improvement, it could be wasteful of scarce resources. Purchase of fire safety equipment and fire abatement technology was expensive. The emphasis on form meant that equipment might be purchased that was 'state of the art' but unworkable within a Thai environment. Fire rescue equipment, for example, needed to be able to function in very tight spaces, spaces that were often too small for equipment able to service high-rise buildings. Inappropriate equipment, however apparently effective on paper, would be a waste of money if it could not be transported down narrow or clogged streets. Kanathat explained the problem:

> [If] the big company sells the equipment, if they want my opinion, they have to change their strategy. OK, they have to come to study, study about Bangkok! Of course, you can sell us equipment [but] you have to have like a supermarket, the big truck, the small, one suitable to us ... Some of them are very big [too big] ... If the fire break out we will call 'hey, move this out', and you see the traffic, how long will take them to get and go for nothing. Not suitable! We have to research to get it right.

Sovereignty, then, worked to reassert Thai regulatory character, which in turn influenced the translation of international standards to the Thai context in a way that signalled expertise, or an ability to manage its own affairs, to outsiders. Even the presence of experts within government was argued to be used for this purpose. They could be used to talk to foreigners about the Thai regulatory system in a language that foreigners understood. Discussing one bureaucrat, Bundit argued, '[The government] use him as the correspondent with the foreigner. To show we have the expert!'

The collection of government statistics on fires well illustrated this emphasis on appearance over substance. According to government statistics, there were only 700 calls per annum to the fire brigade in Bangkok, an extremely low figure when compared internationally with cities of similar size. For Kanathat, the purpose of government collection of these statistics was to demonstrate to the public (both nationally and internationally) that the situation was under control. He explained how this worked:

> I have been to London and I got the statistics there; whole [of] London, same [population] as Bangkok, calls are 100,000 a year. In Bangkok? Guess – 700. If you think this number is good, you are crazy! It's not effective. I went to Hong Kong; it's very small, smaller than Bangkok – how much? Average 50,000. I learned from Osaka, Japan. Very small, like this area, 20,000, but Bangkok, 700. Do you believe this number? ... No! The government don't tell the truth in the statistics to the people. In my opinion, it should be the same about London. [But] if you show the big number, people think there is a fire every day in many places, people die, there is a crisis, because your property – and you – burn. We burnt property a lot, but they don't tell the truth to the people, not the real information to the people.

Kanathat felt that the fire emergency service system was lacking. Lack of communication between the levels of the bureaucracy meant that the size of the problem was unknown. There was no fire safety system, and because of this, there could be an assumption that there was no problem:

> [There is no] central monitoring. I have been to cities in Australia, to Singapore and Hong Kong. You have to install and provide smoke detector, heat detector or whatever. When the smoke is coming, the smoke detector can be checked, they will alarm the building itself, sending a message directly to the fire brigade; isn't that right? This is in every country, mainly in the West. Not in this country!

The challenge, then, was to translate international standards and international expertise in a way that took account of the uniqueness of the Thai context, but in a manner that did not render reforms ineffective or prey to the worst of Thai regulatory character. This meant building on a Thai sense of pride, but retaining the central purpose of reform. Reform needed to be seen as the 'Thai way', not some international implant. But the process of negotiation with politicians was hazardous, as Chaiyuth explained; '... sometimes if you say too much about other countries doing this and that, they [the government] says, "No, we are different".' Chaiyuth described how negotiation worked in the development of regulations concerning the need for safety officers:

> I think we would like industry to be on their own ... So I think that person [the safety officer] should be hired by the company, he should work with the company to build up the system there, to be a technical man for industry. Without him, it would be a big mess. The man would monitor, would check around would put up a fire safety code, do the investigations, provide some training and so on. We would put it that way. Under the regulations we would state his duties, what he is supposed to do.

The government was involved, though, in the training of the safety officers. Coming up with training that was in a 'Thai way' involved drawing on international precedent and then going through a process of negotiation with government. The reforms in Thailand drew not only from the West and Japan, but from a wide range of nations. However, the actual length of the training was a result of a bargaining process within the bureaucracy:

> In fact I pick up the idea [initially] from India, I went to India, I saw the programme there. India they have a safety officer that has to be trained for the whole year, for one year in order to work for industry. At that time I think we had the expert from Finland working with us. Because Finland also have a system and the training has to be 12 weeks or 9 weeks. We checked with the States, and the National Safety Council there, they have a six-week programme. I also checked with the Philippines, they also have something similar, but they can be part-time safety officers. Singapore they also have a programme in 1985. We thought we should have something ... so I proposed six week training, my boss said two weeks, I asked our expert who worked with us at that time to back us up, and he said well this is the average you see in Finland, in Scandinavia it is 9-12 weeks the States 6 weeks, in Singapore 8 weeks or so. So we are optimum.

This process of bargaining could see the process of re-creation within a Thai context as hazardous in terms of the possibility of safety change. In the case of safety committees the translation from international precedent to the Thai context meant changing the authority structure of the committee away from workers, towards management in keeping with the hierarchist underpinning of Thai regulatory character:

> The safety committee idea came from Scandinavia; the Danish officials who worked in Bangkok gave us some of their regulations. But we did not copy them, we modified a little bit. For example, their safety committee they have to have equal number of management and workers. If you have two employers, management, you have to have two workers and they have to chair the meeting. But, over here we gave the power, the right to the management to chair the meeting.

This negotiation process and drawing on the legitimacy of international precedent went further than just negotiations between government and bureaucracy. NGOs could also find their own regulatory system internationally that fitted their more egalitarian view of how regulation should be reformed. They would then use this to lobby government for change. One example here was the reform in workers' compensation. The push for a single independent institution promoted by the NGOs described in Chapter 6 above arose from a German model. Chaiyuth saw this as important in understanding how NGO politics worked:

> ... the workers they had the German experience, you see, they went to Germany they saw the system there they would like to follow this German system. So, they thought it is the best for the country, so that's why they keep pushing since 1994/5, almost 10 years.

However, the concern of activists was around the accountability of the compensation fund. Drawing on a German model to support their demand was a way of giving it legitimacy, but it was not a simple process of following the preferred international model. The weaknesses of regulatory reforms moulded by traditional Thai regulatory character led activists and others to draw on international models that they saw as providing greater potential for improvement. International models were drawn on to support change, but the motivation did not necessarily lie in mimicking international trends, but in challenging a sovereignty under which they felt workers gained little.

Protest, Sovereignty and Globalization

Experience of global social experiments had also led to a resolve by activists to challenge reform imposed from outside. The catalytic experience was the devastation created in rural areas by ADB and World Bank funded dam building projects (Bello, Cunningham and Poh, 1998). The group that arose to challenge these infrastructure projects and the model of development they represented – the Assembly of the Poor described above in Chapter 7 – had as their main aim the prevention of further dam building, the restoration of fish stocks and the repossession of their land. The solutions proposed by some development agencies, such as fish ladders, were seen as ineffective and missed the point. What was needed was an appreciation of the damage development and international interference could bring, not only the benefits.

Part of this damage was the way that imposed development undermined social cohesion by pitting the needs of the city against rural regions. Voravidh explained the process:

> ... they [the government] use this [dam building] to create a division among the people. Lots of people in the town wanted the water. But the people who work in the forest, they said they live with the forest. Once you turn forest into water there's nothing else. You've got water, but what is that ... I don't know. But myself, I would prefer forest to water ... I think we've been living too lavishly. Even the water – you look how many massage shops we have, and how much the massage shop they use water, we have said them you can have [that much] water ... The people that have been living there [in the forest] for ages and now they [the government] said that they should move out because we wanted to construct the dam, we wanted the water.

The social division brought about here included those divisions created by industrial development that required more water as well as the inequity in the impact of industrial disasters on workers' families when compared with the consequences for the elite.

These inequalities were not unique to Thailand and the protest against such injustice drew from an international base. Local activists found international support for their campaigns. Local groups linked together with other NGOs, both within the Asian region, and more, generally to agitate for reform. Jaded explained:

> We built a network. The Asia Monitor Resource Centre is in Hong Kong; in Thailand there is the council for the network in Thailand and Friends of Women and also other groups in Hong Kong, Sri Lanka and Japan. The network from Japan, Korea and Taiwan, Hong Kong, Thailand, Sri Lanka are now trying to contact Indonesia and Philippines to fight for the safety and health issue [there].

In the Kader case, the international network was critical to the success of the campaign, particularly in terms of compensation. In particular, the support from Hong Kong was most welcome as Voravidh explained:

> We've got support from the international movement. The pressure group in Hong Kong [Q: The Asia Monitor Resource Centre?] Yeah, they co-ordinate the people to make a demonstration in front of Kader, which was important ... we found it very effective internationally because the big companies are often afraid of their name. So, we have a cross-link with AMRC. I think it helps a lot – the international networking. Even with a recent case, this case in Chiang Mai, we also have a group of Taiwanese NGOs that said that they could help us ...

But it was not a straightforward case of globalization 'from below'. Considerable support for NGOs and activists in the wake of Kader and subsequent disasters came from both FES and the AFL-CIO, the German and US peak union bodies. The funding for these organizations could be mainstream. Phil Robertson explained that early on, the funding base for the AFL-CIO was largely from USAID, but now it was from an independent endowment, a fund called the National Endowment for Democracy. Both AMRC and AFL-CIO tended to focus their effort at the grassroots level to effect change. This made them popular with grassroots activists. Somyot conceded that, in contrast to some other international agencies, 'perhaps AFL-CIO, they're concerned'.

The need to raise awareness of workers about the negative sides of globalization was critical for activists. In contrast to raising awareness about safety hazards, here the awareness was around the risks that globalization posed, and that it was not itself an inevitable process, nor an accident. Rather, it was a process clearly promoted and augmented by the activities of global institutions such as the International Monetary Fund, which were often criticized by activists. The IMF was simply there to do the bidding of multinationals by making Thai workers more compliant, Somyot argued:

> IMF is useless. They have destroyed the workers' lives. They're concerned over only their money and debt, so the multinational corporation can invest in the cheap labour. There is no regulation for them [here] so that they can exploit our environment; they can destroy our people. That's their concern. They only want Thailand to continue under the fierce competitiveness of the trading in the world so multinational corporations can use Thailand for their [own] concerns.

The sentiment expressed here is one of anger at the strategic and immoral global order. It was the structural adjustment policies of the IMF that came in for the most criticism. Jaded explained:

> We take money from IMF, we need to follow the conditions with them right. It's just like you need to increase VAT, the VAT tax. They've got a privatisation plan for state enterprise, and some of the Thai businesses have to close down because they don't have enough money to run in this situation. A lot of business need to be closed, the workers are out of a job ... the cost of living is going up ... there is an increase in criminals, crime is increased. If the people don't have the money, they become criminal. People start to come out and a lot of kids are out of school because the families don't have the money to keep them there.

However, other institutions were also implicated because they shared the same economic philosophy. The strategic rationale of the policies of these institutions partly lay behind the anger expressed and the fundamental suspicion of motive of these organizations. For Somyot, the World Bank and the IMF were equally to blame for the ills experienced by Thai workers: 'World Bank is the right-hand side of the multinational corporations. IMF is the left-hand side. Both of them are evil.' It was the way these organizations placed a priority on investment and profit, not on the wellbeing of the population, that Bundit argued was most problematic:

> From the IMF side, they don't really care about safety issues, but much more about the income of people in this country. They're talking about whether to change the minimum wage, the salaries of officials, government officials. [They say] you need to do [your policy] according to the inflation and also they're talking about privatisation, re-

structuring, about these issues … Salaries will not go up at the same way … Like, if you were a teacher, you used to have your salary go up say 2 [per cent] per year; now the IMF say, 'No, you cannot do that.'

Activists felt that these organizations had no real sense of what life was like. Bundit continued:

The real situation is that most of the workers have to send money that they earn back to their families. From research, two thirds of the money [used] by rural families comes from industrial workers that they send home. At home, that means that two-thirds of the money is sent to them from their kids, but not now. They are in much more serious trouble because the workers themselves have no jobs.

However, the criticism of the World Bank in terms of health and safety was somewhat surprising. In the area of occupational health and safety, the World Bank, held up as an exemplar by activists of all that was wrong with globalization, had had a number of projects that involved trying to assist the Thai bureaucracy to improve safety. One project funded by the World Bank involved tackling the critical problem of safety in small and medium-sized enterprises, as Chaiyuth explained:

At the moment the World Bank is offering some funds for our ministry to study about how to improve safety and health in workplace. So they have given the ministry US $400,000, something like that, to carry out some study, how to implement the programme, what type of programme you would like to do in the near future. For example, we are proposing a programme for small enterprises, safety and health for small enterprises. We would like a specific programme for that, because we cannot rely on the normal inspection system. We feel that the small micro-enterprises, they need help; they need technical help, they need financial help. So we are discussing with them.

This did not prevent accusations by NGOs of the World Bank being 'out of touch' with the realities of everyday life. The World Bank were shaken by recent globalization protests which saw it, not as a force for good, but as inhumane and siding with the oppressors over the oppressed. Clearly these accusations went beyond Kader, indeed beyond Thailand. They were having an effect, though, on the way global institutions worked within Thailand. In response, the Bank had invited several grass-roots NGOs to meetings with them to discuss common goals. The NGOs were unclear as to the purpose of these consultations. Bundit, from the Arom Pongpangan Foundation, was one who had received several invitations from the World Bank. 'The World Bank [is] now inviting the NGOs and people outside to come to join them at various seminars … it has now started an office in Thailand.' Uncertainty about the purpose of seminars and meetings meant that invitations were not always accepted. Bundit continued: 'The World Bank has been sending me invitations four or five times, but I went there just once.' Secondly, there was also reticence because of the known position of the World Bank on the benefits of global economic reform. The NGO movement, Voravidh explained, was divided on whether to accept support from such a source:

> ... Right now the NGOs or people's organization are divided by the money that the
> World Bank offers through social investment fund. NGOs and grass roots organizations
> are divided by this ... whether they should accept or not accept ...

In the area of occupational health and safety, the global institution with the longest
history in the area is undoubtedly the International Labour Organisation. It was
interesting that activists rarely mentioned them during interviews as having an
important role to play in the wake of Kader. The opinion about the IMF was
certainly negative, as it was seen to be actively promoting poor conditions, but the
ILO was more viewed as irrelevant. Yet it was the one organization that had long
tried to combine a 'top-down' approach to safety reform with programmes that
could engage workers and business on the ground. In terms of providing a
philosophy and practice under which OHS regulation could be effective, the ILO
had had a long involvement with the Thai bureaucracy and was involved in both
review and development of new strategies within NICE. It also saw work with Thai
unions as critical to progress. Despite this, activists had some ambivalence towards
the work of the ILO. For some, it seemed that all the ILO wanted from
collaboration was grassroots information for producing reports, but was unwilling
itself to push for change. Bundit commented, 'When the ILO invites the NGOs,
they want the information from *you.*' Once the information was given, activists
were then supposed to work amongst themselves to solve the problems of safety.
Bundit continued:

> They want the NGOs to talk with them, investigate, yeah, ... They have you to talk with
> the others ... so they arrange a conference and then they sort of ... disappear ... Most of
> the ILO [representatives] come from the government side and most of the people, from
> the unions. [What is important from the ILO side] is the ILO report, is the status thing,
> the number.

Activists felt the ILO had potential, but over-emphasized process and bureaucracy.
Somyot argued that they were soft: 'They are very lazy, I think ... Too much
dialogue! ILO ... they stay in a very good building, air conditioned, they don't care
anything.' Others saw it as a problem of a mindset. Phil Robertson argued that
'The ILO could do a lot more here, but they have to sort of break out of their
bureaucratic reactive mentality in the sense that they tend to sit around and wait for
the government to ask them for help.'

However, from the point of view of those within the ILO, they understood their
approach as trying to effect change at two separate levels, both from the top down
and the bottom up. The top-down approach was primarily through ILO
conventions, since it established government support for the regulatory framework
that included employers and workers as well as government. Kawakami, a local
ILO representative, explained:

> We have developed many guidelines, international labour standards, and different
> conventions [such as] number 155, which is our mother convention or our umbrella
> convention in safety and health. This clearly defines the role of government, of
> employer, and workers. The government should establish the clear registration and

national policy, and also develop the very good inspection services to cover all occupations. Then the employer, they are responsible for ensuring the safe one and healthy workplace for workers. They should establish very good enterprise programme and make sure it is implemented. The workers, they need to co-operate with the employer to implement the safety and health programme. But also worker has the right to participate actively in OHS; they can propose changes. So this is our tool, we are always using this ILO convention whenever I am visiting Thailand, Vietnam and so on. I use this ILO convention as a basis for the developing the regulatory and legal system. This is our tool, the top-down tool.

ILO conventions were viewed not only as a mandate for change, but also an aspirational statement by member countries. Kawakami continued:

> The Southeast Asian countries that have ratified Convention 155 are Vietnam and also Mongolia. Of course, you know still their legal system and perhaps their legislative and inspection services may still not be in the spirit of the ILO convention, not yet. But it means their commitment. So they ratified it, it means they committed themselves to improve OHS through their legislative system. So we very much encourage [them], to help more ... We can help them but at the stage of ratification there is no need to have it in place completely, to adjust their legal system immediately to completely fit into the ILO requirement.

This model clearly aimed to involve the state. For the ILO, a strong OHS system required government involvement. Despite the lack of ratification by Thailand of Convention 155, the ILO was still involved with government regulators in Thailand.[41] They were involved in the setting up of NICE,[42] one of the major occupational health and safety regulators within the Thai bureaucracy. From the bureaucracy's perspective, the ILO was an obvious choice as an agency, with expertise that could assist them to institutionalize health and safety within Thailand. Chaiyuth explained their involvement in the setting up of NICE:

> Well, in fact, they [the ILO] are our partners, in doing so I think firstly, the ILO is the organization that is well respected and secondly, they are our counterparts ... We are members [of the ILO] and they are open for requests from us. You see, I thought it was a good idea ... I had that feeling, you see, when I talked to my boss and said, 'Is it OK?'

---

[41] Interestingly, those countries who saw ratification not as an aspirational statement but as mandating certain legal requirements were unlikely to ratify conventions. This included Thailand as well as Australia and Japan. Kawakami explained this further:

> The most important one [is Convention number] 155; only Vietnam and Mongolia in Southeast Asia have ratified. Australia has not and Japan not. Because this is a big political problem, because some government discuss with some government official in Japan, maybe Japan is also too serious ... they want to fit all the legislative system before ratifying the convention, so that is why it is very difficult for them to ratify ... In the European Union, for example, many countries ratified the 155 Convention, also Latin America ... But I found [in] Asia, ILO convention [is] not very familiar here in Asia. ILO activities started from the European countries and Latin America. They speak Spanish and French so they can get the ideas. But Asia, we are quite different, so ... but now I try to promote the ILO ... importance of ILO conventions.

[42] National Institute for the Improvement of Working Conditions and Environment.

So I talked with a friend within the ILO and said, 'Can you do that?' He said, 'Why not?' So I draft a letter and asked my boss to sign it and send it over ... We bring it up to the ILO office to discuss, and we say, 'Well, could we have a conference or a workshop in the country, tripartite ... to discuss this subject, safety and health for Thailand.'

Bureaucratic support for such initiatives could be more forthcoming than ongoing political support. The involvement of top politicians or the military in the partnership was often spasmodic. NICE, for example, was created during a time of military rule. Chaiyuth argued about the role of the politicians: 'They don't care; they don't care what we are going to do! ... they would come to the meeting, for the opening have picture taken [and then go].' However, this lack of political support was a key difficulty in effecting real change. Further, political interest was often piqued when political authority was threatened. Tripartism allowed for the retention of patriarchal dominance, but was accepted internationally as the right path. This could create problems. When activists tried to go beyond tripartism, for example in the promotion of the five-partite independent institute as outlined in Chapter 6, they could encounter opposition not only from government. The five-partite idea also met with disinterest from the ILO since it went beyond the tripartite model. Yet effective reform needed the freedom to diverge from international norms, as Bundit argued: 'Why should we be like the others if it is not useful?'

In other areas, however, the ILO also understood the need to cut through traditional responses and redundant ways of working. One programme that they had championed had potential to change the traditional model of education and training within Thai regulatory character away from a hierarchical model to a more inclusive and pragmatic approach. As will be remembered from Chapter 6, the use of 'training' to raise awareness about safety issues could be undermined by the approach to education where 'big people talk and little people listen'. It was a problem the ILO had encountered across Asia. In response, they had developed the WISE programme (an acronym for Work Improvement in Small Enterprises), a programme in which education and training were intertwined through the process of reform that worked from a 'bottom-up' model. The programme had two unique features: firstly it only took positive examples of good safety practice from the local context. In regulatory terms, it emphasized local 'best practice', since international examples could be irrelevant – or worse – unhelpful given local resources. Secondly, the programme required participants in a given workplace to collaborate and analyse their own workspaces to come up with practical, low-cost changes. Kawakami explained:

... we develop one WISE training [initially] exclusively for workers and trade unions. We conducted several for the trade union members and workers in many countries: Pakistan, Bangladesh, Thailand and Mongolia. Participants were all trade union members and the workers. So we train them using the WISE training of positive examples, group work and checklist. So after that they have to go back to the factories; they have to convince management of the need for change. Five years ago when I started this project I [worried whether] the trained workers ... could they really convince the management to take some action. But, many of them succeeded because, you know, after the training, workers could identify very practical technical points, so they can give very concrete and clear proposals for safety and health in their workplace, low cost improvements. Even managers are pleased because workers become very practical and propose very concrete ideas much, much better than discussing the general complaints or so on.

From this point WISE was broadened to include employers as well as farmers, through a sister programme WIND:[43]

> I can say I have been involved in WISE and WIND as the participative trainer in many countries in Asia. Thailand, Vietnam, Malaysia, the Philippines and China, Pakistan, Bangladesh. I can say in all countries this method [is] well accepted. Of course some participants may have problem [and make an excuse like] 'Today I have some appointment with business', something like that. But as far as they have no urgent matters, they could keep their interest.

In each case the programme required active engagement by participants, a marked contrast to traditional training sessions. To ensure this, considerable groundwork by the ILO was undertaken before the programme could begin. The following description by Kawakami of how this worked in China shows how the process linked into cultural traits that could further programme aims:

> People in China, they are very much accustomed to the traditional style of training course; it means a lecturer comes and the lecturer speaks for two hours and the people just listen and write things. They are quite accustomed to this sort of training, so two months ago when I was in China my Chinese colleagues advised me, 'You better prepare very carefully,' so I visited the pre-participants workshop with them first to discuss [the programme] with them. I said, 'This training is very different from the conventional one; group work, you know, don't hesitate to speak out, [to voice] your opinion.' Also my Chinese colleagues advised me, 'You'd better take dinner with them, this is Chinese tradition, so during the dinner and you can pay and put some of the whisky or beer please, work together, then this can create a sort of co-operative atmosphere, right?' Then our workshop was very successful. According to my Chinese friend, Chinese people basically talkative. Have you been to China? ... On the street, they speak to each other in a very loud voice. I think they are fighting! They are very talkative. So once you could break their psychological barriers, they like to speak out and the group work should become very, very lively. But [the basic training] always the same. Good examples, group work, checklist, that's all.

The WISE and WIND initiatives are good examples of programmes from a global institution that understands the need for change in traditional ways of working. They are an important initiative. Their mere existence, however, is not sufficient for success. They must be supported at a number of levels. Local communities must see their value and build on the knowledge such programmes bring. In addition, for the WISE programme, employees and employers must be willing to work together constructively. Finally, both programmes require government

---

43   Work Improvement in Neighbourhood Development.

commitment to change. Even the best-designed programme can be distorted by the demands of alternative political agendas, agendas from both national and international institutions.

Conclusion

This chapter continued the analysis of the impact of globalization on regulatory character and reform. Figure 8.1, below, graphically depicts the dynamic of exchange between the global and the local described in Chapters 7 and 8. The figure shows how globalization works independently through separate components of regulatory character. Chapter 7 was concerned with the normative interaction between globalization and regulatory character through valorizing self-reliance as well as a legislative interaction between global rules and formalism at the local level, shown at the bottom left and top right of the figure.

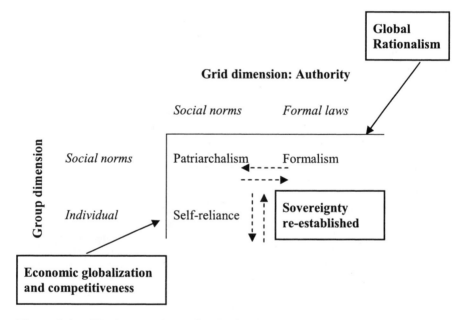

Figure 8.1   The intersections of globalization and regulatory character

This chapter showed how sovereignty was expressed in the response to these global normative and legislative pressures, depicted in Figure 8.1 by the box in the centre of the diagram. In the wake of Kader, sovereignty was re-created through the re-imposition of regulatory character in the response to pressures for economic reform and those to reduce the hazards of industrial development. International expertise and resources were a tool to re-create regulatory character. International rules and institutions had a critical influence on the development of Thai regulations, but the chapter showed the importance of understanding how these were taken up in the Thai context. The response was more than simply mere acceptance of international technical knowledge. Indeed, construing reform purely as a technical problem had serious limitations. National pride could influence how international initiatives were responded to, and a misunderstanding of this pride led to distortions in understanding and communication. Further, there were examples where Thai initiatives in the area of health and safety management had developed beyond international precedents. Despite these innovations, international rules tended to be re-created within Thailand in a manner that was consistent with Thai regulatory character. National pride demanded that rules be presented as consistent with the 'Thai way', but in some instances this meant that the potential within these rules for engendering substantial change could be blunted to emphasize the importance of form over substance or the need to retain status hierarchies of a particular kind.

Nonetheless, there was change. The change was best understood as emanating from the interaction between different elements of the regulatory environment, the economic and political demands, and the growing importance of protest and challenge from NGOs and others wearied – and in some cases angered – by the negative consequences of industrialization and trade. The social divisions created by heavy-handed models of development funded by the World Bank accentuated the need for those at the bottom, internationally, to push for mutually beneficial change. This anger was in part a rejection of the instrumental rationality underlying market development. The model of the activists was clearly strategic and involved networking within the region and more generally to demand reform. Kader activists worked with a number of Asian NGOs who agreed with their perspective of the need for radical change. Globalization, as Falk (1995) has noted, works in two ways: bottom up and top down. However the distinction between the two, particularly if funding for bottom-up strategies was included, can blur. This blurring continued to grow. Both strategies were evident in the reforms after Kader, and both brought together forces both within Thailand and internationally. Whilst activists worked from the grass roots, the World Bank supported initiatives for safety reform within the Thai bureaucracy. Recent protests against globalization had seen attempts by the World Bank to work with the grass roots, leading to the two coming into closer contact. This was viewed warily, since the Bank's support for economic globalization and the individualism that underpinned it cast shadows on its attempts to include activists through funding NGO projects and soliciting input into its own reform policies.

The impact of the ILO, the global institution with the longest history in OHS, was interesting. In some ways it appeared anachronistic, despite this history. This quality stemmed in part because it seemed out of step with the current round of globalization, with its economic philosophy of individualism, a philosophy that seemed to render its bureaucratic approach cumbersome and reactive. Nonetheless, there was sound reasoning behind ILO programmes, as it sought to work both from the top down, through conventions, and from the bottom up through programmes such as WISE and WIND. As an institution with a long history, its successes and failures held many lessons: the problems with including the state in safety reform which, whilst essential, also provides opportunities for manipulation and power games that undermine safety improvement; the need for consensus when consensus may mean both a reactive stance and long-winded and bureaucratic methods that get bogged down in complexity; and finally, the problems of agreeing on a philosophy – in this case tripartism – which is overtaken by both international and national contexts so that it can be made to entrench the national status quo on one hand, and become a straightjacket to inhibit progress on the other.

Chapter 9

Conclusions

The trauma of Kader and the response of both the national and international communities provided a window into the workings of globalization, sovereignty and regulatory change. The insights gleaned from the event have significance not only for Thailand, but also for policymakers and scholars interested in how law, place and globalization interact. The study highlights how globalization creates opportunities for some – at the expense of others. The study, though, provides no easy answers. Simply pushing for stronger laws may not see significant improvement. Rather, reforms that are demanded must take account of place. Regulatory character, as a means to explore the relationship between individuals, norms and laws in a given place, provides a useful starting point. Regulatory character allows a grounded assessment of what legal reform might mean in a given situation and how it may, or may not, influence behaviour.

Certainly, the Kader story resonates with many others that demonstrate the underbelly of globalization highlighted by authors such as Mander and Goldsmith (1996), Greider (1997), Martin and Schumann (1997), and Bello *et al.* (1998). The company itself was a major multinational owned by powerful Thai and regional interests that manufactured toys under licence from the giants of the toy industry in the United States. In this way it contributed to the flow of capital from West to East and East to West. Kader experienced rapid growth throughout East and Southeast Asia, fuelled in part by the burgeoning demand for toys. From factories in Bangkok it spread to the Thai countryside, to Vietnam, Cambodia and China. The toys created by the company were themselves symbols of global culture: Bart Simpson dolls amongst them. The story of Kader, its products, its rise and spread, was repeated countless times throughout the second half of the twentieth century.

The fire that led to catastrophic outcomes for hundreds of Thai working families lent considerable weight to the argument of the scholars above that such globalization brings with it misery and destruction. The elite gain wealth and status, at the expense of those who toil in their factories and workplaces. In the case of Kader, compensation was forthcoming for some victims, yet difficulties in identifying who was present in the factory at the time of the fire, in addition to ongoing challenges in making sure that it was those most in need who gained from the money and support, meant that the impact was less than might have been predicted. Certainly, neither the business itself nor its senior executives seemed to suffer much. Indeed, the outcome of the court case saw a worker sentenced to 10 years jail for smoking a cigarette that started the fire, and all managers charged with various offences found not guilty. A small measure of justice saw the company fined 520,000 baht.[44] One plausible reading of the impact of the Kader fire is that it shows the ubiquitous triumph of capital, with the company simply reinventing itself, by moving to the countryside, a strategy aided by government incentives that sought to relieve the congestion of the city and bring wealth to rural areas. Under this reading, the sole aim for business is to lower costs, including the costs of labour. Investment must then flow to the rural areas of Thailand and the surrounding nations of Vietnam, Cambodia and most importantly China. Thus, the lessons for business that result from Kader were how to reduce economic costs that result from disasters and the ensuing demand for safety improvement, rather than how to reduce the incidence of disasters themselves. Life is cheaper elsewhere. The mobility of capital means that putting these lessons into practice is relatively straightforward. The Marxist analysis of globalization, as Falk (1997) has commented, still has much to commend it.

A liberal response to this state of affairs is also compelling, namely that economic globalization must include within it the demand that those who bring their capital to Thailand also bring with them their standards. After all, if capital can internationalize, why can't standards? Their demand is to require that multinational companies institutionalize standards throughout their operations so that safety is not part of the competitive equation and in doing so, prevent the suffering that disasters like Kader engender. Much of the regulatory literature canvassed in Chapter 2 is dedicated to that end, suggesting methods for punishing, persuading and cajoling multinationals to improve their standards, most recently without the overt involvement of any government, but rather using the power of consumers and activists.

The Kader aftermath described in this book suggests that, to an extent, the standards of the West *are* finding their way into the statute books and practices of businesses in Bangkok. Common problems can find common solutions, even where the problems are those caused by multifaceted global processes. Certainly, building, fire and health and safety standards in Thailand are not the wasteland they are sometimes depicted to be in the West. The research here shows that there were a plethora of initiatives that arose after the Kader event. Various government departments drew on the international pool of safety regulatory techniques to bolster their regulatory framework. Initiatives went beyond government, with both NGO involvement through SA 8000 and quasi-government programmes such as TIS 18001. A simple enumeration of programme initiatives would provide some basis for optimism.

But the picture is a complex one, and simple questions such as those posed at the beginning of the book, 'Is globalization making the situation for workers better or worse in terms of safety?' are not able to be answered with a definitive 'Yes' or 'No.' As the research here shows, any assessment of regulatory change in the context of economic globalization cannot simply map the spread (or lack of spread) of rationalist models of regulation through technocratic policy channels. Nor can such analysis make a priori assumptions about the impact of global economic change on regulatory standards. Regulatory scholarship, if it is to be useful, also

---

44   As at January 2005, equivalent to approximately US $13,500.

must attempt to understand how regulatory techniques interact with the local economic, cultural and political conditions. In short, uniqueness as well as commonality need to come to centre stage. Regulatory change or 'modernization' may well include the adoption of formal standards and procedures that are internationally approved, but local implementation greatly depends on 'regulatory character', that is, the interaction between social norms and formal laws. This book has argued that regulatory character, both as a first order theoretical construct and a second order empirical reality, can help understand the nature of the translation of regulatory techniques from one context to another.

Before turning to regulatory character per se, however, a comment must be made on economic pressures that affect regulatory character. The Kader case showed that reform and compliance in light of regulatory character must take account of both international and local economic demands. To an extent, the analysis above shows, along with others (e.g., Braithwaite and Drahos, 2000), that regulatory standards have internationalized in line with the spread of investment and the business links between West and East. However, the Kader case shows the important step of the impact of economic pressure on how these standards find their way to local influence. This transition was heavily shaped by the demands of both international and local capital. The demands of capital, however, cannot be oversimplified as unitary, with Thailand merely being exploited by international capital as 'rich pickings' in terms of investment opportunities, with such companies having direct control over the local environment. International capital engagement with Thailand necessarily depended on their interaction with local capital. As Hewison (1987) and others have demonstrated, local Thai capital should not be seen as a mere victim of global pressure; it is equally as strategic and self-interested as its Western counterpart.

The Kader aftermath demonstrated the importance of local, not simply global or Western, capital to understanding the trajectory of safety standards under globalization. Most attention in the West has focussed on companies such as Nike, where constant activist attention has prompted it to craft itself as a leader in the area of regulatory compliance, particularly in the area of environmental and safety standards. The contractors who work under licence for Nike are silent or absent in the debate, since Western activism puts responsibility squarely at the feet of Nike. In the case of Kader, from the Thai activists' perspective, however, it was the international toy companies that were incidental to their major concern, namely the activities of Kader itself. In the aftermath of the fire, it was the Thai and regional capital interests and the Thai government, not the Western toy companies, that were at the centre of campaign attention. For Thais, Kader itself was sufficiently high profile and sufficiently culpable so that it was from Kader that compensation was demanded – not their Western counterparts. Further, Thai activists demanded that the Thai government and its regulators should protect their people, not simply Western consumers.

Other disasters at the time of Kader illustrate that Western consumers may also simply not be part of the equation. The explosion that took place at a longan factory near Chiang Mai during the fieldwork for this project is a clear example of a highly risky processing plant with highly ineffective safety practices, where local people suffered greatly. The visibility of this case to the West was extremely low, and the ability of the Western consumer to alter the activities of the companies involved was effectively nil.

Regulatory Character and its Implications

Irrespective of whether the event involves a high-profile Western company or not, this research demonstrates the importance of taking account of the influence of local factors on regulatory reform and regulatory compliance. Regulation occurs in a given place, not in some theoretical or conceptual space. The impact of international regulatory trends, or global rationalism, on behaviour is largely dependent upon local conditions.

Understanding the significance of reforms, then, meant coming to grips with the 'law–practice' gap; more particularly regulatory character, as both a theoretical construct and an empirical reality, moulds how reform and compliance are shaped. The theoretical construct of regulatory character as described in Chapter 3 took as a starting point Hood's (1998) use of cultural theory that grounded analysis within the competing paradigms of hierarchism, individualism, egalitarianism and fatalism. It was argued that regulatory character could be seen to express competing ideals of what regulation was desirable, what regulation should aim to achieve. Each ideal-typical orientation holds within it notions of authority that are alternately hierarchical, individualistic, communitarian or ritualistic.

Regulatory character as used in this work went further than this theoretical base to explore the centrality of the law–practice gap. To do this it incorporated Weberian insights of rationality and rationalization to highlight the importance of understanding of this 'gap' to the study of regulation. Through this extension, it was necessary to understand three relationships in order to achieve a contextual understanding of regulatory change and regulatory compliance. These were: the interaction between social norms and the formal regulatory framework in a given regulatory milieu; the interaction between individuals and social norms; and finally, the interaction between individuals and the formal regulatory framework. Together, these three relationships form the central features of a 'map' of regulatory character.

The first step undertaken in embedding this characteristic analysis as a way of understanding the regulatory response to Kader was to map out a tentative empirical understanding of Thai regulatory character, that was to move from a first order to a second order concept. Contemporary academic literature on Thailand revealed a complex society, nonetheless one infused with a hierarchist relationship between those in positions of power and ordinary individuals. These hierarchist or patriarchal norms could be seen as arising from Thai economic and political history, and were not understood as an essentialist given. Nor could they be seen as unchallenged; the actions of the bureaucracy, the military, labour and rural activists have been woven into successive political upheavals that have moulded, hardened or softened patriarchal control. Further, these patriarchal norms were dualistic. They were seen as both 'legitimate', an understanding of 'who we are and how we behave' embodied in the mantra 'Nation, Religion, King', as well as being cultural or normative resources for strategic improvement of one's own position. Overall, within Thai regulatory character, considerable emphasis is placed on personal relationships, networks and systems of patronage. The predominant relationship in Thai regulatory character was that between self-reliant individuals, skilled in understanding social position, and those in positions of authority.

This relationship affected the other two: the relationships between social norms and formal laws, and that between individuals and formal laws. This was highlighted through the analysis of the translation of both activist demands and international standards into local context. Politicians and the bureaucracy re-established sovereignty through the contours of regulatory character to make sure that regulatory change took account of local power interests. Issues of sovereignty were particularly critical in the area of compensation and health and safety law. Reform to these laws was difficult, and ground was given grudgingly by those in positions of ultimate authority. Not surprisingly, demands that drew on international regulatory trends that could be framed within existing power relations found a more willing audience. A considerable number of such regulatory innovations did find their way into the regulatory framework. Compensation laws were altered to include greater numbers of businesses that were required to pay into the scheme, the demand for Safety Day on 10 May was acceded to, safety officer training was tightened, and safety committees introduced into all workplaces employing more than 10 workers.

The primary relationship within Thai regulatory character was this nexus between patriarchal social norms and self-reliant individuals who work skilfully within networks in order to survive and thrive. The primacy of this social interaction rendered the relationship between both social norms and formal regulatory mechanisms – as well as between individuals and formal mechanisms of redress and protection – highly problematic. At the most extreme, international standards were merely *pak chee roy nah* or 'window dressing' scripted into regulations but used primarily to convince outsiders that Thailand was a good place to do business, a place that had the 'right' regulations. Standards could also be altered, with 'necessary' cost considerations included (such as replacing the requirement for smoke detectors with heat detectors, or allowing the use of non-accredited fire panels). Regulatory reform remained irrelevant to many workers' lives, since their best chance of improving their lot remained with finding powerful people to protect them. Strategies to climb the social hierarchy, such as education, or more recently to succeed in business, were often preferred to pushing for recognition of legal rights.

The irrelevance of the formal regulatory mechanisms to the lives of many workers gave rise to understandable indifference by workers to formal health and safety law. Why use legal redress when the costs were prohibitive? What was the point of a safety committee when there were more pressing needs for survival and the possibility of losing your job if you pushed your demands too forcefully? A safer way was to find out through friends who was a good boss and who was more likely to take better care of your needs. What was the point of a government safety scheme, if the chances of being denied compensation were high? A better plan, and the approach used by Kader victims, was to lobby prominent companies directly for compensation, since they were vulnerable to public pressure, whereas the Thai government remained resistant to such pressure. This indifference to formal strategies was also found within the inspectorate: why place a prohibition notice on a machine if a possible outcome was to be being sued by the owner? A safer path was to use persuasion and if that failed, blame the worker for not taking enough care, or not being 'safety aware'. Perhaps even to accept the manager's offer of lunch was not so bad, after all, at least he was showing some respect to the authority of the inspector.

The relationship between social norms and formal regulatory mechanisms after reform efforts often remained one of control. Tripartism lent itself to corporatism. A tripartite framework did not necessarily mean an improvement, as it could be used to marginalize groups that pushed for more radical change in the aftermath of Kader. The union movement was highly fragmented and so those wishing to stymie far-reaching change easily exploited differences between different unions. Laws and regulations were often structured to retain centralized control. Government doctors dictated who was eligible for compensation, and inspectors' decisions were subject to tripartite committee oversight. The role of those outside the tripartite framework remained critical, then, in the push for change, and their networks with receptive members of the bureaucracy were also important.

This relationship between social norms and formal regulatory mechanisms also led to an emphasis on regulatory form, rather than effectiveness. Formal regulations were used as signals; signals that Thailand was competent, that it had 'made the grade' on the world stage. The popularity of accreditation schemes, such as the ISO 9000 series, illustrated that the symbolic aspect of formal mechanisms, a signal of competence, was important to understand. Reform in the wake of Kader illustrated the way this symbolic dimension of safety regulation worked to increase a sense of Thai identity. Reforms that were acceded to by government and regulators were gleaned from the global stage, not only from the West but also from neighbours such as India, Malaysia and the Philippines. However, the political elite was often convinced of their need by demonstrating that they represented a 'Thai way' and that they would not interfere too much with the accepted way of doing things.

The irrelevance of many formal regulatory initiatives, policies and demands to everyday working life had several ramifications. First, there could be considerable contradiction between the content of policies such as education campaigns and the normative messages sent. Educational content might emphasize the need for safety awareness, but educational form emphasized the sanctity of the social hierarchy. The need to defer to the social hierarchy, at least overtly, was often the primary lesson learned. Contradiction between form and substance could be accepted and normalized. Secondly, when formal regulatory methods *were* enforced there could be resentment expressed, not only by managers but also by workers whose daily rhythm (along with coping mechanisms) was disrupted. However, there were positive aspects to the normative emphasis on relationships rather than regulatory content. Those managers who had worked within an international environment and were convinced that certainly regulatory requirements could improve, could be a powerful means to improve standards more generally.

Activists were well aware of the way regulatory character, and in particular the patriarchal–self-reliance nexus, worked to undermine genuine change. A challenge for activists was to capture public attention as to the importance in pushing for comprehensive reform. This was described in Chapter 6. Victims, those who had borne the brunt of weak, ineffective regulations, were seen as central to change, since they could act as a constant reminder to all workers of what might happen to them if conditions did not improve. However, there continued to be no role for victims in the formal legal framework, despite activist pressure. In the absence of this and other structural changes to the safety framework, the extent that individuals drew on their formal rights to push for redress remained weak. It is for this reason that victim demands formed an important part of the analysis of the aftermath of Kader, since they revealed both the nature of traditional Thai regulatory character and the potential within their reform demands for more meaningful change. Each of the demands made by activists were best understood not as merely demands for adoption of international regulatory techniques, but rather as demands for a change in the underlying form Thai regulatory character should take. Egalitarian views infused local activist demands. Key amongst these was the five-partite regulatory structure that could break open tripartite control within Thailand. Regulation was conceived of as a mechanism to empower workers to enable them to control their own future. Each element of the initial demands by the activists fit within this overall egalitarian scheme: a Safety Day to keep alive the need for improved standards in the mind of the public; safety committees to improve access by workers to information about workplace safety; and, critically, a five-partite occupational health and safety institute that could draw on the to resource adequately a comprehensive health and safety programme, from education to enforcement, empowerment to prosperity for both workers and management.

The only conceivable and available avenue to put this grand vision into effect was law reform. But the government, and more critically the bureaucracy, did not share their vision. For those in authority, improvement in health and safety might be desirable, but it needed to be achieved within the confines of the existing regulatory character. Some within the bureaucracy clearly felt significant change within the current framework was possible, albeit they were frustrated with the slow pace of change. The struggles between the government and the activists were a struggle between competing visions. Activists were fully cognisant of the problems that occurred within a patriarchal regulatory character: the irrelevance of regulations, the non-payment of compensation, the perpetual frustration inherent in the process of taking grievances to court, and the cynicism of the public towards regulatory change. It was not the lack of regulatory techniques in law that continued to concern activists, it was what appeared to them to be the persistent devaluing of worker's lives inherent within traditional Thai regulatory character.

Overall, the reforms that were institutionalized into law as a result of the negotiation between activists and bureaucracy largely reinforced or left untouched traditional Thai regulatory character. Critically, a health and safety institute with wide-reaching powers and an egalitarian ethos never came to fruition, although during the 10-year anniversary of the Kader fire there was an attempt to reignite interest in this vision. Perhaps the institute may eventuate, but at this time it appears unlikely to take the radical form activists proposed. It is more likely to approximate health and safety institutes internationally, with their emphasis on education and research. Such institutes are less threatening and able to be incorporated into existing characteristic patterns of regulation and non-regulation.

A further dimension to regulatory character must also be acknowledged, that of gender. Social norms were gendered, so the impact of regulatory reform – the victories won and any gains activists made – needed to be understood in terms of their different implications for women and men. Traditional regulatory character, premised on the patriarchal self-reliance relationship, meant that women bore the brunt of care in the aftermath of Kader. In the case of Kader, the compensation paid could be less than effective when men were allowed to side-step their responsibilities yet still retain compensation moneys. Further, as patriarchal obligations declined, traditional safeguards for women also changed. Vulnerable women were particularly affected: those with little broader family or economic support and few transferable skills. Further, their traditional role as 'dependable' was increasingly invoked as the obligations on men declined. Without a commensurate increase in legal safeguards, the decline of normative safeguards saw women workers face a challenging future (Timm, 1992). Nonetheless, the strength of women's involvement in the union movement may well see some rise to that challenge (Ungpakorn, 1999).

From the point of view of regulatory character, however, it would be unwise to draw the conclusion that 'nothing changed'. Rather, the reforms need to be appreciated in light of regulatory character. That is, the significance of law and regulatory reform need to be appraised in light of Thai regulatory character. Regulatory character is not an essentialist given. It has changed over time and will continue to do so with the changing economic and political circumstances of Thailand. But in the absence of revolution, the change will build on existing character, rather than radically alter it. For this reason change will be slow, but there will be change nonetheless. Further, change may well occur in any or all of the key relationships of that character. Change may occur in the relationship between individuals and social norms, between those norms and the formal legal and regulatory structure, or by individuals changing how they use the law, for example, away from a strategy to gain political advantage to a means to assert their rights.

More critical perhaps is to recognize that the direction of change is uncertain, as each of the other three ideal types present in Hood's (1998) analysis of administrative culture are present in the Thai context and in the pressures that accompany globalization. The hierarchist present could shift towards greater egalitarianism (the activist demand), embrace the ideals of the market in a manner that valorizes individualism, or drift towards fatalism and ritualism already present in traditional forms of Thai regulatory character. The importance of formal law in each of these scenarios will be important. Activists coming from an egalitarian frame were keen to augment legal rights, however they were not exclusively focussed on formal law, as their direct negotiations with Kader demonstrate. Further, the individualism within the market has been associated historically with the need for more certain law (Weber, [1947] 1964, but see Nelken 2001, 2004). Certainly, analysis in Chapters 5 and 6 showed shifts towards egalitarianism, greater individualism or greater fatalism clearly present in the aftermath of Kader.

Regulatory Character and International Pressure

The potential for movement in one or other direction arose both from international as well as local pressures. Chapters 7 and 8 showed how changes in regulatory character could also arise through international pressure, although this shift was neither unitary nor direct. Further, regulatory character itself could exert a brake on the degree of actual change in local conditions.

Nonetheless, international pressure was vividly felt, as is highlighted in Chapter 7. Fear of loss of investment and the knowledge of the possible transfer of investment and capital away from Thailand to China was a real fear for the government as well as regulators charged with raising standards. Government and bureaucracy responded by embracing elements of individualism that could make Thailand recognizable to foreign investors as a good place to invest. The emphasis on 'investment first', both from the government and from international agencies such as the IMF, illustrates the way that individualism was evident in new regulatory initiatives. Individualism emphasizes the power of atomized individuals in making self-interested choices. Here, regulation rode on the coat-tails of the market. A prominent example here was the TIS 18001 programme that explicitly set out to raise the standards of business in Thailand through competitive advantage. Accreditation and improved standards were argued to be a useful selling point in an increasingly competitive market. Both consumer demand and the demands of exacting overseas companies in their critical decisions about awarding contracts to local firms was seen as a way by the bureaucracy to sell the advantages of the TIS 18001 programme. International institutions also added to this pressure towards individualism. The IMF, for example, was in part funding the TIS initiative, and was keen to ensure that the auditing process be subject to market discipline.

This individualist emphasis was not only present in government response to international pressures. NGO initiatives such as SA 8000 also can be seen to push regulatory character more in the direction of individualism, since it also relies on companies seeing the SA 8000 accreditation as a competitive advantage. It is a programme that clearly sets out to use the power of the market and the self-interest of companies. This was not a clear-cut case, however. The content of the accreditation was clearly intended to empower local workers to communicate to management their safety needs. Further, the auditing regime is clearly hierarchist, with external auditors monitoring compliance and reporting back to SAI. The data presented above further suggests that the presence of external auditors can disempower local managers and local workers, since they disrupt the normal everyday relationships between individuals. Whilst this may sometimes work to workers' benefits (for example, to rectify a longstanding problem), it can also be an unwanted and unwelcome imposition. Finally, should auditing become ritualized, the drift towards fatalism is clearly possible.

Fatalism is an intriguing element of Thai regulatory character. At one level, the emphasis on the form of rules, and their symbolism directed towards external audiences, is characteristic of ritualism. But ritualism and symbolism can be either full or empty of meaning, depending on the audience. Fatalism emphasizes the emptiness of ritual and external form. This only explains the one side of ritualism as it is expressed in the Thai regulatory character. Nonetheless, empty ritualism was clearly present. International pressures could be seen to exacerbate this fatalism. Arms-length demands from international investors, international industry groups and foreign governments that Thai companies adopt certain codes of conduct can easily result in ritualistic compliance. Fatalism also combined with pressure of the market towards individualism, a combination that provided a means for those in positions of authority to be excused of even their traditional patriarchal responsibilities. Here, ritualism is not found in rules, but in the ritualism of norms. Norms of deference, once responded to by norms of noblesse oblige, become replaced with norms of indifference.

Finally is egalitarianism. The egalitarianism pushed for by local activists, for example, was also present in some international initiatives. The WISE programme of the ILO had egalitarian underpinnings, with the emphasis on collaboration between workers and management to solve the problems of safety cognizant of local conditions. The emphasis on good examples from the local context, rather than simply the imposition of standards from outside, meant that empowerment was more evident in the philosophy and practice of the programme.

Global pressures intersected with local pressures, then, to push regulatory character in different directions. In the case of Kader, competing pressures that pushed this character towards greater levels of individualism and fatalism were met by the egalitarian demands of national and international NGOs. As Figure 8.1 showed, the pressures of the global market most easily intersected with individualism, which in the Thai context meant placing greater demands on the self-reliance of Thai workers. This individualism could in turn be used to produce fatalism with respect to patriarchal norms, including those of reciprocity. At another level, global rationalism could build on the existing ritualism within Thai regulatory frameworks.

Overall, the study illustrates how globalization intersects with local reform initiatives, both in terms of hard economic realities of investment and disinvestment, but also in terms of character. In this way, globalization is experienced as not just an economic reality, but also as an exhortation to a set of norms and beliefs of the values of individualism. Control is extended through both economic and normative means (Anghie, 2000), however, this control is mediated through regulatory character. This can lead to classic examples of 'unintended consequences', such as the pressure for self-reliance under governance strategies leading to the workers and others seeking patronage through traditional characteristic ties and relationships.

Resonance and Regulatory Character

What is important about this study is not only that it demonstrates that reform is dependent on context, nor that it demonstrates how regulation cannot be abstracted to a set of 'best practice' forms that will simply need reiterating in each national context. Commonalities as well as uniqueness are both important aspects of the study. The theoretical construct of regulatory character is central to this ability to connect both common and unique aspects of a given situation. It is a theoretical and empirical method by which both the uniqueness of context as well as its commonality with other locales can be explored. There are clear areas of resonance between the Kader experience and other areas of regulatory reform. 'Thai style' regulatory compliance is resonant of notions of *katcha* within Pakistan and even 'she'll be right' within Australia, although each has a different cultural gloss. Further, procrastination in reform and reform implementation is not novel. Finally, the use of regulations for strategic purposes unrelated to compliance with regulatory goals can arguably be seen as the reason for the push to deregulation and economic globalization in the first place. Regulatory scholars reading the study will find much that resonates with their own research of the challenges of regulatory reform.

Nonetheless, a grounded understanding of regulatory character in Thailand was important to the study and this importance is well illustrated by the possible outcomes of ignoring it and focussing exclusively on the generic component of globalization and regulatory change. Ignorance of Thai regulatory character would lead to a misunderstanding of why reforms were ineffective either in the short or, as in the case of compensation, in the long term. Further, promotion of the best the world has to offer in a technical sense may lead to much money being spent for little effect. There is a real chance, too, of regulatory colonialism: of the imposition of rules without engagement in the political process and full of unwritten assumptions about the 'right' way of acting (see Anghie, 2000). This is the stuff of resentment. So too is an unreflective linking between patriarchalism and corruption. The connection between regulatory character and 'corruption' warrants much closer attention. Indeed, the notion of corruption does not sit equally easily within Hood's (1998) master categories. The idea of corruption as undesirable resonates most easily with individualism, whereas patriarchalism could view it as normal, as could fatalism, within a framework where rules are ritually observed and effective political action relates to subverting rules.

Certainly, however, there are also problems with an exclusive focus on regulatory character, in isolation from an appreciation of the global regulatory context. As Braithwaite and Drahos (2000) have documented, the international regulatory landscape provides rich pickings for NGOs intent on reform of entrenched government and business practice. Nonetheless, examples of effective regulatory regimes are more diverse than the literature sometimes allows. The 'five-partite' model of safety regulation championed by Thai activists provides an example from which others might learn. This book is a timely reminder of the need to preserve tension within our understanding of regulation and regulatory reform. Without this, regulatory scholarship that becomes too preoccupied with prescribing regulatory techniques may unwittingly become part of the problem, rather than part of the solution working towards a global system where disasters such as Kader become less and less frequent occurrences.

What is needed is to review regulatory change and regulatory compliance in light of regulatory character. When this is understood, lessons can clearly be learnt from other contexts, particularly those that share great similarities in regulatory character. These similarities, or resonance, between one context and another are clearly present. As Hood (1998) argues in his work, the master tropes of hierarchism, individualism, fatalism and egalitarianism are found across the globe, from north to south and east to west. It is unsurprising then, that different contexts will resonate with each other in terms of their regulatory framework, their strengths and their weaknesses. Regulatory character provides a filter through which the appropriateness of regulatory innovations can be understood, and their likely shortcomings. One further point needs to be made here. That is, that 'appropriateness' may mean different things at different times. As Kader showed, in some cases, 'appropriate' may mean working within the regulatory character – in another, it may mean identifying a critical reform that challenges the certainties within the current way of working. As Hood (1998) points out, however, each underlying world-view holds within it known problems. Kader certainly shows the difficulties with a hierarchist underpinning to regulatory character, but this does not mean that individualism inherent within global economic reform nor egalitarianism championed by activists is problem-free.

The extension on Hood's (1998) work in this book adds a further dimension: one that is critical to regulation, namely, the interaction between social norms and formal regulatory mechanisms. To an extent, the work here is more Weberian than Hood's and Douglas' cultural theory. Hierarchism as it was expressed in Thailand was a hierarchism that emphasized social norms over and above formal laws. Other contexts may emphasize the hierarchism within rules, with rules having greater authority than norms, more in the vein of Weber's classical form of bureaucracy. There may well be resonance between these two forms of regulatory character, yet there are likely to be differences too, certainly greater differences than between two hierarchist forms of regulatory character in different places that both emphasize norms, or two that emphasize formal regulatory rules.

The Kader story demonstrates one final aspect of regulation that can never be ignored, namely the reality that regulation, regulatory change and regulatory compliance are processes, not simply the existence or absence of rules or techniques. Perhaps this is not such a new conclusion. Nonetheless, this study reveals the complex nature of the process as one that takes place between individuals, norms and formal rules. The processes both of reform and of compliance in the wake of Kader bring with them some cause for optimism. Nonetheless, the challenges that remain are considerable. This should not tempt us to prescribe solutions, rather to sharpen our understanding of regulation and reform as a process – one that cannot be divorced from local character. It is an empathetic, albeit critical understanding of the interaction between regulations and their context that should form the basis of regulatory scholarship.

Appendix 1:

Reflections on Research Methods

In the early 1990s when this research was in its infancy, questions about globalization and its impact on working conditions within rapidly industrializing environments had a high profile within both political and academic debate. The debate was multi-faceted, with part of this interest in working conditions stemming from the increased investment by Australian manufacturers in operations within the region, with the subsequent loss of investment and employment within Australia. The interest in working conditions within Asia was, then, part altruism and part self-interest, since an aspect of the debate concerned a fear that conditions within Australia too, would decline. These debates coincided with my own research at the time into the responses of Australian companies to the deaths of their workers (Haines, 1997), which had given me some insight into the logic some companies used when they argued that, for profitability reasons, they would have to move their operations overseas. Their justification rarely stemmed directly from the death of their employees (my interest at the time), although increasing expectations on their behaviour by government, in the form of the full range of regulatory demands (including but not limited to occupational health and safety and environment) did. This raised significant questions for me about the levels of safety standards when Western companies move their operations overseas, questions I was unable to explore within the confines of that research.

Research into the impact of globalization on working standards is a difficult issue to explore, as it has no easy boundaries. Further, much work on globalization appeared ideological, based on a priori decisions about its value and consequences, so a clearly defined study that could mine the nature of regulatory change in the face of globalization was essential.

When the Kader fire occurred, the worst fears about globalization appeared to be realized. It appeared from reports filtering through to Australia that MNCs were not only willing to exploit the weakest within their own national boundaries, but also internationally. Understanding whether this was indeed the case, or if regulatory standards would develop over time that would be able to stem the devastation wrought by such events, seemed critical, but the vehicle to be able to explore this was not clear. I was attending a union training conference on globalization and safety in June 1993 where a survivor from the Kader factory spoke. It was a moving and awful story that stuck with me, and it was from that moment that this current research began. It became clear to me that, in similar vein to my earlier work (Haines, 1997, 1999), one means to explore the impact of globalization on regulatory standards was to explore, in depth, individual cases of disaster and their aftermath. From this time, material on the fire, media reports, activist reports and published literature were collected and filed away whilst other research commitments were completed.

The research presented in this book is best understood as an instrumental case study (Stake, 1998). The Kader case is critical to the book, yet a central feature of the work is to understand how the forces of globalization intersect with local conditions to influence regulatory change. The Kader fire is a heuristic device, in the same manner as the deaths of employees in my earlier work (Haines, 1997), with the event having both intrinsic interest but also used as a means to shed light on critical social and regulatory processes.

The fieldwork that forms the basis of this book took place predominantly during two trips to Bangkok in 1999 and 2000, as well as a trip to Hong Kong in 2002. The visits to Bangkok included ethnographic work as well as a series of semi-structured interviews with a range of key informants about the Kader case and the Kader campaign. Further interviews were undertaken, based on the initial interviews in 1999, to broaden understanding of how the Kader event intersected with ongoing regulatory reform initiatives. Thus, the informants were purposively chosen to gain as broad an understanding of the fire and its aftermath as possible. The purpose of this sample was not only to clarify key events that took place after the fire, but also to understand different interpretations and understandings of the event, the campaign, reform measures and their significance (Stake, 1998, p. 97). Interviews were undertaken with government officials from three separate government bureaucracies (NICE, TISI and MASCI), NGOs and union activists (both national and international), business people and global institutions such as the ILO. Documentation, including legislation and research reports, such as those undertaken by Arom Pompangan, the Asia Disaster Preparedness Centre (ADPC), the ILO and academics from the Economics Faculty at Chulalongkorn University, were also accessed whilst in the field. Finally, seminars addressing occupational health and safety in the region were attended, one at the newly formed OHSEI, a research institute established by the Danish Government through their Danish trade union movement's aid agency, LO-TCO, and the other an activist seminar on the Chiang Mai disaster where activists met with victims' families and local leaders to form a response to the tragedy.

The field research was supplemented with material available in Australia. This included written references including Voravidh Charoenloet (1998), 'The Situation of Health and Safety in Thailand', dossier No. 5, April, Asia Monitor Resource Center Toy Campaign; International Confederation of Free Trade Unions (undated), *From the Ashes; A Toy Factory Fire in Thailand: An Expose of the Toy Industry*, ICFTU, Belgium; Casey Cavanagh Grant and Thomas J. Klem (1994), 'Toy Factory Fire in Thailand Kills 188 Workers', *National Fire Prevention Authority Journal*, January/February, pp. 42–9; Peter Symonds (1997), *Industrial Inferno: The Story of the Thai Toy Factory Fire*, Labour Press Books, Bankstown (Australia). Web-based research was also critical. A full archive of the *Bangkok Post* exists on the web and was a critical source of information. Email links were also established with many informants whilst in the field so that material could be checked and updated throughout the research. In many ways, this research itself is a product of globalization.

Finally, a note must be made of language. I do not speak Thai. For some scholars I consulted in the early stages of my research this meant I would be ill-equipped to undertake the research. At the beginning I was inclined to agree, not wanting to undertake unproductive and unhelpful research. However, over time it became clear that research in non-Western settings specifically concerned with regulation and its reform were few, and the questions raised by globalization and the response of regulatory scholars demanded research be done in these settings. In short, if no-one else was willing to do this research, then I would. Once this had been decided, I was surprised at the amount of English language material that was available, and grateful for the wealth of support I received. Major pieces of legislation, such as the *Labour Protection Act* (1998) and *Factory Act* (1969, amended in 1972, 1975, 1979 and 1992) are available in English. Many of those interviewed also spoke English. Thai government bureaucracies also make a limited amount of their material available in English on their various websites. Invaluable assistance was given to me by Thai colleagues and contacts who provided me with material, much of it in English, and I was assisted by an excellent interpreter who understood not only the language, but also the regulatory context. My solution to my language inadequacies was to be as open as I could during fieldwork to observations, comments, sights, expressions, thoughts and conversations. I took every opportunity during my fieldwork to discuss my ideas with those living and working in Thailand. The visit to the Southeast Asian Research Centre in Hong Kong was also designed to check my facts, ideas and thoughts about Thailand with the excellent group of scholars working there, most notably Kevin Hewison. It should be clear from this that I owe many a debt of gratitude, and I extend to all who gave of their ideas, time and resources my grateful thanks.

Appendix 2:

Tsunami Postscript

As the publication of this book was nearing the final stages, a disaster of monumental proportions occurred, affecting not only Thailand, but also Indonesia, Sri Lanka, the Maldives, India, Myanmar, Malaysia and Somalia. On 26 December 2004 an earthquake measuring 9.0 on the Richter scale, its epicentre off the coast of Indonesia in the Indian Ocean, created a tsunami that caused, at the latest estimate, the loss of 226,000 lives, over 5,000 of them within Thailand. At first glance, the disparities between the trauma of the Kader fire and the devastation that is unfolding following this latest catastrophe seem worlds apart. Kader resulted from factors known to create unacceptable hazards. In every sense of the word, the Kader fire was preventable. Whilst there were some reports that more could have been done to prevent the devastation from the tsunami, the location of the earthquake, its size and the devastation it caused were extraordinary. The tsunami and the outpouring of support it generated seem to eclipse the Kader story.

Yet parallels can be drawn between the two events. As at the time of writing, the Thai government's response to the tsunami bears the hallmarks of a Thai approach to disaster, hallmarks of their 'regulatory character'. The decision by the Prime Minister Thaksin Shinawatra to refuse international aid, saying Thais had the resources to cope with the disaster themselves, the reports of warnings ignored by the head of the meteorological department (currently under investigation), and reports of tourist victims being dealt with in a manner that means identification is more possible when compared with the mass disposal of bodies of Thai victims, are all part of the tsunami aftermath. They resonate with elements of the Kader story, where Thai pride featured prominently in the reform initiatives, identification of victims was hampered by poor record-keeping, and warnings of hazards with the building before the fire occurred were ignored.

The resonance between the two events suggests that the experience of those involved in Kader and its aftermath may provide some lessons, at least for those involved in the rebuilding of communities and for those fighting to re-establish their lives and their communities in the wake of the tsunami. First and foremost, the Kader story reiterates the importance of political context to the aftermath of any disaster. For those outside the region wishing to provide support and assistance, there needs to be recognition that there is no such thing as unmediated access to local communities, no 'distortion free communication' with victims of the disaster that can produce long-term solutions to the problems of rebuilding. International assistance and the desires of the global community to provide much needed assistance inevitably will be moulded by the local context.

International NGOs, in particular, need to be wary of making promises that they will be able to provide necessary support for communities without involving government. Government will be involved. The Thai government, for example, has a legitimate and ongoing concern for Thai communities devastated by the tsunami. Individual Thai citizens, too, may well have a more immediate concern with what their government and local leaders are doing, than concern with a particular international NGO. Further, and despite protestations to the contrary, international NGOs do not have the ongoing commitment to any given place necessary to sustain any one community in the long term. The spotlight will move on, and with it, donor concerns and donor dollars. International NGO attention will follow.

What is at issue, then, is not whether international NGOs will or will not have a relationship with national governments and local authorities, but what kind of relationship that will be. The Kader story showed the importance of NGOs (both international and local) in providing an alternative vision of society, both to government and to the Thai people. This vision included a difference in norms: a change from hierarchical values to a more egalitarian vision. This flowed on to change perceptions that law should function as a support for individual and community needs. Certainly, well-placed NGOs are in a position to provide much needed resources, but perhaps the best form of support in the reconstruction effort is that which engenders a more robust relationship between Thai people, their local communities and their government – not one that presumes that Thais have few resources of their own, or that government assistance necessarily will be bureaucratic and self-interested.

Clearly, however, the Kader story also shows the difficulties in engendering good government policies and practices in the aftermath of disaster. It also shows the importance of taking account of both substantive and strategic elements of government action. There was a concern shown for the Kader victims, both by some politicians and bureaucrats. Substance provided by the norms of patriarchalism meant that some support was forthcoming for victims. Law reform to strengthen safety also occurred. Appealing to the best that government has to offer and working to bring this to fruition seems logical. Yet, there must also be an acknowledgement of the way disasters provide both opportunities and threats for political gains or losses and status enhancement or decline. Newspaper reports in the Thai media demonstrate that political concerns are well and truly in place during the current crisis. Certainly, Thaksin has shown a genuine concern for the affected regions. He has also bolstered Thai pride in his rejection of foreign aid. His refusal to allow Thais to be placed in the position of helpless victims either as individuals or as a country increased his stature in the elections on 6 February 2005, when he won a resounding victory.

Responding to a disaster suits Thaksin's managerial style, yet the long-term effects on the most vulnerable people in Thailand remain unclear. Burmese immigrants, even those legitimately in the country, have found themselves on the receiving end of scapegoat policies. They are fearful of going to government for assistance for fear of being branded as looters, and subsequently being deported. Other 'outsiders', such as traditional fishing communities, also may find land confiscated for tourist 'redevelopment' in the wake of the tsunami.

Finally, mention must be made of the relationships that local people have that are able to sustain them. Orphaned children taken in by relatives, and hospitality workers provided with support by family members to tide them over through the current crisis, show how family relationships remain critical to long-term survival for those affected by the tsunami. Yet again, however, the Kader example suggests caution in suggesting that family can or will provide all necessary support. The use of compensation money provided by the Kader company was used by some to augment family income, but in other cases the capacity of men to take a second wife and absolve themselves from ongoing responsibility for their children meant that ageing grandmothers were left with sole responsibility for raising young children, without any compensation support. Similar stories of both the use and misuse of compensation money received by families received in the wake of the tsunami are to be expected.

Disasters of all types bring out the best and worst in individuals, communities and governments. Certainly, the stories of heroism and acts of kindness between strangers, as well as the outpouring of support both locally and across the globe for those affected, attest to the best of human nature. However, stories of Thai bureaucrats ignoring warnings for fear of scaring tourists, reports of paedophiles praying on lost and orphaned children, the emergence of Thai scam letters appearing on email in-trays, and the deportation of Burmese 'looters' by the Thai authorities, show the darker side of the aftermath of disaster. It is equally important to acknowledge and understand both sides. Grounded understanding and reflective action must accompany generosity and good intentions. To succeed in rebuilding areas devastated by the tsunami, those wanting to assist – NGOs, governments, government coalitions and UN agencies – are dependent upon their local knowledge. Reflective use of this knowledge is essential to sustainable long-term rebuilding of communities. Without this, armed only with good intentions, individual initiatives to help may end in becoming part of the problem and a drain on already scarce local resources.

Bibliography

Note: Entries with authors' names beginning with 'Mc...' are alphabetized as if spelled 'Mac...'

ADPC (1994), *Strengthening Disaster Management Strategies in Thailand*, Project of the Royal Thai Government (under THA/88/004) United Nations Development Programme, March.

Anghie, A. (2000), 'Time Present and Time Past: Globalization, International Financial Institutions and the Third World', *International Law and Politics*, Vol. 32, pp. 243–90.

Aoki, K. and Cioffi, J. (1999), 'Poles Apart: Industrial Waste Management Regulation and Enforcement in the United States and Japan', *Law and Policy*, Vol. 21(3), pp. 213–45.

Asia Monitor Resource Center (1997), Report on Regional Meeting: 'Remembering Kader: Promoting Occupational Health and Safety, Workers Rights and the Rights of Industrial Accident Victims in Asia', Bangkok, 10–13 May 1997.

Asia Monitor Resource Center (1998), Toy Campaign: The People United will never be Defeated, April, dossier No. 5 compiled by the Hong Kong Toy Coalition and the Asia Monitor Resource Center.

Asian Disaster Preparedness Center (see ADPC).

Australian Broadcasting Commission (2001), 'Esso Fined $2m for Longford Blast', Monday July 30, available at www.abc.net.au/pm/indexes/2001/pm_archive_2001_Monday30 July2001.htm. Accessed 28 January 2005.

Ayres, I. and Braithwaite, J. (1992), *Responsive Regulation: Transcending the Deregulation Debate*, Oxford University Press, Oxford.

Baldwin, R. and Cave, M. (1999), *Understanding Regulation: Theory Strategy and Practice*, Oxford University Press, Oxford.

Banfield, E.C. (1958), *The Moral Basis of a Backward Society*, Free Press, Glencoe, Illinois.

Bauman, Z. (1998), *Globalization: The Human Consequences*, Polity Press, Cambridge.

Baumol, W. and Blinder, A. (1988), *Economics: Principles and Policy* (4th edn), Harcourt Brace Janovich, San Diego.

Beck, U. (1995), *Ecological Enlightenment: Essays on the Politics of the Risk Society*, Humanities Press, New Jersey.

Bello, W., Cunningham, S. and Poh, L.K. (1998), *A Siamese Tragedy: Development and Disintegration in Modern Thailand*, White Lotus, Bangkok.

Bierne, P. (1983), 'Cultural Relativism and Comparative Criminology', *Contemporary Crisis*, Vol. 7, pp. 371–91.

Block, R., Roberts, K., Ozeki, C. and Roomkin, M. (2001), 'Models of International Labor Standards', *Industrial Relations*, Vol. 40(2) pp. 258–92.

Braithwaite, J. (1985), *To Punish or Persuade: Enforcement of Coal Mine Safety*, State University of New York Press, Albany.

Braithwaite, J. and Drahos, P. (2000), *Global Business Regulation*, Cambridge University Press, Cambridge.

Brown, A. (1997), 'Locating Working Class Power', in K. Hewison (ed.), *Political Change in Thailand: Democracy and Participation*, Routledge, London, pp. 163–78.

Brown, A. (2001), 'After the Kader Fire in Thailand', in J. Hutchison and A. Brown (eds), *Organising Labour in Globalising Asia*, Routledge, London, pp. 127–46.

Brown, A., Bundit Thanachaisetavut and Hewison, K. (2002), 'Labour Relations and

Regulation in Thailand: Theory and Practice' Working Paper Series No 27, July, City University of Hong Kong.

Bundit Thanachaisethavut (1995), 'Trade Union Structure and Tripartite Systems in Thailand', Arom Pongpangan Foundation and Friedrich Ebert Stiftung, unpublished monograph.

Burk, J. (1988), *Values in the Marketplace: The American Stock Market Under Federal Securities Law*, Walter de Gruyter & Co, Berlin.

Castells, M. (1996), *The Rise of the Network Society*, Blackwell, Oxford.

Castells, M. (1997), *The Power of Identity*, Blackwell, Oxford.

Castells, M. (1998), *The End of the Millennium*, Blackwell, Oxford.

Chai-Annan Samudavanija (1997), 'Old Soldiers Never Die, They are Just Bypassed: The Military, Bureaucracy and Globalism', in K. Hewison (ed.), *Political Change in Thailand: Democracy and Participation*, Routledge, London, pp. 42–57.

Chua, T. and Wei Ling, W. (1993), 'Help! Is There a Way Out?' *Asian Labour Update*, Vol. 12, pp. 1–8.

Connors, M. (2002), 'Framing the "People's Constitution"', in D. McCargo (ed.), *Reforming Thai Politics*, Nordic Institute of Asian Studies Press, Leifsgade, Copenhagen, pp. 37–55.

Cooney, S. (2000), 'Testing Times for the ILO: Institutional Reform for the New International Political Economy', *Comparative Labour Law and Policy*, Vol. 20, pp. 365–99.

Cooney, S., Lindsey, T., Mitchell, R. and Zhu, Y. (2002), 'Labour Law and Labour Market Regulation in East Asian States: Problems and Issues for Comparative Inquiry', in S. Cooney, T. Lindsey, R. Mitchell and Y. Zhu (eds), *Labour Law and Labour Market Regulation in East Asia: Themes and Issues in Comparative Law*, Routledge, London.

Cooney, S. and Mitchell, R. (2002), 'What is Labour Law Doing in East Asia', in S. Cooney, T. Lindsey, R. Mitchell and Y. Zhu (eds), *Labour Law and Labour Market Regulation in East Asia: Themes and Issues in Comparative Law*, Routledge, London.

Cotterrell, R. (1998), 'Why Must Legal Ideas be Interpreted Sociologically?', *Journal of Law and Society*, Vol. 25(2), pp. 171–92.

Cotterrell, R. (2001), 'Is There a Logic of Legal Transplants?', in D. Nelken and J. Feest (eds), *Adapting Legal Cultures*, Hart Publishing, Oxford, in association with the Onati International Institute for the Sociology of Law, pp. 70–92.

Curran, D. (1993), *Dead laws for Dead Men: the Politics of Federal Coal Mine Health and Safety Legislation*, University of Pittsburgh Press, Pittsburgh, PA.

Dezalay, Y. and Garth, B. (2001), 'The Import and Export of Legal Institutions: International Strategies and National Palace Wars', in D. Nelken and J. Feest (eds), *Adapting Legal Cultures*, Hart Publishing, Oxford, in association with the Onati International Institute for the Sociology of Law, pp. 241–55.

Diller, J. (1999), 'A social conscience in the global marketplace? Labour dimensions of codes of conduct, social labelling and investor initiatives', *International Labour Review*, Vol. 138(2), pp. 99–129.

Dilokvidhyarat, L. and Chaleonlert, V. (2000), 'Economic Crisis, Trade Union Movement and Occupational Health and Safety in Thailand', paper presented at Asian Workers Institute for Occupational Health, Safety and Environment, Bangkok, 6–7 December.

Dixon, N.F. (1976), *On the Psychology of Military Incompetence*, Jonathon Cape, London.

Doneys, P. (2002), 'Political Reform through the Public Sphere: Women's Groups and the Fabric of Governance', in D. McCargo (ed.), *Reforming Thai Politics*, Nordic Institute of Asian Studies Press, Leifsgade, Copenhagen, pp. 163–82.

Douglas, M. (1966), *Purity and Danger: An Analysis of the Concepts of Pollution and*

Taboo, Routledge, London, reprinted 1996.

Douglas, M. (1992), *Risk and Blame: Essays in Cultural Theory*, Routledge, London.

Dunkley, G. (1997), *The Free Trade Adventure: The Uruguay Round and Globalism – A Critique*, Melbourne University Press, Melbourne.

Durkheim, E. (1933, 1964), *The Division of Labour in Society*. Free Press of Glencoe, New York.

Engel, D. (1978), *Code and Custom in a Thai Provincial Court*, Published for the Association for Asian Studies by The University of Arizona Press, Tucson, Arizona.

Espeland, W. (1998), *The Struggle for Water: Politics, Rationality and Identity in the American Southwest*, University of Chicago Press, Chicago.

Falk, R. (1995), *On Humane Governance: Towards a New Global Politics*, Polity, Cambridge.

Falk, R. (1997), 'State of Siege: Will Globalization Win Out?' *International Affairs*, Vol. 73(1) pp. 123–36.

Foo, G. and Lim, L. (1989), 'Poverty, Ideology and Women Export Factory Workers in Southeast Asia', in H. Ashfar and B. Agarwal (eds), *Women, Poverty and Ideology in Asia: Contradictory Pressures, Uneasy Resolutions*, Macmillan Press, London, pp. 212–33.

Freidman, M. and Freidman, R. (1996), 'The Power of the Market', in G. Agyrous and F. Stilwell, *Economics as a Social Science*, Pluto Press, Sydney.

Frost, S. and Wong, M. (2001), 'Monitoring Mattel in China', *Asian Labour Update*, Vol. 39 (April–June). Available at www.amrc.org.hk/Arch/3701.htm. Accessed 28 January 2005.

Fung, A., O'Rourke, D. and Sabel, C. (2001), 'Realizing Labor Standards: How Transparency, Competition, and Sanctions Could Improve Working Conditions Worldwide', *Boston Review*, Vol. 26, pp. 1–20. Accessed 5 January 2005.

Geertz, H. and Geertz, C. (1975), *Kinship in Bali*, University of Chicago Press, Chicago.

Giddens, A. (1990), *The Consequences of Modernity*, Polity Press, Cambridge.

Giddens, A. (1995), 'Politics and Sociology in the Thought of Max Weber', in *Politics, Sociology and Social Theory*, Polity Press, Cambridge.

Gill, S. and Law, D. (1988), *The Global Political Economy: Perspectives, Problems and Policies*, Harvester Wheatsheaf, New York.

Goodin, R.E. (1992), 'The Green Theory of Agency', in R. Goodin, *Green Political Theory*, Polity Press, Cambridge, pp. 113–68.

Grabosky, P.N. (1994a), 'Green Markets: Environmental Regulation by the Private Sector', *Law and Policy*, Vol. 15, pp. 419–48.

Grabosky, P.N. (1994b), 'Beyond the Regulatory State', *Australian and New Zealand Journal of Criminology*, Vol. 27, pp. 192–7.

Grant, Casey Cavanagh, and Klem, Thomas J. (1994), 'Toy Factory Fire in Thailand Kills 188 Workers', *National Fire Prevention Authority Journal*, (January/February).

Greider, William (1997), *One World, Ready or Not: The Manic Logic of Global Capitalism*, Touchstone Books, New York.

Gunningham, N. (1991), 'Private Ordering, Self-Regulation and Futures Markets: A Comparative Study of Informal Social Control', *Law and Policy*, Vol. 13(4), pp. 297–326.

Gunningham, N. and Grabosky, P. (1998), *Smart Regulation: Designing Environmental Policy*, Clarendon Press, Oxford.

Gunningham, N. and Johnstone, R. (1999), *Regulating Workplace Safety: Systems and Sanctions*, Oxford University Press, Oxford.

Haines, F. (1997), *Corporate Regulation: Beyond 'Punish or Persuade'*, Clarendon Press, Oxford.

Haines, F. (1999), 'Innocent Deaths and Regulatory Failure: A Case Study of Change in the Absence of Punishment', *International Journal of the Sociology of Law*, Vol. 27, pp. 23–50.

Haines, F. (2000), 'Towards Understanding Globalization and Control of Corporate Harm: A Preliminary Criminological Analysis', *Current Issues in Criminal Justice*, Vol. 12(2), pp. 166–80.

Haines, F. and Lewis, C. (2004), 'Kader, compensation and justice: the need for a comprehensive analysis', in S. Pickering and C. Lambert (eds), *Global Issues, Women and Justice,* Institute of Criminology, Sydney Series No 19, Institute of Criminology, Sydney, pp. 230–58.

Haines, F. and Sutton, A. (2000), 'Criminology as Religion: Profane Thoughts about Sacred Values', *British Journal of Criminology*, Vol. 40(1), pp. 146–62.

Haines, F. and Sutton, A. (2003), 'The Engineer's Dilemma: A Sociological Perspective on the Juridification of Regulation', *Crime, Law and Social Change*, Vol. 39(1), pp. 1–22.

Hancher, L. and Moran, M. (1998), 'Organizing Regulatory Space', in R. Baldwin, C. Scott and C. Hood (eds), *A Reader in Regulation*, Oxford University Press, Oxford, pp. 148–73.

Harding, A. (2001), 'Comparative Law and Legal Transplantation in South East Asia', in D. Nelken and J. Feest (eds), *Adapting Legal Cultures*, Hart Publishing, Oxford, in association with the Onati International Institute for the Sociology of Law, pp. 199–222.

Harvey, D. (1989), *The Condition of Postmodernity*, Blackwell, Cambridge.

Held, D., McGrew, A., Godblatt, D. and Perraton, J. (1999), *Global Transformations: Politics, Economics and Culture*, Polity, Cambridge.

Hellman, J., Jones, G. and Kaufmann, D. (2000), '*Seize the State, Seize the Day'*: State Capture, Corruption and Influence in Transition*, World Bank Policy Research Working Paper No. 2444, The World Bank, Washington.

Hewison, K. (1989), *Bankers and Bureaucrats: Capital and the Role of the State in Thailand*, Monograph Series 34, Yale Center for International and Area Studies, New Haven.

Hewison, K. (1996), 'Thailand: Regime Change', in G. Rodan (ed.), *Political Oppositions in Industrialising Asia*, Routledge, London, pp. 72–94.

Hewison, K. (1997), 'The Monarchy and Democratisation', in K. Hewison (ed.), *Political Change in Thailand: Democracy and Participation*, Routledge, London, pp. 58–74.

Hewison, K. (2001), Thailand: Class Matters, Southeast Asia Research Centre Working Paper Series, No 8, City University of Hong Kong.

Hewison, K. (2002a), 'The World Bank and Thailand: Crisis and Social Safety Nets', *Public Administration and Policy*, Vol. 11(1), pp. 1–21.

Hewison, K. (2002b), 'Responding to Economic Crisis: Thailand's Localism', in Duncan McCargo (ed.), *Reforming Thai Politics*, Nordic Institute of Asian Studies Press, Leifsgade, Copenhagen, pp. 143–61.

Hewison, K. and Brown, A. (1994), 'Labour and Unions in an Industrializing Thailand', *Journal of Contemporary Asia*, Vol. 24(4), pp. 483–514.

Higgott, R. (1999), Coming to Terms with Globalisaton: Non state Actors and Agenda for Justice and Governance in the Next Century, GHC Working Paper Series 99/3. Available at www.humanities.mcmaster.ca/~global/wps/higgott.PDF. Accessed 2 May 2003.

Higgott, R. (2000), 'Contested Globalization: The Changing Context and Normative Challenges', *Review of International Studies*, Vol. 26, pp. 131–53.

Hirst, P. and Thompson, G. (1996), *Globalization in Question: The International Economy and the Possibilities of Governance*, Polity Press, Cambridge.

Hood, C. (1998), *The Art of the State: Culture, Rhetoric and Public Management*, Clarendon Press, Oxford.

Hooker, M.B. (1988), 'The "Europeanization" of Siam Law 1855–1908', in M.B. Hooker (ed.), *Laws of South-East Asia, Vol II: European Laws in South-East Asia*, Butterworth Co. (Asia), Singapore, pp. 535–76.

Hopkins, A. (1995), *Making Safety Work: Getting Management Commitment to Occupational Health and Safety*, Allen and Unwin, St Leonards.

Hutchison, J. and Brown, A. (2001), 'Organising Labour in Globalising Asia: An Introduction', in J. Hutchison and A. Brown (eds), *Organising Labour in Globalising Asia*, Routledge, London, pp. 1–26.

Industry Commission (1994), 'Workers' Compensation in Australia', Report No. 36, 4 February.

International Confederation of Free Trade Unions (undated), *From the Ashes; A Toy Factory Fire in Thailand: An Expose of the Toy Industry*, ICFTU, Belgium.

International Monetary Fund (1999), 'Progress Report: Developing International Standards', IMF Policy Development and Review Department, March. Available at www.imf.org/external/np/rosc/progrev.pdf. Accessed 7 May 2003.

International Monetary Fund and The World Bank (2002), 'Market Access for Developing Country Exports – Selected Issues', Approved by Timothy Geithner and Gobind Nankani, 26 September. Available at www.imf.org/external/np/pdr/ma/2002/eng/092602.pdf. Accessed 6 May 2003.

Jayasuriya, K. (2001), 'Governance, Post Washington Consensus and the New Anti-Politics', in T. Lindsey and H. Dick (eds), *Corruption in Asia: Rethinking the Governance Paradigm*, Federation Press, Annandale, Ch. 2.

Jettinghoff, A. (2001), 'State Formation and Legal Change: On the Impact of International Politics', in D. Nelken and J. Feest (eds), *Adapting Legal Cultures*, Hart Publishing, Oxford, in association with the Onati International Institute for the Sociology of Law, pp. 99–117.

Johnstone, R. (1997), *Occupational Health and Safety Law and Policy, Text and Materials*, Law Book Company, North Ryde.

Kagan, R. (2000), 'Introduction: Comparing National Styles of Regulation in Japan and the United States', *Law and Policy*, Vol. 22(4), pp. 225–44.

Kahn-Freund, O. (1974), 'On Uses and Misuses of Comparative Law', *Modern Law Review*, Vol. 31, pp. 1–27.

Keesing, R. (1991), 'Culture and Asian Studies', *Asian Studies Review*, Vol. 15(2), pp. 85–92.

Keyes, Charles (1987), *Thailand, Buddhist Kingdom as Modern Nation-state*. Westview Press, Boulder.

Kitamura, Y. (2000), 'Regulatory Enforcement in Local Government in Japan', *Law and Policy*, Vol. 22(4), pp. 305–18.

Kobrua Suwannathat-Pian (2002), 'The Monarch and Constitutional Change since 1972', in D. McCargo (ed.), *Reforming Thai Politics*, Nordic Institute of Asian Studies Press, Leifsgade, Copenhagen, pp. 57–71.

Kolko, G. (1963), *The Triumph of Conservatism*, Free Press of Glencoe, New York.

Kolko, G. (1965), *Railroads and Regulation*, Princeton University Press, Princeton.

Lae Dilokvidhyarat and Voravidh Chareonloert (2000), 'Economic Crisis, Trade Union Movement and Occupational Health and Safety in Thailand', paper presented at Asian Workers Institute for Occupational Health, Safety and Environment, Bangkok, 6–7 December.

Laird, J. (2000), *Money, Politics, Globalisation, and Crisis: The Case of Thailand*, Graham Brash Pte Ltd., Singapore.

Levine, D. (1985), *The Flight from Ambiguity: Essays in Social and Cultural Theory*, University of Chicago Press, Chicago.

Lindsey, T. (2001), 'History Always Repeats? Corruption, Culture and "Asian Values"', in T. Lindsey, and H. Dick (eds), *Corruption in Asia: Rethinking the Governance Paradigm*, Federation Press, Annandale, Ch. 1.

Lindsey, T. and Dick, H. (2001), *Corruption in Asia: Rethinking the Governance Paradigm*, Federation Press, Annandale.

McCargo, D. (1997), 'Electoral Politics: Commercialisation and exclusion', in K. Hewison (ed.), *Political Change in Thailand: Democracy and Participation*, Routledge, London, pp. 132–48.

McCargo, D. (2002a), 'Introduction: Understanding Political Reform in Thailand', in D. McCargo (ed.), *Reforming Thai Politics*, Nordic Institute of Asian Studies Press, Leifsgade, Copenhagen, pp. 1–18.

McCargo, D. (2002b), 'Thailand's 2001 General Elections: Vindicating Reform?', in D. McCargo (ed.), *Reforming Thai Politics*, Nordic Institute of Asian Studies Press, Leifsgade, Copenhagen, pp. 247–59.

McCluskey, M. (1998), 'The Illusion of Efficiency in Workers' Compensation "Reform"', *Rutgers Law Review*, Vol. 50(3), pp. 657–941.

MacDonald, S. and Vollrath, T. (2005) 'The Forces Shaping World Cotton After the Multifiber Arrangement' *Economic Outlook Report from the Economic Research Service'*, United States Department of Agriculture, available at http://www.ers.usda.gov/publications/cws/apr05/cws05c01/cws05c01.pdf. Accessed 8 June 2005.

Maisrikrod, S. and McCargo, D. (1997), 'Electoral Politics: Commercialisation and Exclusion', in K. Hewison (ed.), *Political Change in Thailand: Democracy and Participation*. Routledge, London, pp. 132–48.

Mander, J. and Goldsmith, E. (1996), *The Case against the Global Economy: And for a Turn Toward the Local*, Sierra Books, San Francisco.

Martin, H. and Schumann, Harald, (1997), *The Global Trap: Globalization and the Assault on Democracy and Prosperity*, Pluto Press, Sydney.

Marx, K. (1976), *Capital*, Vol. 1, Penguin, London.

Meidinger, E. (2002), 'Law Making by Global Civil Society: the Forest Certification Prototype', electronic paper available at
http://law.buffalo.edu/homepage/eemeid/scholarship/GCSEL.pdf. Accessed 28 January 2005.

Mills, C.W. (1963), 'Two Styles of Social Science Research', in *Power, Politics and People: the Collected Essays of C. Wright Mills* (edited and with an introduction by Irving Louis Horowitz), Oxford University Press, New York.

Mittelman, J. (1994), 'The Globalisation Challenge: Surviving at the Margins', *Third World Quarterly*, Vol. 15(3), pp. 427–43.

Mitter, S. (1994), 'On Organising Women in Casualising: A Global Overview', in S. Rowbothom and S. Mitter (eds), *Dignity and Daily Bread: New Forms of Economic Organising Among Poor Women in the Third World and the First*, Routledge, London, pp. 14–52.

Mulder, N. (2000), *Inside Thai Society: Religion, Everyday Life, Change.* Chiang-Mai, Silkworm Books.

Murray, J. (2001a), 'The Sound of One Hand Clapping? The "Ratcheting Labour Standards" Proposal and International Labour Law', *Australian Journal of Labour Law*, Vol. 14, pp. 306–32.

Murray, J. (2001b), 'A New Phase in the Regulation of Multinational Enterprises: The Role of the OECD', *Industrial Law Journal*, Vol. 30(3), pp. 255–70.

Napaporn Athivanicharyapong (1997), 'Lives and Families of the Workers After Kader's Tragedy', Arom Pongpangan Foundation, Unpublished Report, 10 May.

Naruemon Thabchumpon (2002), 'NGOs and Grassroots Participation in the Political Reform Process', in D. McCargo (ed.), *Reforming Thai Politics*, Nordic Institute of Asian Studies Press, Leifsgade, Copenhagen, pp. 183–99.

Nelken, D. (1994), 'Whom can you Trust? The Future of Comparative Criminology', in D. Nelken (ed.), *The Futures of Criminology*, Sage, London.

Nelken, D. (2001), 'Towards a Sociology of Legal Adaptation', in D. Nelken and J. Feest (eds), *Adapting Legal Cultures*, Hart Publishing, Oxford, in association with the Onati International Institute for the Sociology of Law, pp. 7–54.

Nelken, D. (2004), 'Using the Concept of Legal Culture', *Australian Journal of Legal Philosophy*, vol 29, pp. 1-26.

Nottage, L. (2001), 'The Still-Birth and Re-birth of Product Liability in Japan', in D. Nelken and J. Feest (eds), *Adapting Legal Cultures*, Hart Publishing, Oxford, in association with the Onati International Institute for the Sociology of Law, pp. 147–85.

OECD (2000), 'Reducing the Risk of Policy Failure: Challenges for Regulatory Compliance', paper prepared by Christine Parker, Kirsi Kuuttiniemi, But Klaasen, Jefferson Hill and Scott Jacobs.

Ohmae, K. (1995), *The End of the Nation State*, Free Press, New York.

O'Rourke, D. (2000), 'Monitoring the Monitors: A Critique of PricewaterhouseCoopers (PwC) Labour Monitoring', available at http://nature.berkeley.edu/orourke/PDF/pwc.pdf. Accessed 28 January 2005.

Pasuk Phongpaichit and Baker, C. (1995), *Thailand: Economy and Politics*, Oxford University Press, Oxford.

Pasuk Phongpaichit and Baker, C. (1997), 'Thailand in the 1990s', in Kevin Hewison (ed.), *Political Change in Thailand: Democracy and Participation*, Routledge, London, pp. 21–41.

Pasuk Phongpaichit and Baker, C. (1998), *Thailand's Boom and Bust*, Silkworm Books, Chiang Mai.

Pasuk Phongpaichit and Baker, C. (2000), *Thailand's Crisis*, Silkworm Books, Chiang Mai.

Pasuk Phongpaichit and Sungsidh Piriyarangsan (1994), *Corruption and Democracy in Thailand*, Silkworm Books, Chiang Mai.

Pasuk Phongpaichit, Sungsidh Piriyarangsan and Nualnoi Treerat (1998), *Guns, Girls, Gambling and Ganja: Thailand's Illegal Economy and Public Policy*, Silkworm Books, Chiang Mai.

Paterson, J. (2000), *Behind the Mask: Regulating Health and Safety in Britain's Offshore Oil and Gas Industry*, Ashgate Dartmouth, Aldershot.

Pearce, F. and Tombs, S. (1990), 'Ideology, Hegemony and Empiricism: Compliance Theories of Regulation', *British Journal of Criminology*, Vol. 30(4), pp. 423–43.

Penchan Charoensuthiphan (2003), 'Union Heads to Pursue Case in Court', *Bangkok Post*, April 21.

Poggi, G. (1990), *The State: Its Nature, Development and Prospects*, Stanford University Press, Stanford.

Prapaiparn Dasaneyavaja (2000), 'Seven-Year Trial May End This Year', *Bangkok Post*, May 10.

Pravit Rojanaphruk (2005) "300,000 Textile, Garment Jobs at Risk" *The Nation*, May 30, 2005, available at http://thailabour.org/news/05053002.html. Accessed June 8, 2005.

Prudhisan Jumbala and Maneerat Mitprasat (1997), 'Non-governmental Development

Organisations: Empowerment and Environment', in K. Hewison (ed.), *Political Change in Thailand: Democracy and Participation*, Routledge, London, pp. 195–216.

Quarantelli, E. (1993), 'Community Crises: An Exploratory Comparison of the Characteristics and Consequences of Disasters and Riots', *Journal of Contingencies and Crisis Management*, Vol. 1, pp. 67–8.

Quarantelli, E. (1995), 'Draft of a Sociological Research Agenda for the Future: Theoretical, Methodological and Empirical Issues', Disaster Research Center Preliminary Paper No. 228.

Reason, J. (1997), *Managing the Risks of Organizational Accidents*, Ashgate, Aldershot.

Reichman, N. (1998), 'Moving Backstage: Uncovering the Role of Compliance Practices in Shaping Regulatory Policies', in R. Baldwin, C. Scott and C. Hood (eds), *A Reader on Regulation*, Oxford University Press, Oxford, pp. 325–46.

Reiss, A.J. (1984), 'Consequences of Compliance and Deterrence Models of Law Enforcement for the Exercise of Police Discretion', *Law and Contemporary Problems*, Vol. 47, pp. 91–102.

Riggs, F. (1961), *The Ecology of Public Administration*, Asia Publishing House, New York.

Sassen, S. (1998), *Globalization and Its Discontents: Essays on the New Mobility of People and Money*, The New Press, New York.

Schmidt, J.D. (2002), 'Democratization and Social Welfare in Thailand', in Duncan McCargo (ed.), *Reforming Thai Politics*, Nordic Institute of Asian Studies Press, Leifsgade, Copenhagen, pp. 91–104.

Self, P. (1993), *Government by the Market*, Macmillan, London.

Sellars, C. (1997), *Hazards of the Job: from Industrial Disease to Environmental Health Science*, University of North Carolina Press, Chapel Hill.

Selznick, P. (1992), *The Moral Commonwealth: Social Theory and the Promise of Community*, University of California Press, Berkeley.

Sewell, W. (2002), 'A Theory of Structure: Duality, Agency and Transformation', in L. Spillman (ed.), *Cultural Sociology*, Blackwell, Oxford, pp. 324–8.

Smith, A. (1776, 1970), *The Wealth of Nations*, Penguin, Harmondsworth.

Social Security Office, Thailand (1999), 'Annual Report'. Extract was available at www.asean-ssa.org/ah_goto.asp?page=objectives.asp&country=Thailand. Accessed 6 May 2003.

Stake, R. (1998), 'Case Studies', in N. Denzin and Y. Lincoln (eds), *Strategies of Qualitative Enquiry*, Sage, Thousand Oakes, pp. 86–109.

Stigler, G (1975), *The Citizen and the State: Essays on Regulation*, University of Chicago Press, Chicago.

Strange, S. (1996), *The Retreat of the State: The Diffusion of Power in the World Economy*, Cambridge University Press, Cambridge.

Suehiro, A. (1989), *Capital Accumulation in Thailand: 1855–1985*, The Centre for East Asian Cultural Studies, Tokyo.

Surin Maisrikrod and McCargo, D. (1997), 'Electoral Politics: Commercialisation and Exclusion', in K. Hewison (ed.), *Political Change in Thailand: Democracy and Participation*, Routledge, London, pp. 132–48.

Suriyasarn Busakorn (1993), 'Roles and Status of Thai Women from Past to Present', available at www.busakorn.addr.com/women/ThaiWomenRoles-Status.htm. Accessed 26 January 2005.

Symonds, Peter, (1997), *Industrial Inferno: The Story of the Thai Toy Factory Fire*, Labour Press Books, Bankstown, Australia.

Tamada, Y. (1991), 'Itthiphon and Amnat: An Informal Aspect of Thai Politics', *Southeast Asian Studies*, Vol. 28(4), pp. 455–66.

Tanase, T. (2001), 'The Empty Space of the Modern in Japanese Law Discourse', in D.

Nelken and J. Feest (eds), *Adapting Legal Cultures*, Hart Publishing, Oxford, in association with the Onati International Institute for the Sociology of Law, pp. 187–98.

Teubner, G. (1998a), 'Juridification: Concepts, Aspects, Limits, Solutions', in R. Baldwin, C. Scott and C. Hood (eds), *A Reader on Regulation*, Oxford University Press, Oxford.

Teubner, G. (1998b), 'Legal Irritants: Good Faith in British Law or How Unifying Law Ends up in New Divergences', *Modern Law Review*, Vol. 61, pp. 11–32.

Thitinan Prongsudhirak (1997), 'Thailand's Media: Whose Watchdog?', in K. Hewison (ed.), *Political Change in Thailand: Democracy and Participation*, Routledge, London, pp. 217–32.

Tian Chua and Wong Wei-Ling (1993), 'Help! Is There a Way Out?' *Asian Labour Update*, Issue 12, July, Asia Monitor Resource Centre, Hong Kong.

Timm, M. (1992), 'Law vs. Custom in Thailand', *IDRC Reports*, Vol. 20(2), pp. 23–4.

Trebilock, M. and Howse, R. (1995), *The Regulation of International Trade*, Routledge, London.

Unger, D. (1998), *Building Social Capital in Thailand: Fibers, Finance and Infrastructure*, Cambridge University Press, Cambridge.

Ungpakorn, Ji Giles (1999), *Thailand: Class Struggle in an Era of Economic Crisis*, Monograph, Asia Monitor Resource Center and Worker's Democracy Book Club, Hong Kong and Bangkok.

Voravidh Chareonloet and Lae Dijokvidhyarat (2000), 'Economic Crisis, Trade Union Movement and Occupational Safety and Health in Thailand', paper for discussion at the team conference: The Impact of Globalization on Occupational Health, Safety and Environment, organized by Asian Workers Institute for Occupational Health Safety and Environment, Thailand, 6–7 December 2001.

Voravidh Charoenloet (1998), 'The Situation of Health and Safety in Thailand', dossier No. 5, April, Asia Monitor Resource Centre Toy Campaign, Hong Kong.

Wallerstein, I. (1995), *After Liberalism*, New Press, New York.

Waters, M. (1995), *Globalization*, Routledge, London.

Weber, M. (1922, 1993), *The Sociology of Religion*, Beacon Press, Boston.

Weber, M. (1947, 1964), *The Theory of Social and Economic Organization*, The Free Press, New York.

Weber, M. (1948, 1991) *From Max Weber: Essays in Sociology* (ed. by H. Gerth and C. Wright Mills), Routledge, London.

Weber, M. (date not known; Engl. trans. 1958), 'The Three Types of Legitimate Rule', in M. Truzzi (ed.) (1971), *Sociology: The Classic Statements*, Routledge, London, pp. 180–95.

Weiss, L. (1998), *The Myth of the Powerless State: Governing the Economy in the Global Era*, Polity Press, Cambridge.

Wells, C. (1995), *Negotiating Tragedy: Law and Disasters*, Sweet and Maxwell, London.

Williams, R. (2002), 'Base and Superstructure', in L. Spillman (ed.), *Cultural Sociology*, Blackwell, Oxford, pp. 58–62.

Woodiwiss, A. (1998), *Globalisation, Human Rights and Labour Law in Pacific Asia*, Cambridge University Press, Cambridge.

World Bank (1998), *Annual Report*, available from http://www.worldbank.org/html/extpb/annrep98/. Accessed 26 January 2005.

Wyatt, D.K. (1984), *Thailand: A Short History*, Silkworm Books, Chiang Mai.

Index

Note: References followed by *n* indicate footnotes; those followed by *f* indicate figures; those followed by *t* indicate tables.

4